Foreign Trade Regimes and Economic Development:
SOUTH KOREA

Foreign Trade Regimes and Economic Development:

*A Special Conference Series
on Foreign Trade Regimes
and Economic Development*

VOLUME VII

NATIONAL BUREAU OF ECONOMIC RESEARCH
New York   1975

SOUTH KOREA

by **Charles R. Frank, Jr.**

PRINCETON UNIVERSITY
AND THE BROOKINGS INSTITUTION

Kwang Suk Kim

KOREA DEVELOPMENT INSTITUTE

Larry E. Westphal

NORTHWESTERN UNIVERSITY

DISTRIBUTED BY Columbia University Press
New York and London

NATIONAL BUREAU OF ECONOMIC RESEARCH

*A Special Conference Series on Foreign Trade Regimes
and Economic Development*

To
the Memory of
Thomas F. Olmsted
1929–1975

Library of Congress Card Number: 74–82375
ISBN for the series: 0–87014–500–2
ISBN for this volume: 0–87014–507–X

Printed in the United States of America
DESIGNED BY JEFFREY M. BARRIE

Relation of the Directors of the National Bureau to
Publication of the Country Studies in the Series on
Foreign Trade Regimes and Economic Development

The individual country studies have not passed through the National Bureau's normal procedures for review and approval of research reports by the Board of Directors. In view of the way in which these studies were planned and reviewed at successive working parties of authors and Co-Directors, the National Bureau's Executive Committee has approved their publication in a manner analogous to conference proceedings, which are exempted from the rules governing submission of manuscripts to, and critical review by, the Board of Directors. *It should therefore be understood that the views expressed herein are those of the authors only and do not necessarily reflect those of the National Bureau or its Board of Directors.*

The synthesis volumes in the series, prepared by the Co-Directors of the project, are subject to the normal procedures for review and approval by the Directors of the National Bureau.

Contents

Tables

Figures

Co-Directors' Foreword

This volume is one of a series resulting from the research project on Exchange Control, Liberalization, and Economic Development sponsored by the National Bureau of Economic Research, the name of the project having been subsequently broadened to Foreign Trade Regimes and Economic Development. Underlying the project was the belief by all participants that the phenomena of exchange control and liberalization in less developed countries require careful and detailed analysis within a sound theoretical framework, and that the effects of individual policies and restrictions cannot be analyzed without consideration of both the nature of their administration and the economic environment within which they are adopted as determined by the domestic economic policy and structure of the particular country.

The research has thus had three aspects: (1) development of an analytical framework for handling exchange control and liberalization; (2) within that framework, research on individual countries, undertaken independently by senior scholars; and (3) analysis of the results of these independent efforts with a view to identifying those empirical generalizations that appear to emerge from the experience of the countries studied.

The analytical framework developed in the first stage was extensively commented upon by those responsible for the research on individual countries, and was then revised to the satisfaction of all participants. That framework, serving as the common basis upon which the country studies were undertaken, is further reflected in the syntheses reporting on the third aspect of the research.

The analytical framework pinpointed these three principal areas of research which all participants undertook to analyze for their own countries.

Subject to a common focus on these three areas, each participant enjoyed maximum latitude to develop the analysis of his country's experience in the way he deemed appropriate. Comparison of the country volumes will indicate that this freedom was indeed utilized, and we believe that it has paid handsome dividends. The three areas singled out for in-depth analysis in the country studies are:

1. *The anatomy of exchange control:* The economic efficiency and distributional implications of alternative methods of exchange control in each country were to be examined and analyzed. Every method of exchange control differs analytically in its effects from every other. In each country study care has been taken to bring out the implications of the particular methods of control used. We consider it to be one of the major results of the project that these effects have been brought out systematically and clearly in analysis of the individual countries' experience.

2. *The liberalization episode:* Another major area for research was to be a detailed analysis of attempts to liberalize the payments regime. In the analytical framework, devaluation and liberalization were carefully distinguished, and concepts for quantifying the extent of devaluation and of liberalization were developed. It was hoped that careful analysis of individual devaluation and liberalization attempts, both successful and unsuccessful, would permit identification of the political and economic ingredients of an effective effort in that direction.

3. *Growth relationships:* Finally, the relationship of the exchange control regime to growth via static-efficiency and other factors was to be investigated. In this regard, the possible effects on savings, investment allocation, research and development, and entrepreneurship were to be highlighted.

In addition to identifying the three principal areas to be investigated, the analytical framework provided a common set of concepts to be used in the studies and distinguished various phases regarded as useful in tracing the experience of the individual countries and in assuring comparability of the analyses. The concepts are defined and the phases delineated in Appendix A.

The country studies undertaken within this project and their authors are as follows:

Brazil	Albert Fishlow, University of California, Berkeley
Chile	Jere R. Behrman, University of Pennsylvania
Colombia	Carlos F. Díaz-Alejandro, Yale University
Egypt	Bent Hansen, University of California, Berkeley, and Karim Nashashibi, International Monetary Fund
Ghana	J. Clark Leith, University of Western Ontario

India   Jagdish N. Bhagwati, Massachusetts Institute of Technology, and T. N. Srinivasan, Indian Statistical Institute

Israel   Michael Michaely, The Hebrew University of Jerusalem

Philippines   Robert E. Baldwin, University of Wisconsin

South Korea   Charles R. Frank, Jr., Princeton University and The Brookings Institution; Kwang Suk Kim, Korea Development Institute, Republic of Korea; and Larry E. Westphal, Northwestern University

Turkey   Anne O. Krueger, University of Minnesota

The principal results of the different country studies are brought together in our overall syntheses. Each of the country studies, however, has been made self-contained, so that readers interested in only certain of these studies will not be handicapped.

In undertaking this project and bringing it to successful completion, the authors of the individual country studies have contributed substantially to the progress of the whole endeavor, over and above their individual research. Each has commented upon the research findings of other participants, and has made numerous suggestions which have improved the overall design and execution of the project. The country authors who have collaborated with us constitute an exceptionally able group of development economists, and we wish to thank all of them for their cooperation and participation in the project.

We must also thank the National Bureau of Economic Research for its sponsorship of the project and its assistance with many of the arrangements necessary in an undertaking of this magnitude. Hal B. Lary, Vice President-Research, has most energetically and efficiently provided both intellectual and administrative input into the project over a three-year period. We would also like to express our gratitude to the Agency for International Development for having financed the National Bureau in undertaking this project. Michael Roemer and Constantine Michalopoulos particularly deserve our sincere thanks.

JAGDISH N. BHAGWATI
Massachusetts Institute of Technology

ANNE O. KRUEGER
University of Minnesota

Acknowledgments

When Charles Frank was engaged by the Co-Directors of this series to write the book on Korea, he learned that Larry E. Westphal and Kwang Suk Kim were already at work on a parallel study sponsored by the World Bank. To avoid duplication, the three of them agreed to collaborate, and the present volume represents their joint efforts.

Kim did most of the research for chapters 2, 3, 4, and 5, and also wrote the first drafts. Westphal and Kim produced chapters 6 and 10, and Frank contributed the remaining chapters. All three authors participated in the planning of each other's work and in the revision of first drafts.

Much of the material in chapters 6 and 10 was drawn from the Westphal and Kim contribution to the World Bank study. Their essay, "Industrial Policy and Development in Korea," emphasizes the methodology of measuring effective incentives and contains considerably more detailed analysis than it was thought necessary to include in the National Bureau's series.

We are grateful to the World Bank and to Bela Balassa, editor of *Development Strategies in Semi-Industrialized Countries,* for permission to make use of the Westphal and Kim essay in this book. We are also grateful to Balassa for his helpful guidance at every stage of our research and for his comments on several draft chapters.

The authors thank Thomas Olmsted and his colleagues at the USAID mission to Korea for their full support and cooperation. They also acknowledge the Ford Foundation grant of 1971 that enabled Kim to spend a year at Princeton working closely with his coauthors. Upon his return home, Kim was named a senior fellow of the Korea Development Institute. The Institute and its president, Mahn-je Kim, were very helpful to the authors. The Korean officials who offered their services are too numerous to be listed here.

The compilation of the 1955 input-output table in Chapter 10 was supported by grants from the University Committee on Research in the Humanities and Social Sciences and the Council on International and Regional Studies, Princeton University. Sae Min Oh of the Bank of Korea's staff oversaw the task. Much of the computation of the growth contributions was financed by the Research Program in Economic Development, the Woodrow Wilson School, Princeton University. The Research Program in Economic Development provided general assistance including office space, secretarial help, and research assistants. Northwestern University granted Westphal a quarter's paid leave to permit time for further computations and writing.

Hal Lary read each draft of this volume very carefully and made numerous suggestions which greatly improved the end result. Jagdish Bhagwati and Anne Krueger provided expert guidance and intellectual stimulation. They gave us many helpful comments on earlier versions of the manuscript. T. N. Srinivasan, who read the next to last draft, passed on a variety of useful ideas. All of our colleagues associated with the National Bureau project are to be thanked for the insight of their suggestions, which were offered at the group sessions on research strategy.

A special acknowledgment is due Alice Ann Navin, without whose valuable assistance, the input-output analysis and effective incentive calculations could not have been done so expeditiously. Rekka Nadkarni furnished expert and extremely valuable help to Charles Frank in the computer programming and analysis in chapters 8 and 9. Kyi-Ja Kang tabulated statistical materials and performed computations for Kwang Suk Kim.

Many draft chapters were typed by Dorothy Rieger of Princeton's Research Program in Economic Development. Claudette Simpson also helped with the typing of several revised chapters. The final draft was typed by Rosemary Taromino.

The authors alone are responsible for all errors and omissions.

Principal Dates and Historical Events in South Korea

1904	Effective takeover of government by the Japanese in Korea.
1910	Korea formally annexed to Japan.
1945	Liberation of Korea by American and Russian troops; country split along 38th parallel; U.S. military government installed in South Korea.
1947	First stage of land reform; properties expropriated after departure of Japanese landlords are redistributed.
May 1948	National Assembly elections, rightist parties in the majority.
July 1948	Syngman Rhee elected President of South Korea by the National Assembly.
Aug. 1948	End of rule by U.S. military government.
1949	Second stage of land reform; expropriation and redistribution of land from farms greater than three chongbos (about three hectares).
June 1950	Beginning of war between North and South Korea.
Sept. 1950	General MacArthur lands with UN troops at Inchon.
Nov. 1950	UN troops reach the Yalu River but are thrown back by Chinese troops who enter the war.
March 1951	Seoul retaken by UN troops.
July 1951	Peace talks begin at Kaesong; battlefront stabilized.
July 1953	Korean War armistice signed.
March 1960	Opposition parties walk out of National Assembly over charges of fraud.
April 1960	Student demonstrations lead to resignation of President Rhee.

July 1960   New National Assembly elections; Chang Myon chosen as prime minister by the Assembly.

Jan. 1961   Devaluation of the won from 65 to 100 won to the U.S. dollar.

Feb. 1961   Devaluation of the won from 100 to 130 won to the U.S. dollar.

May 1961   Military coup from which General Park Chung Hee emerges as head of ruling junta.

June 1961   Unification of the multiple exchange rate system.

Jan. 1963   Return to multiple exchange rates.

Oct. 1963   National Assembly elections followed by Assembly elections of Park Chung Hee as president.

May 1964   Devaluation from 130 to 257 won to the U.S. dollar; exchange rate fluctuates.

March 1965   Reunification of the multiple exchange rate system.

Aug. 1965   Exchange rate pegged at 271 won to the U.S. dollar.

Sept. 1965   Interest rate reform; loan rate on regular commercial bank loans raised from 16 to 26 percent.

Jan. 1967   Controlled flotation of the domestic currency upward from 271 won to the dollar.

May 1967   Reelection of Park Chung Hee as president.

July 1967   Reform of the import control system by switch from the positive-list to a negative-list system.

1967   Tariff reform.

April 1971   Third election of Park Chung Hee as president.

June 1971   Devaluation from 326 to 370 won to the U.S. dollar; exchange rate pegged.

1971   Further tariff reforms.

Jan. 1972   Exchange rate floated upward in controlled fashion from 370 won to the U.S. dollar.

June 1972   Exchange rate pegged at about 400 won to the U.S. dollar.

Aug. 1972   Financial reforms and initiation of price stabilization program.

Sept. 1973   Further tariff reforms.

Foreign Trade Regimes and Economic Development: SOUTH KOREA

Chapter 1

Introduction

The economy of South Korea has grown very rapidly since 1963. The average annual rate of growth of GNP between 1963 and 1972 was about 9.6 percent. Exports have grown even faster, from $87 million in 1963 to $1.6 billion in 1972, and to about $3.2 billion in 1973. The annual rate of growth of exports averaged 38.9 percent between 1963 and 1972 and reached a peak of almost 100 percent in 1973, a very remarkable rate of increase.

This volume examines the relationship between trade and exchange rate policies and the rapid growth of South Korean output and trade. Of particular interest are the attempts to liberalize trade policy and the exchange rate system and the effects of these efforts on resource allocation and growth.

There are a few easy explanations that might be given for the growth of Korean trade. For example, South Korea's economy was devastated by both World War II and the Korean War. Between 1953 (when the Korean War ended) and 1960, exports averaged only 1.1 to 2.4 percent of GNP, although a country of South Korea's population and income might have been expected to reach a much higher level of exports, perhaps one of at least 10 or 15 percent of GNP. Thus one explanation of South Korea's export performance is to say that what appears to be growth is really a case of "catching-up" to some "normal" level. By 1971, however, South Korean exports had surpassed the level that is usual in countries of similar population and income.[1] Exports reached about 26 percent of GNP in 1973 and showed little tendency toward less rapid expansion. While early growth of exports might be attributed in part simply to "catching-up," continued growth remains to be explained. Furthermore, South Korea lacks the readily exportable primary products commonly

1

found in other countries of similar size and income. Almost all her exports
are manufactured and as a fraction of GNP they are exceedingly high compared with the proportion of manufactures exported by other less developed
countries.

Other easy explanations could be imagined: for example, South Korea's
exports may have been boosted by war in Viet Nam. In fact, only a tiny fraction of South Korea's exports have been destined for Viet Nam or were in any
way related to the hostilities there. Alternatively, one might attribute South
Korea's export growth to government targets. While such targets have played
a role, it is unlikely that they are the sole or even the major reason exports
grew so rapidly. Unless incentives to export accompany targets, firms will be
driven out of business if continuously forced to export, at a loss, an increasing
proportion of their output.

Growth in income has also been explained in various ways. The most
commonly accepted easy explanation is that South Korean growth is due to
very high levels of foreign aid. Foreign aid has been important, especially
from 1953 to 1963. Domestic savings averaged only about 3 percent of GNP
during those years, while foreign savings (imports of goods and services less
exports of goods and services financed mostly by foreign aid grants) averaged 9 percent of GNP. Approximately three-quarters of total investment
was financed by foreign aid. Those were the years, however, when economic
growth was relatively slow in South Korea. The rate of growth of GNP averaged about 5 percent. After 1964 domestic savings grew very rapidly, rising
from about 4 percent of GNP to almost 17 percent in 1970. The fraction of
total investment financed domestically rose from less than one-third in 1963
to about 63 percent in 1970. Furthermore, beginning in 1965, foreign capital
imports took less the form of foreign aid and more the form of commercial
loans. By 1969, well over half of all foreign loan agreements in that year were
commercial. The period of decreasing reliance on foreign aid, 1964 to 1970,
was also a period of accelerated growth, the annual rate over the period averaging close to 11 percent.

No doubt foreign assistance has been important to South Korea's economic growth. But to attribute rapid growth solely to massive foreign aid
would be a mistake, for South Korea's economic policies have played a role
too. They have ensured the effective use of foreign resources while increasing
the domestic contribution to the process of growth.

In this volume we shall concentrate on the function of trade and exchange rate policies. South Korea has followed a set of policies which are
unusual compared with those of most less developed countries. Instead of
emphasizing import substitution, most policy initiatives have promoted exports. A wide variety of export incentive schemes has been devised, and the
exchange rate has been adjusted frequently and dramatically. During most of
the period since 1967, exchange rate policy has been based on the gliding peg.

Chapter 2 of this volume is a brief economic history of South Korea since World War II. It is largely descriptive and intended as general background for the rest of the book.

Chapter 3 deals with phases I and II of the Bhagwati-Krueger scheme.[2] Phase I begins with the end of World War II and ends with the Korean War armistice signed in 1953. The government was directly involved in trade and controlled what little private trade existed. There was a multiplicity of exchange rates and a flourishing black market in foreign exchange and military payment certificates. Phase II lasted from the end of the Korean War until 1960. It was a period of increasingly sophisticated control mechanisms and complicated procedures which were invented to assist barter trade and to facilitate trade payments.

Chapter 4 covers two Phase III attempts at liberalization, the first from 1961 to 1962, the second from 1964 to 1965. A steep devaluation declared in 1961 was followed by an abortive effort to unify exchange rates and to liberalize trade policy. But a bad crop in 1962 combined with the expansionary fiscal policies of the military government, which had ousted the reformist civilian administration in May 1961, led to a return in 1963 to a Phase II regime with multiple rates and stringent controls on trade.

A much more successful attempt to realize a Phase III liberalization began in May 1964 with a devaluation of the won close to 50 percent and continued through September 1965, when domestic interest rates were substantially raised. The multiple exchange rate system was unified, trade restrictions were eased, and tax administration reformed.

Chapter 4 also covers 1966, the first year of a Phase IV regime in which efforts were made to consolidate reforms. Chapter 5 analyzes the continuation of the Phase IV regime from 1967 to early 1973. During this period, tariffs were revised and the trade control program was changed in 1967 from a positive-list to a more liberal negative-list system. The won was allowed to "glide" from early 1968 to mid-1971, i.e., it floated downward at a determined rate which was meant to be consistent with rates of inflation in Korea and in her major trading partners. The won was again devalued in June 1971 and was floated again during the first half of 1972. In August 1972, a new set of reforms involved price stabilization, pegging the exchange rate at about 400 won to the dollar. There was also a tendency during this period to resort to the old price-distorting practices whenever the balance of payments was under pressure. Trade controls were alternately strengthened and relaxed. The number and level of export subsidy measures increased until early 1973.

Chapter 6 is an analysis of Korea's export growth and treats this subject in some detail. Besides discussing the import-intensity of export production, we also analyze the role of exchange rates, export subsidies, and other incentives in stimulating exports. The degree to which exports are responsible for the growth of the South Korean economy, sector by sector, is described by means of various decomposition techniques. South Korea's growth patterns are compared with those of other countries to demonstrate the relatively predominant role of exports in the South Korean economy.

Foreign capital inflows have been very important in South Korea's growth. Immediately after the Korean War, most of the capital inflow consisted of foreign aid grants. By the mid-1960s, private commercial loans became important. Chapter 7 analyzes the part played by foreign capital in South Korea's growth and the efficiency of the foreign capital inflow.

In Chapter 8, we develop an econometric model of the South Korean economy. The estimation of the model involves the testing of a number of hypotheses concerning the role of exchange rates and commercial policy variables on aggregate behavioral relationships in the economy. Chapter 9 uses the econometric model to determine whether alternative sets of commercial policies would have resulted in more or less growth over the decade of the 1960s. The simulations in Chapter 9 examine the optimality of South Korea's exchange rate policy, tariff levels, and levels of export subsidy in a macroeconomic framework.

In Chapter 10, we discuss the efficiency of the South Korean trade and exchange rate regime. The analysis of efficiency involves first the measurement of nominal protection rates by means of a survey of price comparisons of world market and domestic prices. The nominal protection rates are used to estimate the effective protection of some 150 sectors of the economy. We go beyond measures of effective protection to estimates of rates of effective subsidy which include a wide range of taxes and subsidies to industry in addition to tariff rates. In Chapter 10 we also investigate the labor and capital intensity of South Korea's exports and the effect of valuation at domestic prices, or at international prices, on the growth and structure of the economy.

Chapter 11 provides an overview. The first two sections examine the effects of rapid growth on employment and income distribution. Since these topics are not closely related to trade policy, they do not readily lend themselves to treatment in the main text. We felt, however, that a book on Korean development would be sorely inadequate if it omitted discussion of employment and income distribution.

The next six sections of Chapter 11 consider the factors responsible for growth in Korea with particular reference to trade and exchange rate policies. We draw on the results of research presented in the preceding chapters as much as possible. To a certain extent, however, we must take a broader view of the growth process in order to provide a proper context for the analysis of the role of exchange rates and trade policy. Thus we talk about education and literacy, political regimes, the influence of Japanese culture, and other important factors that help to determine economic policies. Furthermore, we cannot hope to be definitive within this volume even with respect to trade and exchange rate policies because of limitations on data, time, and research capacity. Therefore, some of the observations in Chapter 11, even those involving trade and exchange rate policy, are speculative.

The final section of Chapter 11 offers some caveats about generalizing from the South Korean experience and drawing lessons for other countries. The special factors operating in Korea are extremely important to keep in mind.

NOTES

1. See Bhagwati and Cheh (1972). See also the analysis of exports in Chapter 6.

2. For a description of the Bhagwati-Krueger five-phase scheme, see Bhagwati and Krueger (1970) and also the description of the phases in Appendix A.

Chapter 2

Economic Growth in South Korea since World War II

ECONOMIC DISORGANIZATION FOLLOWING LIBERATION

The Japanese occupation of Korea ended on August 15, 1945 and was supplanted in part by a U.S. military government. The immediate postwar period was characterized by extreme economic disorganization and stagnation caused by the sudden separation of the Korean economy from the Japanese economic bloc, and by the partition of the country along the 38th parallel.

Under colonial rule from 1910 to 1945, the Korean economy became highly dependent upon Japan for capital, technology, and management. Of the total authorized capital of business establishments in Korea, the Japanese owned approximately 94 percent, as of 1940.[1] Japanese engineers and technicians employed in manufacturing, construction, and public utilities in 1944 constituted about 80 percent of the total technical manpower in Korea. The proportion of Korean engineers and technicians was particularly small in the metal and chemical industries (11 to 12 percent).[2] The relative number of Korean business establishments was very small in high-technology industries— about 10 percent in the metal and chemical industries and 25 percent in the machinery industry. Most Korean establishments were small and used simpler technology than the Japanese. Furthermore, establishments in Korea were mainly subsidiaries of Japanese companies. Therefore, the sudden retreat of the Japanese and the separation of the economy from the Japanese economic bloc brought about a suspension of many production activities in Korea.

Partition also had deleterious effects on the South Korean economy. In 1940, Korea's total population was 23.5 million people, 15.6 million in the South and 7.9 million in the North. Approximately 92 percent of average annual power generation, however, had come from plants in the North and most

6

of the country's mineral resources were located there too. In 1940, the North produced about 90 percent of Korea's output of metal products and 83 percent of its chemical products (Table 2-1). By contrast, the South accounted for 72 percent of machinery production, 85 percent of textile production, 64 percent of processed food output, and 89 percent of printing and publishing output in the same year. Thus, metals, electric power, and chemical industries were located mainly in North Korea at the time of liberation, while light industries and machinery production tended to be located in the South.

The number of industrial establishments and employment in South Korea declined sharply after 1945 when the Japanese left and when firms closed for lack of electricity. The industrial survey of November 1946 showed that the number of manufacturing establishments had dropped by 43.7 percent since

TABLE 2-1

Manufacturing Output and Employment, 1940 and 1948

(output in millions of 1948 constant won)

	Manufacturing Output in 1940[a]		South Korea's Share	South Korea's Manufacturing Output, 1948	Manufacturing Workers, 1948 (000)
	All Korea	South Korea			
Metal	49.2(9.3)	4.9(2.0)	(10.0)	2.2(4.2)	4.9(3.7)
Machinery	19.3(3.6)	13.9(5.6)	(72.0)	3.4(6.4)	14.4(11.0)
Chemicals	181.5(34.2)	30.7(12.4)	(16.9)	15.2(28.8)	32.6(24.9)
Textiles	72.8(13.7)	61.5(24.8)	(84.5)	21.6(41.0)	60.4(46.1)
Foods	118.8(22.4)	76.0(30.6)	(64.0)	6.6(12.5)	9.0(6.9)
Ceramics	15.7(3.0)	4.3(1.7)	(27.4)	1.4(2.7)	5.6(4.3)
Printing	7.0(1.3)	6.2(2.5)	(88.6)	1.6(3.1)	2.4(1.8)
Handicrafts	7.6(1.4)	4.9(2.0)	(64.5)	0.7(1.3)	1.8(1.4)
Other	59.0(11.1)	45.7(18.4)	(77.5)	0.0	0.0
Total	530.9(100.0)	248.1(100.0)	(46.8)	52.6(100.0)	131.1(100.0)
Central government operated				11.6(22.1)[b]	37.8(28.8)[b]
Local government operated				6.8(12.9)[b]	25.6(19.5)[b]
Private				34.2(65.0)	67.8(51.7)
Total				52.6(100.0)	131.1(100.0)

NOTE: Figures in parentheses are percentages.
SOURCE: Bank of Korea, *Economic Statistics Yearbook, 1949,* pp. 1-47-1-48.
a. Data for 1940 were recompiled by Bank of Korea to obtain manufacturing output for South Korea.
b. These shares were large because the government took over Japanese firms after August 1945. Most of those firms were later sold to private interests.

1944. Manufacturing employment was 59.4 percent lower. In 1948 total manufacturing output in South Korea was only about one-fifth of the 1940 level (Table 2–1) and had declined sharply in every major sector. (Manufacturing output is likely to have been much lower in 1946, but data are not available.)

In addition to the drastic decline in domestic manufacturing, severe food shortages developed after the war. Population increased rapidly because of the immigration of refugees from the North and the repatriation of Koreans from Japan and other countries. Since domestic grain output was not enough to feed the increased population, the U.S. military government imported about 670 thousand metric tons of food (including wheat, barley, rice, and powdered milk) from May 1946 to January 1948.

Uncontrolled expansion of the money supply before and after liberation set off a hyper-inflation. Currency in circulation expanded by about 6.7 times between the end of 1941 and August 15, 1945.[3] After the liberation, it expanded 77 percent between August 15 and November 1, 1945 and by about 15 times in the four years and four months from August 15, 1945 to the end of 1949. Prices rose very rapidly. The Seoul retail price index increased about 123 times from June 1945 to June 1949.

The U.S. military government attempted to control inflation by announcing maximum prices on essential goods and by rationing. These measures were not successful and were accompanied by increased black market activities. When this became apparent, the government relaxed the controls.

ECONOMIC GROWTH AND TRADE, 1946 TO 1953

Neither national income data nor an overall industrial production index is available for the period 1946 to 1953. Production indexes are available, however, for major commodities as shown in Table 2–2.

Although the average production index for the major commodities is an unweighted, simple average, it gives a rough indication of the growth rate of production. Starting from a very low base in 1946, the postwar recovery of production was fairly rapid. The average production index shown in Table 2–2 increased about two and a half times from 1946 to 1949. Electric power generation and tungsten production for export increased sharply. Heavy industry, however, recovered much more slowly, especially iron and steel and chemicals.

The Korean War again brought a sharp drop in industrial production in 1950 and 1951. By 1952 industrial production began to pick up again as the fighting gradually stalemated along the present demilitarized zone. Although hostilities did not cease until 1953, by that time the average production index (excluding tungsten) had slightly surpassed the 1949 level. The recovery, however, was uneven. Tungsten production increased spectacularly, but production

TABLE 2–2
Production Indexes of Major Commodities, 1946 to 1953
$(1946 = 100)$

Commodity	1947	1948	1949	1950	1951	1952	1953
Rice	115	123	122	121	94	77	117
Wheat and barley	90	95	123	127	74	106	125
Anthracite coal	169	281	347	222	44	175	269
Tungsten ore	353	394	413	112	327	1,106	2,347
Salt	87	113	225	208	99	241	238
Processed marine products	72	61	118	52	61	61	78
Cigarettes and tobacco	237	296	367	280	316	480	433
Raw silk	100	91	92	46	66	70	112
Cotton yarn	109	115	247	191	111	188	257
Cotton cloth	119	79	230	198	116	154	216
Paper and paper products	83	84	213	150	62	266	261
Laundry soap	7	141	197	164	268	316	310
Cement	172	212	225	108	68	339	390
Chinaware	107	150	419	303	274	356	330
Nails	598	595	865	716	225	569	1,114
Transformers	93	74	41	14	53	51	57
Light bulbs	163	162	127	49	35	30	68
Electric power	109	217	291	182	140	282	327
Average index (unweighted)	155	184	259	180	135	270	392
Average index (unweighted) excluding tungsten	143	171	250	184	124	221	277

SOURCE: Various indexes, Bank of Korea, *Annual Economic Review,* 1955; various annual output figures, ibid.

of a number of commodities, such as coal and cotton cloth, did not reattain the 1949 level.

From 1946 to 1953, the average production index increased about 3.9 times (2.8 times if tungsten is excluded). Despite its rapid growth, however, industrial production in South Korea by 1953 was still far below the level achieved in 1940. We can infer from the data presented above that by 1953 total industrial production was probably not much more than one-third of the 1940 level.

Table 2–3 gives merchandise exports and imports (excluding aid imports) from 1946 to 1953. Since all export and import data for that period were tabulated in won, we can show the trend in Korea's trade in real terms only by deflating the export and import current price figures, using for this purpose the Seoul wholesale price index.

South Korea's exports and imports in 1946 were negligible since the country was only beginning to recover from World War II. By 1949 exports

TABLE 2–3

Merchandise Exports and Imports, 1945 to 1953

(millions of won)

	Current Prices[a]		Seoul Wholesale Price Index (1947 = 100)	1947 Constant Prices	
	Exports	Imports		Exports	Imports
1946	0.05	0.16	55.0	0.09	0.29
1947	1.11	2.09	100.0	1.11	2.09
1948	7.20	8.86	162.9	4.42	5.44
1949	11.27	14.74	222.8	5.06	6.62
1950[b]	32.57	5.21	348.0[c]	9.36	1.50
1951	45.91	121.83	2,194.1[d]	2.09	5.55
1952	194.96	704.42	4,570.8	4.27	15.41
1953	398.72	2,237.01	5,951.0	6.70	37.59

NOTE: Table includes recorded private and government trade only. Aid-financed imports, transactions with North Korea, and smuggling are excluded.

SOURCE: Bank of Korea, *Annual Economic Review, 1955.*

a. Exports and imports were valued in won according to f.o.b. export or c.i.f. import prices until March 1951; thereafter, according to domestic market prices (tariffs, domestic taxes, and trade margins were subtracted from domestic prices to estimate the price of imports).

b. Imports and exports through Inchon and Seoul customs offices were not included because records were lost during the war.

c. Average index for June 1950.

d. Average index for April–December in Pusan.

and imports were still quite small, about $17 million and $22 million, respectively.[4] Although the Korean War severely disrupted trade patterns, exports by 1953 exceeded the 1949 level by more than 32 percent and imports were almost six times greater than in 1949.[5]

Nearly all of South Korea's exports during this period were primary products. Agricultural and fishery products generally declined from about 80 percent of total annual exports in 1946 to only some 10 to 15 percent during 1951–1953 because fishing was limited during the Korean War. On the other hand, exports of mineral products, mainly tungsten but also graphite, copper, kaolin, and talc, expanded sharply from about 10 percent of the total in 1946 to about 80 percent from 1951 to 1953.

Major imports in this period were food grains and manufactured goods. In 1946, 1952, and 1953, food grain imports accounted for 34 to 44 percent of total nonaid imports. In other years, when grain imports were not as high, manufactured goods imports accounted for 39 to 59 percent of total imports.

POST–KOREAN WAR RECONSTRUCTION

The Korean Armistice took effect on July 27, 1953. According to government estimates, war damages to industrial offices, plant and equipment, public facilities, private dwellings, and transport equipment (exclusive of military installations) in South Korea were approximately $3.0 billion. This amount was almost equal to estimated GNP for 1952 and 1953 combined.[6] In addition, about one million civilians were killed during the war.

After the Korean War, real GNP grew rapidly from 1953 to 1957, averaging about 5 percent per annum. The only relatively bad year was 1956 when agricultural production declined almost 6 percent (Table 2–4). Mining

TABLE 2–4

**Annual Percentage Growth of GNP and Major Sectors,
1954 to 1972**

(1970 constant prices)

Year	GNP	Agriculture, Forestry, & Fishery	Mining & Mfg.	Social Overhead & Services
1954	5.5	7.6	11.2	2.5
1955	5.4	2.6	21.6	5.7
1956	0.4	−5.9	16.2	4.0
1957	7.7	9.1	9.7	5.8
1958	5.2	6.2	8.2	3.5
1959	3.9	−1.2	9.7	7.5
1960	1.9	−1.3	10.4	2.8
1961	4.8	11.9	3.6	−1.1
1962	3.1	−5.8	14.1	8.9
1963	8.8	8.1	15.7	7.4
1964	8.6	15.5	6.9	3.0
1965	6.1	−1.9	18.7	9.9
1966	12.4	10.8	15.6	12.6
1967	7.8	−5.0	21.6	13.8
1968	12.6	2.4	24.8	15.4
1969	15.0	12.5	19.9	14.6
1970	7.9	−0.9	18.2	8.9
1971	9.2	3.3	16.9	8.9
1972	7.0	1.7	15.0	5.8

SOURCE: Bank of Korea, *Economic Statistics Yearbook, 1973,* pp. 298–299.

and manufacturing output grew by about 15 percent per annum. By contrast, the period 1958 to 1960 was one of declining GNP growth, averaging less than 4 percent. Since population increased about 2.9 percent per annum, per capita income barely changed. The growth of mining and manufacturing averaged only about 9 percent per annum from 1958 to 1960, less than two-thirds of the rate in the preceding four-year period. One of the causes of the slowdown from 1958 to 1960 was a financial stabilization program that had been forcefully applied in 1957 and 1958.

Most of South Korea's imports from 1953 to 1960 were financed by foreign aid grants from two sources: the United Nations Korea Reconstruction Agency (UNKRA), which had been providing relief through the United Nations Civil Assistance Command in Korea (UNCACK) during the war, and the United States bilateral assistance program. UNKRA assistance from 1953 to 1960 totaled approximately $120 million, and official U.S. aid during the same period amounted to $1,745 million, including $158 million of PL 480 goods. Foreign aid from both UNKRA and the United States was used for importing food and essential industrial raw materials as well as capital goods. Between 1954 and 1960, foreign assistance, excluding donations by foreign voluntary organizations, financed more than 70 percent of total imports. From 1956 to 1958 imports financed by U.S. aid exceeded 80 percent of total imports. About 74 percent of South Korean investment was financed by foreign aid from 1953 to 1960.

Rapid economic growth from 1953 to 1957, largely induced by substantial injections of foreign assistance, was accompanied by rapid inflation (Table 2–5). The wholesale price index increased more than three and one-half times between 1953 and 1957, an average annual rate of inflation of almost 40 percent. Concern with inflation led to an agreement between the South Korean government and the Office of the Economic Coordinator (the U.S. ICA Mission to Korea) on a financial stabilization program which was implemented from 1957. The annual rate of domestic inflation started to decline from that year. Price stability was achieved in 1958–1959 (wholesale prices even declined slightly in 1958). After the student revolution in April 1960, the new government abandoned the stabilization program in its first months in office. Wholesale prices rose by about 11 percent in 1960.

Commodity exports declined substantially during the period of rapid economic growth in the 1950s. By 1957 they were less than one-half the 1953 level in dollar terms (Table 2–6). During the stabilization period, exports began a recovery, but did not reach the 1953 level until 1961. In any case, during the whole period 1953 to 1960, exports of goods and services were negligible, ranging from 1.1 to 2.4 percent of GNP (Table 2–7 and Figure 2–1). Exports continued to be primarily mining, agricultural, and fishing products. Imports of goods and services were substantial, ranging from 8.8 to 14.3 per-

TABLE 2-5

Major Price Indexes at Midyear, 1953 to 1972

(1970 = 100)

Year	GNP Deflator	Wholesale Price Index	Wholesale Price of Foods	Wholesale Price Index Excluding Foods	Seoul Consumer Price Index
1953	5.7	8.2	8.1	8.3	7.5
1954	7.5	10.5	6.5	13.9	10.2
1955	12.4	19.1	15.4	21.5	17.3
1956	16.2	25.1	24.7	26.2	21.2
1957	19.5	29.2	28.4	30.6	26.1
1958	19.4	27.3	23.3	30.3	25.3
1959	19.9	28.0	20.4	32.5	26.4
1960	21.8	31.0	24.4	35.2	28.6
1961	25.1	35.1	28.9	39.0	30.9
1962	28.6	38.4	32.6	41.9	32.9
1963	36.8	46.3	44.8	46.3	39.7
1964	48.6	62.3	61.4	61.5	51.4
1965	52.6	68.5	60.4	73.0	58.4
1966	60.1	74.6	65.3	79.8	65.4
1967	68.5	79.4	70.9	84.1	72.5
1968	76.6	85.8	79.7	89.3	80.6
1969	86.7	91.6	89.3	93.0	88.7
1970	100.0	100.0	100.0	100.0	100.0
1971	111.5	108.6	115.0	105.7	112.3
1972	127.7	123.8	137.5	117.5	125.6

SOURCE: Bank of Korea, *Economic Statistics Yearbook,* pp. 4 and 262–265 in *1973*; pp. 328–329 in *1970*.

a. From 1953 to 1959 these figures are the wholesale price indexes of grains and the wholesale price indexes excluding grains converted from a 1965 to a 1970 base.

cent of GNP or, on the average, almost seven times export earnings. Food grains and manufactured goods were the most important imports.

MILITARY GOVERNMENT, 1961 TO 1963

A military coup in May 1961 overthrew the Chang Myon government that had come to power following the student revolution of April 1960. The military government controlled the economy from May 1961 to the end of 1963. Stagnation developed in the South Korean economy from the spring of 1960

TABLE 2–6

Balance of Payments, 1953 to 1972

(millions of U.S. dollars)

Year	Com- modity[a] Exports	Com- modity Imports	Services Net	Net Goods & Services	Official Grant Aid	Net Capital Inflows	Gold & Foreign Exchange Holdings[b]
1953	40	347	28	−279	193	112	109
1954	24	241	37	−180	139	28	108
1955	18	327	43	−266	240	−3	96
1956	25	380	24	−331	298	14	99
1957	19	390	−17	−388	355	18	116
1958	17	344	16	−311	319	−7	146
1959	20	273	25	−228	229	−17	147
1960	33	305	10	−262	256	−1	157
1961	41	283	44	−198	207	19	207
1962	55	390	43	−292	200	19	169
1963	87	497	7	−403	208	108	131
1964	119	365	25	−221	141	27	136
1965	175	420	46	−199	135	−17	146
1966	250	680	107	−323	122	196	245
1967	335	909	157	−417	135	293	356
1968	486	1,322	170	−666	121	476	391
1969	658	1,650	198	−794	98	717	553
1970	882	1,804	119	−803	82	626	610
1971	1,132	2,178	28	−1,018	64	834	568
1972	1,676	2,250	33	−541	52	330	740

SOURCE: Bank of Korea, *Economic Statistics Yearbook*, pp. 266–267 and p. 271 in *1971*; pp. 222–223 and p. 219 in *1973*.
    a. Customs clearance data f.o.b. includes exports to Viet Nam through U.S. procurement.
    b. End of year figures.

to the early part of 1962, mainly because of the political and social instability that followed two upheavals in a little over a year's time. The military government, anxious to revitalize the economy, adopted a very expansionary set of fiscal and monetary policies. These policies brought back inflation in 1962 which accelerated in 1963 (Table 2–5). From 1960 to 1963 the average rate of inflation was about 15 percent per annum. These same policies, however, stimulated growth. Although 1962 was a bad year for agriculture, mining and manufacturing output increased by 14.1 percent. In the next year, which was good for both agriculture and industry, GNP increased by 8.8 percent.

TABLE 2–7

GNP, Exports, and Imports, 1953 to 1972

(billions of 1970 constant won)

Year	GNP	Exports[a]	Exports[a] as Percent of GNP	Imports[a]	Imports[a] as Percent of GNP	Exports Less Imports
1953	844	17.0	2.0	109.4	12.9	−92.4
1954	890	10.3	1.1	78.1	8.8	−67.8
1955	938	12.9	1.4	104.8	11.2	−91.9
1956	942	11.5	1.2	122.4	13.0	−110.9
1957	1,014	15.6	1.5	144.8	14.3	−129.2
1958	1,067	19.7	1.9	125.3	11.7	−105.6
1959	1,108	22.9	2.1	102.6	9.3	−79.7
1960	1,130	27.4	2.4	117.5	10.4	−90.1
1961	1,184	38.2	3.2	106.6	9.0	−68.4
1962	1,221	43.0	3.5	141.2	11.6	−98.2
1963	1,328	46.2	3.5	179.2	13.5	−133.0
1964	1,442	57.1	4.0	133.3	9.2	−76.2
1965	1,530	80.3	5.2	149.6	9.8	−69.3
1966	1,719	122.3	7.1	237.9	13.8	−115.6
1967	1,853	166.0	8.9	320.7	17.3	−154.7
1968	2,087	235.0	11.3	468.0	22.4	−233.0
1969	2,400	310.1	12.9	583.8	24.3	−273.7
1970	2,589	381.2	14.7	642.4	24.8	−261.2
1971	2,827	459.4	16.3	773.6	27.4	−314.2
1972	3,024	643.3	21.3	801.2	26.5	−157.9

SOURCE: Bank of Korea, *Economic Statistics Yearbook, 1973,* pp. 260–261.

a. Export and import figures are taken from Korea's national income accounts data in 1970 constant prices. Both exports and imports include services and goods.

During 1961 and 1962, the military government enacted many economic reforms including budget and tax reforms, a reform of the foreign exchange control system, and in June 1962 a currency reform.[7] A new budget and accounting law was enacted, and various tax laws were revised to increase domestic tax revenues and, at the same time, to promote business internal saving.

The military government became increasingly concerned about earning foreign exchange and raising domestic savings since U.S. grant aid was reduced after 1960. South Korea's foreign exchange holdings, which had been increasing through 1960, gradually declined from 1961 to 1963 owing to the reduction in U.S. aid and the expansionary policies of the military government (Table 2–6). The government increased controls on imports and imple-

FIGURE 2–1

Behavior of Key Economic Aggregates

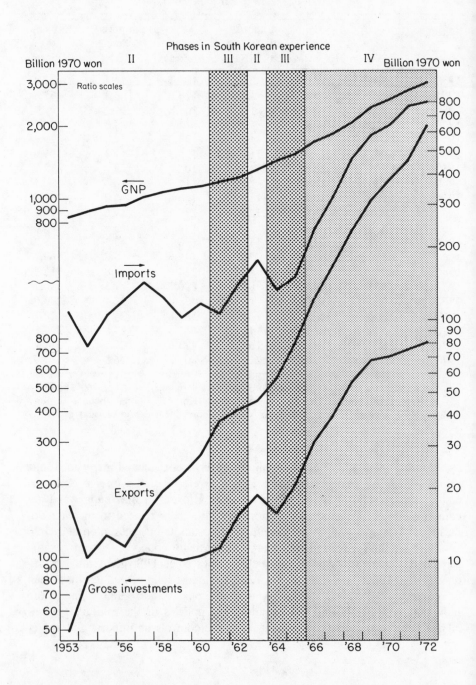

mented export incentive schemes such as tax exemptions. Measures were also taken to encourage the inflow of foreign loans and foreign direct investment. Since domestic savings averaged only 4.3 percent of GNP from 1961 to 1963 (Table 2–8 and Figure 2–1), foreign capital imports and grant aid financed the bulk of investment which was 12 percent of GNP during the period.[8]

Commodity imports declined in 1961, but increased sharply between 1961 and 1963 as the result of the expansionary policies. Export growth was substantial over the period 1961 to 1963; the average annual rate of growth from 1960 to 1963 was about 38 percent. The trade deficit, however, was still very large and grew rapidly from 1961 to 1963. Imports increased from $283

TABLE 2–8

GNP, Domestic Savings, and Gross Investment, 1953 to 1973

Year	GNP (1970 constant billion won)	Domestic Savings[a] (1970 constant billion won)	(percent of GNP)	Gross Investment[b] (1970 constant billion won)	(percent of GNP)
1953	843.5	−32.3	−3.8	49.1	5.8
1954	890.2	24.2	2.7	83.2	9.3
1955	938.2	9.1	1.0	91.9	9.8
1956	942.2	−3.9	−0.4	98.4	10.4
1957	1,014.4	−16.5	−1.6	103.9	10.2
1958	1,067.2	4.4	0.4	101.1	9.5
1959	1,108.3	26.3	2.4	97.0	8.8
1960	1,129.7	19.4	1.7	100.9	8.9
1961	1,184.5	46.9	4.0	108.5	9.2
1962	1,221.0	58.5	4.8	149.2	12.2
1963	1,328.3	55.9	4.2	181.0	13.6
1964	1,442.0	82.6	5.7	151.2	10.5
1965	1,529.7	139.2	9.1	199.5	13.0
1966	1,719.2	201.8	11.7	302.1	17.6
1967	1,853.0	257.5	13.9	387.1	20.9
1968	2,087.1	326.2	15.6	533.2	25.5
1969	2,400.5	408.9	17.0	655.6	27.3
1970	2,589.3	427.9	16.5	677.2	26.2
1971	2,826.8	405.4	14.3	721.6	25.5
1972	3,023.6	467.4	15.5	637.4	21.1
1973	3,522.7	813.5	23.1	893.6	25.4

SOURCE: Bank of Korea.
a. Domestic savings exclude transfers from abroad, and changes in grain inventories which are more a function of the level of the fall harvest than of desired savings in the form of inventories, but include statistical discrepancy.
b. Excludes grain inventory changes.

million to $497 million and the trade deficit from $242 million to $410 million or 15.6 percent of GNP.

Although commodity exports had been growing rapidly since 1959, they started from a very low base and did not become significant until 1963, totalling more than $87 million or about 3.3 percent of GNP. The same year also saw a phenomenal rise in the importance of manufactured exports to more than 50 percent of the total; the major items being plywood, woven cotton fabrics, clothing, and iron and steel.

The First Five-Year Plan announced in 1961 reflected the basic economic policies of the military government. The annual growth target was 7.1 percent for 1962 to 1966. It listed priorities in the following order:

(1) an increase in energy supply, including electric power and coal;
(2) an increase in agricultural production and in farmers' incomes;
(3) expansion of key industries and social overhead capital;
(4) national land conservation and development through utilization of idle resources, particularly manpower;
(5) an improvement in the balance of payments through the expansion of exports;
(6) promotion of technology.

CIVILIAN GOVERNMENT AND ECONOMIC REFORM, 1964 TO 1966

A nominally civilian government emerged from the general election in early 1964 after three years of military government. South Korean GNP continued to grow rapidly from 1964 to 1966, averaging about 9 percent. The rate of inflation in wholesale prices increased to almost 35 percent in 1964, the steepest rise since 1956, but declined to 10 percent in 1965 and to 9 percent in 1966. Rapid economic growth and a reduced rate of inflation in this period were brought about by reforms in 1964 and 1965 and by a stabilization program introduced in late 1963. The main feature of the program was a strict limit on expansion of the money supply, which imposed ceilings on the annual and quarterly increases in the four major sources of "high-powered money," namely, central bank finance of government deficits, bank reserves, fertilizer loans, and foreign sector deposits. Since government deficit financing through central bank channels had been the major factor underlying the monetary expansion in 1961–1963, the government eliminated all deficits from its general budget beginning in 1964 and engaged only in periodic short-term borrowing.

As Chapter 4 explains, the government reformed the exchange rate in 1964 in order to increase incentives for export and to restrain demand for imports. In September 1965, the government announced an interest rate reform that substantially raised interest rates on both bank time deposits and loans. As a result, bank time and savings deposits increased very rapidly, thus enlarging the supply of loanable funds. The interest rate reform, however, created a large interest differential between domestic bank and foreign loans, making the latter particularly attractive.

The government made a serious effort beginning in 1965 to increase tax collections through administrative improvements and minor changes in rates. It also worked out a comprehensive tax reform program in 1966 for implementation in 1967. Government tax revenues gradually expanded from 7.3 percent of GNP in 1964 to 10.8 percent in 1966. Domestic revenues, which had been less than half of total central government revenues until 1958 and about 65 percent in 1964, financed about 75 percent of total central government expenditures in 1966 while counterpart funds originating in U.S. assistance financed the balance.

The ratio of domestic savings to GNP also increased rapidly from 4.2 percent in 1964 to 11.7 percent in 1966. Both private and government savings expanded, the one because of the interest rate reform of 1965 and the other because of the tax drive in 1965 and 1966. The proportion of gross domestic investment financed by domestic saving expanded from 31 percent in 1963 to 66 percent in 1966. The trade balance was also greatly improved, since exports increased continuously by more than 40 percent a year while the rate of increase in imports substantially declined after the devaluation in 1964.

The improvement in the trade balance together with the enlarged inflow of foreign capital brought about a gradual increase in foreign exchange holdings over the period. For this reason, the government gradually loosened import controls.

CONTINUATION OF RAPID GROWTH, 1967 TO 1971

Rapid growth of the economy continued from 1967 to 1971 with considerably more price stability than there had been throughout most of the period since World War II. Basic economic policy was generally guided by the Second Five-Year Plan and the Overall Resources Budget for annual implementation of the plan. For this reason, it is important to present the basic targets and directions of the second plan, announced in mid-1966.

The plan set an annual growth target of 7 percent from 1967 to 1971. The basic objective was "to promote the modernization of the industrial structure and to build the foundations for a self-supporting economy." The plan described the major targets as follows:

(1) The emphasis will be placed on attainment of food self-sufficiency, reforestation, and development of marine resources;

(2) The basis for accelerated and diversified industrialization will be broadened by giving emphasis to investment in such industries as chemicals, machinery, and iron and steel;

(3) Further improvement in the balance of payments situation will be made by achieving a $700 million level of exports (including $550 million commodity exports) in 1971 on the one hand and by promoting import substitution on the other hand;

(4) Population increases will be restricted as much as possible by promoting family planning, while at the same time maximum efforts will be made to increase employment;

(5) A further sharp focus will be placed on increasing farm productivity and income through diversification of farming; and

(6) The level of technology and productivity will be raised by the promotion of scientific and management skills and by improvement of manpower resources.

The actual performance of the economy from 1967 to 1971 far exceeded the original targets in almost all major sectors. The government revised them almost every year through the annual Overall Resources Budget according to actual performance in earlier years and new forecasts.

South Korean real GNP attained an average annual growth rate of more than 10 percent from 1967 to 1971, exceeding the planned figure by a wide margin. Exports of goods and services overshot the original goal by 1968, since both commodity and service exports expanded rapidly owing to an intensified government export drive and an increase in service earnings from construction workers and troops in Viet Nam. The commodity export target which had been set at $550 million for 1971 was actually exceeded by 1969. Commodity exports in 1971 reached $1,132 million and exports of commodities and services exceeded 16 percent of GNP. By 1971, exports of manufactures reached 86.0 percent of total commodity exports. Plywood, woven cotton fabrics, iron and steel, and clothing continued to be major exports. Electrical machinery, footwear, and wigs also became important.

Despite the rapid increase in commodity exports, the trade balance was not significantly improved during this period because of a concomitant increase in imports. The growth of imports reflected gradual over-valuation of the won as domestic prices rose, enlarged inflows of foreign loans, trade liberalization, and increased imports of raw materials for exports. However, South Korea's foreign exchange holdings continued to accumulate rapidly after 1966, mainly because of inflows of both short-term and long-term foreign loans including cash loans beginning in 1965. The rapid accumulation of foreign exchange holdings generated a large expansion in the money supply. Consequently, a major problem in the annual stabilization programs during this period was the neutralization of the additions in bank reserves brought about by the inflow of foreign exchange. The major instruments used to sterilize reserves were increases in bank reserve requirements, compulsory deposits into the Bank of Korea Stabilization Account, and sales of Bank of Korea stabilization bonds.

SLOWDOWN, 1971 TO 1972, NEW REFORMS, AND RECOVERY, 1973

From late 1971 through the first half of 1972, industrial production and construction slowed considerably. Growth of GNP in 1972 fell to 7.0 percent from 9.2 percent in 1971, despite a recovery toward the end of the year. Gross domestic investment, which declined from 25.5 percent of GNP in 1971 to 21.1 percent in 1972, dropped absolutely by about 12 percent. This slowdown was caused to some extent by a slackening in the growth of Korea's major export markets, the United States and Japan. Korean export firms were also hurt by a 10 percent surcharge imposed by the United States on most manufactured imports.

A financial squeeze on a number of South Korean firms was another cause of the slowdown. Many firms that produced primarily for domestic markets had borrowed heavily abroad to finance the import of capital goods for expansion of capacity. As the official rate for the won went from 317 to the dollar in December 1970 to about 400 won by June 1972 and as the Japanese yen and other key currencies appreciated in relation to the dollar in late 1971 and early 1972, the won value of foreign debts held by domestic firms increased by much more between the end of 1970 and mid-1972 than any inflation in profits. Also, many domestic firms had borrowed heavily and on a very short-term basis in the unorganized money markets where rates of interest approached 50 to 60 percent per annum.

The government responded to the problems caused by retarded economic expansion with an Emergency Presidential Decree for Economic Stabilization and Growth dated August 3, 1972. The decree promulgated a set of economic reforms, predicated, for the most part, on the assumption that resumption of rapid economic growth required financial relief for ailing industrial firms. The changes included the following:

(1) Most outstanding unorganized money-market loans to the business sector were converted into medium-term and long-term loans at relatively low interest rates. To enforce this measure, the government required both unofficial moneylenders and debtor firms to report all outstanding loans and debts. All unorganized money-market loans, except small ones of less than 300,000 won,

were frozen for terms ranging from six months to three years, with extended repayment periods after that. During the freeze, debtor firms were to pay only 1.35 percent monthly interest, regardless of the interest rate originally contracted, which generally ranged from 3 to 5 percent per month.

(2) Both bank deposit and loan rates were reduced as of August 3, 1972, the rate on one-year time deposits from 16.8 to 12 percent per annum and the ordinary bank loan rate from 19 to 15.5 percent. In addition, the government granted approximately 200 billion won to the banking system for the replacement of high-interest, short-term loans to the business sector with low-interest, long-term bank loans, and for special long-term loans for specified major industries.

(3) The government authorized special accelerated depreciation rules, allowing 40 to 80 percent more depreciation for specified major industries. In addition, a 10 percent investment credit was granted for new investment in the utilization of domestic resources.

(4) The government announced that the foreign exchange rate would be stabilized at 400 won to the dollar.

The August 1972 reforms marked the beginning of a radically different approach to economic policy in South Korea. From 1964 until 1972, wholesale price inflation had averaged more than 10 percent a year. In the face of this inflation, a number of measures were taken to stimulate savings and use of the banking system and to maintain the international competitiveness of the economy. Most significant of these measures was the maintenance of very high bank deposit rates and frequent devaluations. The new policy stressed price stabilization, low interest rates, and a stable exchange rate. It was recognized, however, that to switch from a regime of rapid inflation, high interest rates, and frequent devaluations to a more stable regime could only be accomplished at the cost of financial disaster for most industrial firms in South Korea, which were heavily indebted, unless special measures were taken. Thus the government sponsored a massive debt roll over, not only of loans in the nationalized banking sector but of private, unorganized money-market loans as well.

The basic plan was to concentrate much of foreseen price increases in 1972 and pursue a rigid stabilization program in 1973. In 1972 utility and fuel prices were raised so that these government monopolies would not require future subsidy. As of August 1972, however, the government announced that utility prices would be frozen indefinitely. The money supply increased sharply in the last half of 1972 as credit was expanded to accommodate the internal debt roll over, but the government announced a price stabilization plan for 1973 which included limited increases in the money supply and a reduction in the rate of growth of government expenditures. The government pledged its efforts to hold the rate of inflation of wholesale prices to 3 percent or less.

Many of the government pronouncements were aimed at cutting expectations of future price increases which, if successful, was expected to help stabilization.

Although GNP grew slowly in 1972, exports increased sharply, by 48 percent, from $1,132 million in 1971 to $1,676 million. Imports, however, grew only 3.5 percent in 1972, compared with a 21 percent increase in the previous year. Since service receipts also expanded rapidly because of increased tourism, the overall balance of payments deficit on current account (net goods and services) was reduced from $1,018 million in 1971 to $541 million in 1972. Gold and foreign exchange reserves reached $740 million at the end of the year, an increase of about $170 million over 1971.

This improvement in the balance of payments was made possible by the combination of two factors: (1) Enhanced international competitiveness of Korean industries due to gradual devaluation of the won from 317 to about 400 to the dollar between December 1970 and June 1972, and the relative appreciation of the Japanese yen and other key currencies based on the Smithsonian Agreement; and (2) the slowdown in domestic economic activities which not only reduced the demand for imports but also induced domestic industries to expand into foreign markets.

In 1973, the growth of real GNP increased to 16.5 percent. The mining and manufacturing sectors grew about 30 percent while exports exceeded the previous year's total by nearly 100 percent. The price stabilization plan, however, was endangered by very high prices for imported fuels, grains, and industrial raw materials.

The continued growth of the economy of South Korea and its export potential seem to be assumed among South Korean government officials and businessmen. They often talk of GNP of $1,000 per capita and exports exceeding $10 billion by the early 1980s. If the performance over the last decade continues unabated, these optimistic expectations are certain to be fulfilled.

NOTES

1. Only the manufacturing establishments whose capital exceeded one million won are included in this estimate. The total authorized capital of such companies in Korea at the end of 1940 amounted to approximately 1,725 million won. See the Bank of Korea, *Annual Economic Review of Korea,* 1948, pp. 1–100.

2. Ibid.

3. Money supply figures for this period, including bank deposits, are not available. But according to the end-of-year money supply estimated by the Bank of Korea in 1955, currency in circulation gradually declined from 74 percent of the money supply in 1945 to 58 percent in 1949.

4. These dollar values of exports and imports were estimated by applying the average official exchange rate of 0.68 won to one U.S. dollar in 1949 to the current price won values of exports and imports in Table 2–3.

5. Exports for 1950 were inflated because of large exports by consignment from Pusan to Japan just after the outbreak of war. Thus the decline between 1950 and 1951 is somewhat overstated.

6. Nathan and Associates (1954) estimated South Korea's GNP for 1952 and 1953 at $1,384 million and $1,721 million.

7. The currency denomination was changed from hwan to won at 10:1.

8. Both domestic savings and gross investment discussed in this chapter are exclusive of grain inventory changes.

Chapter 3

Development of the Trading and Exchange Rate System: Phase I, 1945 to 1953, and Phase II, 1953 to 1960

After World War II and during the Korean War, private foreign trade was almost nonexistent apart from a small amount of private barter. The government was the major exporter of a limited range of primary products, and imports were strictly controlled. Nearly all imports were financed by grant assistance or won redemptions by the United Nations Command during the Korean War, and the government itself was the major importer both before and during the war. A multiplicity of exchange rates applied to a variety of transactions, and a black market in U.S. currency and military payment certificates flourished. By the end of the Korean War, the official exchange rate represented a serious over-valuation of the won despite six major devaluations since 1945. The official rate applied to a very narrow range of transactions and was less than one-quarter of the free market rate on export dollars. We would describe the period 1945 to 1953 as a Bhagwati-Krueger Phase I regime "characterized by heavy reliance on quantitative controls leading to an increasingly over-valued exchange rate."

The first six or seven years after the Korean War brought sporadic growth of real GNP, widely fluctuating exports, rapidly growing imports, and an increasing trade deficit financed by UN and U.S. grant assistance. The trade and payments regime required increasingly complex measures to obviate an over-valued exchange rate.

The multiplicity of exchange rates increased after the war. Rates on foreign exchange loans varied by type of commodity imported. Foreign exchange certificates issued for earning exchange through exports were traded on the free market and resulted in separate rates for a variety of types of export, the most important distinction being drawn between Japanese export dollars and other export dollars. Foreign exchange was allocated by various auction and bidding procedures, by lottery, and by an exchange tax system. Advance deposits were required for certain imports.

A variety of export promotion schemes was used during this period: a deposit system to avoid exchange risk, an export-import link system, direct export subsidies, a variety of preferential loans for exporters and export producers, and tariff exemptions. An increasingly complex system for import quotas evolved and tariffs were raised in 1957. Thus the period 1953 to 1960 can be described, in terms of the Bhagwati-Krueger scheme, as Phase II. In this chapter we attempt to describe the trade and exchange regime during the Phase I period, 1945–1953, and the Phase II period that followed.

DEVELOPMENT OF THE BARTER SYSTEM, 1946 TO 1953

In 1946 and 1947, barter trade took place at South Korean ports between foreign merchants (mainly Chinese from Hong Kong and Macao) and Korean exporters. The Koreans, who lacked both experience and capital, acted mainly as brokers for the foreign merchants.

In June 1947, the Chosun Exchange Bank was established for the purpose of stimulating and facilitating private foreign trade. One technique was to encourage the evolution of barter trade into a more efficient form of trade called "trust shipping." Under this system, an exporter submits the documents for export goods (after shipment is made) to the Chosun Exchange Bank. Having collected 10 percent of the value of the goods as a guarantee, the bank delivers the shipping documents to the skipper of the ship. He in turn hands them to a foreign exchange bank in the importing country which passes them on to the importer. Once the importer sells the goods, he buys and ships the goods ordered by the Korean exporter for importation into South Korea and submits the shipping documents to a foreign exchange bank in his country. The shipping documents are then delivered to the exporter through Chosun Exchange Bank channels and his 10 percent guarantee deposit is returned.

The Chosun Exchange Bank established relations with foreign exchange banks in other countries and developed a variety of additional trade settlement procedures. In 1949, South Korea's trade with Japan began to be settled by back-to-back letters of credit (L/Cs) and escrow L/Cs, which were means of assisting barter trade through commercial banks. In the case of back-to-back L/Cs, a Korean exporter, upon receiving notice of a bank letter of credit from importer A in Japan, opened a reciprocal L/C to A in Japan on the basis of the original L/C. Thus the Korean exporter could use his export proceeds only for importing from A in Japan. The escrow L/C method allowed the exporter to use his export proceeds for importing from traders other than A in Japan. The Korean exporter deposited his export proceeds into an escrow account in Japan and was able to use the deposit to pay for his imports from any Japanese trader. In June 1950, the Korea-Japan Open Account was established in accordance with the "Financial Agreement for Trade" between the Republic of Korea and Occupied Japan. South Korea's trade with Japan was settled through the Open Account without any foreign exchange payment until a deficit of $2.5 million was accumulated. After establishment of the Open Account, South Korea's trade with Japan became more important than its trade with Hong Kong, and the trade settlement method was changed to a regular L/C basis.

The sudden outbreak of war on June 25, 1950 reduced foreign trade for some time. Export goods stocked at Pusan were shipped to Japan on consignment, but other export activity virtually ceased because of war damage, transportation bottlenecks, domestic inflation, and other economic disruptions. Though there was practically no private import trade in the latter part of 1950, it became very active in 1951 when the government began to encourage imports to meet wartime shortages.

THE BANK OF KOREA, 1950

In 1950, the Chosun Exchange Bank was absorbed by the newly formed Bank of Korea. The Bank of Korea Law promulgated a new foreign exchange control system that required all private foreign exchange holdings to be deposited at the Bank of Korea where they were insured against exchange loss through their denomination in dollars.

Foreign exchange deposit accounts were classified into four categories: government, export, general, and special. Government accounts received deposits of government-owned foreign exchange. Export accounts contained deposits of foreign exchange by registered exporters and industrial end-users who had acquired foreign exchange through auctions and loans from the Bank of Korea. General accounts held deposits by foreign diplomatic organizations, foreign firms, religious organizations, and individual foreigners and residents approved by the Monetary Board. Special accounts were established for deposits of U.S. currency and military payment certificates.

The Bank of Korea generated foreign exchange assets of its own through dollar redemption of won advances made to UN forces during the Korean War, and through foreign exchange earnings from tungsten exports, the sale of which was a government monopoly. Redemption of won advances by the United Nations Command was the most important source of foreign exchange during the Korean War. Foreign exchange from this source amounted to $62 million in 1952 and $122 million in 1953, or about 62 and 70 percent of total foreign exchange receipts in those years. In addition to receiving foreign exchange from these two sources, the Bank of Korea acted as a broker for the sale of U.S. aid dollars for imports of private-use commodities after the Korean War.[1]

EXCHANGE RATES, 1945 TO 1963

The first official rate was set at 0.015 won[2] to one U.S. dollar in October 1945, equivalent to the yen exchange rate in Japan. It was raised to 0.05 won to the dollar in July 1947. The official rate did not apply to private trade during most of the period; rather, trade was conducted through the deposit system of the Bank of Korea which involved dollar-denominated deposits. In any case, most trade was barter. The official rate applied only to settlements of military government liabilities against the private sector and other minor transactions until late 1952 when it was extended to some private transactions.

As tables 3–1 and 3–2 show, the official exchange rate was adjusted many times as domestic prices rose rapidly between 1945 and 1953. Despite these frequent adjustments, the price-deflated exchange rate exhibited no noticeable trend because of the rapid inflation. The price-deflated rate reached a peak of about 252 won to the dollar (in 1965 won) in early 1949 and another peak in May–June of 1950,[3] but the price-deflated rate during the Korean War and even after the December 1953 devaluation of 300 percent was far below its prewar highs.

From December 1948, a separate exchange rate was established for depositing won into the Counterpart Fund Special Account, in accordance with the "Agreement on Aid between the United States and the Republic of Korea," signed on December 10, 1948.

Under the original "Agreement between the Government of U.S.A. and the ROKG Regarding Expenditures by Forces under Command of the Commanding General, Armed Forces of the Member States of the United Nations," won advances to UN forces for local currency expenditures were to be repaid in dollars by the United Nations Command (UNC) at the official exchange rate effective on the date of such advances from the Bank of Korea. Although the agreement applied to advances made from the time the agreement was signed in July 1950, not many redemptions occurred until the "Agreement on Economic Coordination between the· ROK and the Unified Command" was signed in May 1952. Even after that, the redemption of won advances was delayed, mainly because of a dispute between the Korean Government and United Nations Command over the applicable exchange rate.[4]

In February 1953, however, a new agreement stipulated that new won advances would be redeemed within 20 days of the month following an advance. The Combined Economic Board (CEB), which had been established in accordance with the Agreement on Economic Coordination, settled on an exchange rate of 18 won to the dollar for the redemption of won advances made prior to January 7, 1953. The CEB also agreed to readjust the exchange rate on won advances whenever increases in domestic prices made the rate unrealistic. Generally, the exchange rate applied to redemption of won advances was negotiated with each particular redemption. Negotiated rates were usually more favorable to the United Nations Command than the official exchange rate but much lower than the free market rates.

ALLOCATION OF FOREIGN EXCHANGE AND MULTIPLE RATES, 1952 TO 1960

The large inflow of U.S. grant aid, United Nations Korean Reconstruction Agency (UNKRA) assistance, and government receipts of foreign exchange from United Nations Command (UNC) sources created difficulties in allocating foreign exchange to various industrial sectors that lasted for some time after the war. Since private exports were very small compared with total receipts of foreign exchange, most imports in the 1950s had to be financed either by U.S. aid or by government-held foreign exchange (KFX).

UNKRA and U.S. aid (excluding technical assistance) amounted to approximately $1.9 billion, or about 72 percent of total imports from 1953 to 1960. Of this amount, a large proportion was allocated to private traders and end-users for imports of raw materials, semifinished products and investment goods. In addition to this official aid fund for commercial imports, the government allocated a large amount of government-held KFX to private traders and industries for commercial imports. The UNC also sold dollars directly to the private sector as a means of procuring won currency from November 1954 to August 1955. The major means of allocation in the early post-Korean War period was a system of special foreign exchange loans and a bidding system for sales of KFX and UNC and U.S. aid dollars.

Special foreign exchange loans to private traders, first instituted in December 1952, were finally discontinued in July 1954. Loans totaled approximately $96.1 million and financed about 45 percent of total imports (or 75 percent of private imports) in the same period. The special foreign exchange loans were financed mainly by foreign exchange receipts from redemption of won advances and tungsten exports. There were two different special loan funds. The first was allocated by industry to exporters and raw material end-users on the basis of export performance and raw material needs. The

TABLE 3–1

Nominal Exchange Rates of Won to U.S. Dollar in South Korea, 1945 to 1970

(current won to the U.S. dollar)

Effective Date	Agreed Rates			Free Market Rates[a]					Wholesale Price Index[e] (1965 = 100)
	Official Exchange Rate	Counterpart Deposit Rate	UN Finance Office[b]	Japan Export Dollars[c]	Other Export Dollars[c]	Other Dollars on Import A/C[d]	U.S. Greenbacks	MPC	
Oct. 1, 1945	0.015	—	—	—	—	—	—	—	0.016
July 15, 1947	0.05	—	—	—	—	—	—	—	0.171
Oct. 1, 1948	0.44	—	—	—	—	—	0.74	0.5	0.297
Dec. 15, 1948	0.45	0.45	—	—	—	—	na	na	0.327
June 14, 1949	0.9	0.45	—	—	—	—	2.17	1.64	0.357
Nov. 1, 1949	0.9	0.5	—	—	—	—	2.55	1.93	0.475
Dec. 1, 1949	0.9	0.6	—	—	—	—	2.83	2.31	0.511
Jan. 1, 1950	0.9	0.8	—	—	—	—	3.48	2.57	0.565
Apr. 1, 1950	0.9	0.9	—	—	—	—	2.98	2.35	0.597
May 1, 1950	1.8	1.1	—	—	—	—	2.28	2.03	0.592
May 15, 1950	1.6	1.1	—	—	—	—	2.28	2.03	0.592
June 10, 1950	1.6	1.4	—	—	—	—	2.42	1.79	0.615
June 15, 1950	1.8	1.4	—	—	—	—	2.42	1.79	0.615
June 25, 1950	1.8	1.8	—	—	—	—	2.42	1.79	0.615
Oct. 1, 1950	1.8	2.5	2.5	—	—	—	2.58	2.27	1.11
Nov. 1, 1950	2.5	2.5	2.5	—	—	—	3.42	3.32	1.27
Dec. 1, 1950	2.5	4.0	2.5	—	—	—	6.12	4.32	1.47
Mar. 11, 1951	2.5	4.0	6.0	—	—	—	na	na	2.77
May 1, 1951	2.5	6.0	6.0	—	—	—	9.83	6.38	2.74
Nov. 10, 1951	6.0	6.0	6.0	—	—	—	18.21	12.85	4.52
Avg. 1952	6.0	6.0	6.0	—	—	—	na	na	8.41
Aug. 28, 1953	6.0	18.0	18.0	—	—	—	26.4	17.6	10.8
Dec. 15, 1953	18.0	18.0	18.0	—	—	—	38.7	29.3	11.8

Nov. 10, 1954	18.0	18.0	77.7	74.0	51.5	65.6	53.0	17.3
Dec. 13, 1954	18.0	31.0	80.9	78.0	65.4	71.1	57.6	17.8
Jan. 10, 1955	35.0	43.0	92.3	83.5	59.8	77.2	62.9	23.6
Apr. 18, 1955	35.0	50.0	75.6	46.6	46.6	74.8	60.5	24.1
June 27, 1955	35.0	48.0	80.2	56.3	59.0	75.3	57.7	27.7
Aug. 8, 1955	35.0	51.0	95.0	82.0	75.0	80.2	66.2	32.3
Aug. 15, 1955	50.0	50.0	95.0	82.0	75.0	80.2	66.2	32.3
Avg. 1956	50.0	—	107.0	100.8	84.7	96.6	81.0	36.6
Avg. 1957	50.0	—	112.3	105.7	84.5	103.3	84.5	42.5
Avg. 1958	50.0	—	122.5	101.5	89.3	118.1	102.9	39.9
Avg. 1959	50.0	—	139.9	124.7	113.5	125.5	114.9	40.8
Jan. 20, 1960	50.0	50.0	164.1	132.0	119.0	132.0	122.3	42.4
Feb. 23, 1960	65.0	65.0	171.8	138.7	129.3	144.9	129.2	43.2
Jan. 1, 1961	100.0	100.0	156.3	141.6	132.0	139.8	120.6	48.2
Feb. 2, 1961	130.0	130.0	147.9	145.4	—	148.3	128.9	50.6
Avg. 1962	130.0	130.0	NT	NT	—	134.0	126.5	56.0
Avg. 1963	130.0	130.0	169.8		—	174.5	147.8	67.5
May 3, 1964	256.5	256.5	314.0		—	285.6	236.2	95.0
Mar. 22, 1965	256.5	256.5	279.0		—	316.0	263.0	97.0
Avg. 1966	271.3	271.3			—	302.7	277.3	108.8
Avg. 1967	270.7	270.7			—	301.8	276.3	115.8
Avg. 1968	276.6	276.6			—	304.1	278.1	125.2
Avg. 1969	288.2	288.2			—	323.6	302.1	133.7
Avg. 1970	310.7	310.7			—	342.8	333.2	145.9

NOTE: MPC—military payment certificates; na—not available; NT—no transactions.

SOURCE: Bank of Korea; Korean Traders Association; USAID, Korea Mission.

a. Monthly and annual averages.

b. Rate applied from Oct. 1, 1950 to Aug. 15, 1955; rate paid UN soldiers raised to 50 won Nov. 10, 1954; rate for other UN transactions raised to 31 won Dec. 13, 1954; the two rates made identical Jan. 10, 1955.

c. Figures represent: nonpreferential dollar rate until 1955; export dollar rate on L/Cs, Dec. 1955 to Jan. 1961; and the rate on export dollar certificates, Feb. 1961 to May 1961. Export dollar rate from 1963 represents the effective free market rate (i.e., the official rate plus export premium). Export premium market ended with exchange rate reform, March 1965.

d. Separate rate on missionary and service dollars effective from Sept. 1954 to Jan. 1961.

e. Seoul index, 1945 to 1954; national index thereafter. Monthly and annual averages.

31

TABLE 3–2

Price-Level-Deflated Exchange Rates of Won to U.S. Dollar in South Korea, 1945 to 1970

(1965 constant won to the U.S. dollar)

Effective Date	Agreed Rates			Free Market Rates[a]				
	Official Exchange Rate	Counterpart Deposit Rate	UN Finance Office[b]	Japan Export Dollars[e]	Other Export Dollars[e]	Other Dollars on Import A/C[d]	U.S. Greenbacks	MPC
Oct. 1, 1945	93.8	—	—	—	—	—	—	—
July 15, 1947	29.2	—	—	—	—	—	—	—
Oct. 1, 1948	148.1	—	—	—	—	—	249.2	168.4
Dec. 15, 1948	137.6	137.6	—	—	—	—	na	na
June 14, 1949	252.1	126.1	—	—	—	—	607.8	459.4
Nov. 1, 1949	189.4	105.3	—	—	—	—	536.8	406.3
Dec. 1, 1949	176.1	117.4	—	—	—	—	553.8	452.1
Jan. 1, 1950	159.3	141.6	—	—	—	—	615.9	454.9
April 1, 1950	150.8	150.8	—	—	—	—	499.2	393.6
May 1, 1950	304.1	185.8	—	—	—	—	385.1	342.9
May 15, 1950	270.3	185.8	—	—	—	—	385.1	342.9
June 10, 1950	260.2	227.6	—	—	—	—	393.5	291.1
June 15, 1950	292.7	227.6	—	—	—	—	393.5	291.1
June 25, 1950	292.7	292.7	—	—	—	—	393.5	291.1
Oct. 1, 1950	162.2	225.2	225.2	—	—	—	232.4	204.5
Nov. 1, 1950	196.9	196.9	196.9	—	—	—	269.3	261.4
Dec. 1, 1950	170.1	272.1	170.1	—	—	—	416.3	293.9
Mar. 11, 1951	90.3	144.4	216.6	—	—	—	na	na
May 1, 1951	91.2	219.0	219.0	—	—	—	358.8	232.0
Nov. 10, 1951	132.7	132.7	132.7	—	—	—	402.9	284.3
Avg. 1952	71.3	71.3	71.3	—	—	—	na	na
Aug. 28, 1953	55.6	166.7	166.7	—	—	—	244.4	163.0
Dec. 15, 1953	152.5	152.5	152.5	—	—	—	328.0	248.3

32

Nov. 10, 1954	104.0	104.0	104.0	449.1	427.7	427.7	379.2
Dec. 13, 1954	101.1	101.1	174.2	454.4	438.2	367.4	299.4
Jan. 10, 1955	76.3	148.3	182.2	391.1	353.8	253.4	327.1
Apr. 18, 1955	74.6	145.2	207.5	313.7	193.4	193.4	310.4
June 27, 1955	65.0	126.4	173.3	289.5	203.2	213.0	271.8
Aug. 8, 1955	55.7	108.4	157.9	294.1	253.9	232.2	248.3
Aug. 15, 1955	154.8	154.8	154.8	294.1	253.9	232.2	248.3
Avg. 1956	136.6	136.6	—	292.3	275.4	231.4	263.9
Avg. 1957	117.6	117.6	—	264.2	248.7	198.8	243.1
Avg. 1958	125.3	125.3	—	307.1	254.4	223.8	296.0
Avg. 1959	122.5	122.5	—	342.9	305.6	278.2	307.6
Jan. 20, 1960	117.9	153.3	—	387.0	311.3	280.7	311.3
Feb. 23, 1960	150.5	150.5	—	397.6	321.1	299.3	335.4
Jan. 1, 1961	207.5	207.5	—	324.3	293.8	273.9	290.0
Feb. 2, 1961	256.9	256.9	—	292.3	287.4	—	293.1
Avg. 1962	232.1	232.1	NT	NT	NT	—	239.3
Avg. 1963	192.6	192.6	251.6	—	—	—	258.5
May 3, 1964	270.0	270.0	330.5	—	—	—	300.6
Mar. 22, 1965	264.5	264.5	287.6	—	—	—	325.8
Avg. 1966	249.4	249.4	—	—	—	—	278.2
Avg. 1967	233.8	233.8	—	—	—	—	260.6
Avg. 1968	220.9	220.9	—	—	—	—	242.9
Avg. 1969	215.6	215.6	—	—	—	—	242.0
Avg. 1970	213.0	213.0	—	—	—	—	235.0

Final column:

Nov. 10, 1954	306.4
Dec. 13, 1954	323.6
Jan. 10, 1955	266.5
Apr. 18, 1955	251.0
June 27, 1955	208.3
Aug. 8, 1955	205.0
Aug. 15, 1955	205.0
Avg. 1956	221.3
Avg. 1957	198.8
Avg. 1958	257.9
Avg. 1959	281.6
Jan. 20, 1960	288.4
Feb. 23, 1960	299.1
Jan. 1, 1961	250.2
Feb. 2, 1961	254.7
Avg. 1962	225.9
Avg. 1963	219.0
May 3, 1964	248.6
Mar. 22, 1965	271.1
Avg. 1966	254.9
Avg. 1967	238.6
Avg. 1968	222.1
Avg. 1969	226.0
Avg. 1970	228.4

NOTE: MPC—military payment certificates; na—not available; NT—no transactions. These figures are the nominal exchange rates shown in Table 3–1 deflated by the wholesale price index (1965=100) included in the same table.

SOURCE: Bank of Korea; Korean Traders Association; USAID, Korean Mission.

a. Monthly and annual averages.

b. Rate applied from Oct. 1, 1950 to Aug. 15, 1955; rate paid UN soldiers raised to 50 won Nov. 10, 1954; rate for other UN transactions raised to 31 won Dec. 13, 1954; the two rates made identical Jan. 10, 1955.

c. Figures represent: nonpreferential dollar rate until 1955; export dollar rate on L/Cs, Dec. 1955 to Jan. 1961; and the rate on export dollar certificates, Feb. 1961 to May 1961. Export dollar rate from 1963 represents the effective free market rate (i.e., the official rate plus export premium). Export premium market ended with exchange rate reform, March 1965.

d. Separate rate on missionary and service dollars effective from Sept. 1954 to Jan. 1961.

second was allocated to major domestic industries for imports of capital goods. The loans were to be repaid in dollars after 60 days for imports from Japan and after 90 days for imports from other areas.

In the allocation of special foreign exchange loans, borrowers were required to make an initial deposit at the Bank of Korea in won equal to the loan at the official exchange rate. In the case of the first special loan fund, when shipping documents were delivered, the borrowers were required to make an additional deposit equal to the difference between the official exchange rate and a special rate for each commodity, depending on the domestic-price/import-price ratio. These special rates ranged from 15.5 to 29.6 won to the dollar compared with an official rate of 6.0 won to the dollar from November 1952 until the end of the war in 1953. The official exchange rate was applied in the case of the second loan fund.

From August 1953, however, all applicants to the first loan fund were required to deposit 20 won per dollar and those to the second loan fund 18 won per dollar at the time of loan allocation. In addition to these requirements, first loan fund applicants were to make a one-year time deposit of 4 won per dollar and second loan fund applicants were to make a notice deposit of 4 won per dollar.

After this system was discontinued, foreign exchange was allocated by competitive bidding. Bidding accomplished the sale of $5 million of KFX on October 18, 1954 and of nearly $40 million of UNC and U.S. military aid dollars from November 29, 1954 to August 8, 1955. In 1954, bids for won per dollar ranged from 46.1 to 69.3 won while the official rate remained at 18.

From August 29, 1955 until May 1957, the official means of allocating KFX was by lottery at the official exchange rate. From May 1957 to August 1958 a modified bidding system was reestablished. Foreign exchange was allocated to those applicants who offered the largest advance won deposits when the total amount of such advances was equal to or less than the total amount of foreign exchange to be allocated at the official exchange rate. If total advance deposits exceeded the won equivalent of the total value of foreign exchange to be allocated, allocation was first made to industrial end-users and traders with a past record of importing respective commodity items in the allocation of U.S. aid, nonproject dollars. Remaining funds were then allocated to other applicants, with priority given to those who were willing to purchase the most national bonds.

After August 1958, the bidding system of allocating foreign exchange was replaced by a combined foreign exchange tax and bidding system in accordance with the Temporary Foreign Exchange Tax Law of 1958. Under the tax system, a basic tax rate of 15 won per dollar was applied to *all* foreign exchange purchases. In the allocation of foreign exchange for commercial imports only, foreign exchange was allocated to those applicants who paid the biggest additional tax (above the basic rate) by using a competitive bidding system. Only licensed exporters and importers were eligible for the foreign exchange sales while industrial end-users were not.

These complicated methods of allocating foreign exchange created an effective exchange rate for most imports that was substantially above the official rate. The major exception was in the allocation of project-related U.S. aid funds where the counterpart deposit rate was applied. The exchange rate for counterpart deposits was almost the same as the official exchange rate except for the first eight months of 1955 (Table 3–1).

For some time after the Korean War the official exchange rate was only applicable to government transactions, project-related foreign assistance, sales of foreign exchange to students studying abroad, and after August 1955, sales of won to the United Nations Command. The official rate was, however, important to the South Korean government since it was the rate applied to won redemptions from and won sales to the United Nations Command. For this reason, the government resisted devaluation of the official exchange rate. Strong pressure was applied, however, by the United States, using its leverage by delaying release of aid funds and special foreign exchange stabilization grants as incentives to devaluation. The result of all this pressure was two big devaluations. The official exchange rate was raised from 6.0 won to the dollar to 18.0 won on December 15, 1953. The rate of 18.0 won to the dollar was maintained through August 15, 1955, when the rate was changed to 50.0 won. The official rate of 50.0 won was in effect until February 1960 (Table 3–1), when it was raised to 65.0 won to the dollar.

Special exchange rates applied to export earnings. The rates on exports were much better for exporters than the official rate. These rates emerged because of import entitlements attached to certificates earned for exports to various areas under various types of financing. The certificates were traded in a free market.

Two basic rates applied to export earnings: one on Japan export dollars usable only for imports from Japan and another on other export dollars. The free market rate on foreign exchange earned from exports to Japan was higher than the rate on foreign exchange earned from export to other countries, as shown in Table 3–1. The difference was caused by government attempts to limit imports from Japan to the amount earned from exports there.

The difference between Japan and other export dollars was even further accentuated. A higher free market rate prevailed for preferential export dollars (those linked to imports of popular items) than for general export dollars from 1953 to August 1955. A higher rate also prevailed for export dollars on a letter of credit (L/C) basis than on export dollars on a documents-against-payment (D/P) basis from August 1955 to January 1961. The free market rates on Japan and other export dollars shown in the table represent the rates on nonpreferential export dollars through August 1955 and thereafter rates on export dollars on an L/C basis.

In addition to export dollar rates, there was a free market rate on dollars used for missionary transactions and service payments and receipts[5] which was much lower than the rate on export dollars.

Multiple exchange rates on export and other dollars were formed in the curb markets prior to 1957 and the system was given legal support from December 1957 onwards. In other words, the Monetary Board ruled that foreign exchange could formally be transferred from one trader's import account in the Bank of Korea to another's, and that missionary dollars could be transferred to export accounts with the government's approval. Starting in December 1957, the Bank of Korea actually acted as a broker for transactions of privately owned foreign exchange at the market exchange rate.

The multiplicity of exchange rates and means of allocating foreign exchange from 1953 to 1960 is staggering to comprehend: special foreign exchange loans of two types, bidding, lottery, foreign exchange tax systems, won redemption rates, a counterpart deposit rate, a variety of export dollar rates, special rates for missionary transactions, and prior to August 1955, two rates for sales of won by the Bank of Korea to the UNC, one for conversion of UN soldiers' pay and another for all other transactions. Other rates shown in Table 3–1 are black market rates for U.S. currency and U.S. military payment certificates (MPC).

TARIFFS

In 1946, a uniform tariff rate of 10 percent was imposed by the United States Military Government on all imports except those financed by foreign assistance. In early 1949, the government began a tariff reform program that culminated in a new law on customs duties effective January 1950. The aims of the new system were to increase government tariff revenue and to provide greater protection for domestic industries. The new customs code listed more than a thousand import items and specified the tariff rate applicable to each. The new simple average of all tariff rates was around 40 percent. The basic structure of tariff rates was as follows:

(1) no duties on food grains and noncompetitive equipment and raw material imports required for industrial, educational, cultural, and sanitation facilities;

(2) a 10 percent duty on essential goods for which domestic production was small relative to demand and on unfinished goods not produced in Korea;

(3) a 20 percent duty on unfinished goods produced in Korea;

(4) a 30 percent duty on finished goods not produced in Korea;
(5) a 40 percent duty on finished goods produced in Korea;
(6) 50 to 90 percent duties on semiluxury goods; and
(7) more than 100 percent duty on luxury goods.

Under the new tariff system, the same tariff rates applied to both commercial and aid-financed imports after September 1950. Duties from aid-financed imports became an important source of government revenue during and after the Korean War.

In 1952, the government announced tariff exemptions on imports of machinery and equipment required for certain major industries, including electric power, shipbuilding, metal working, machinery, chemicals, oil refining, textiles, mining, and fishing. For the shipbuilding, machinery, and mining industries, tariff exemptions were expanded to imports of required raw materials.

In 1957, changes in tariff rates resulted in a 4.1 percentage point increase in the simple average rate. Since the structure of domestic production changed significantly after 1950, some adjustments of tariff rates were made to protect domestic industries. The basic structure of tariff rates remained the same, however: lower rates on raw materials than on semifinished goods, and lower rates on noncompetitive finished goods than on competitive finished goods.

IMPORT CONTROLS

An import and export licensing system was instituted in April 1946. The stated purpose of the system was to prevent the import of nonessential goods and the export of essential domestic products. Until the import quota system was adopted in February 1949, the government simply announced imports that could be licensed and those that were prohibited. There was no attempt to control the quantity of any imports which could be licensed.

When the import quota system was instituted, the government began to control both the types and quantities of imports on the basis of a comprehensive commodity demand and supply program. The quota system was applied quarterly from 1949 to 1953 and semiannually after November 1953. Importable commodities were classified at three levels (section, group, and item). Substitution of item quotas within the same group was usually possible with the approval of the Ministry of Commerce and Industry. Import quotas were also specified separately with respect to imports from Japan and imports from other areas.

After devaluation in August 1955, the Ministry of Finance announced that the import quota system would be replaced by a more flexible system of import licensing. The semiannual trade program which was subsequently drawn up contained a list of items that could be imported under license. In 1956 the program included a list of automatically approved items for which licenses would be issued by the Ministry of Finance without authorization by the Ministry of Commerce and Industry (MCI). The program also listed restricted items that did require the MCI's permission. Items that were neither restricted nor automatically approved were presumed to be prohibited from import. In the trade program for the first half of 1957, the government added many new items for import and included a detailed specification for each imported item.

The trade program was applicable only to South Korea's normal trade transactions, and excluded United States aid-financed imports. Such imports were administered by the Ministry of Reconstruction in accordance with the annual project and nonproject assistance programs agreed upon between the South Korean government and the USAID mission. Therefore, the Ministry of Commerce and Industry had to prepare the semiannual trade program in coordination with the U.S. commodity assistance program.

EXPORT PROMOTION

The multiple exchange rate system, which favored exporting, arose from the grant of import entitlements to holders of foreign exchange earned by export, or from the export-import link system as it is known in South Korea. The first such scheme was the preferential export system adopted in June 1951. Under this system, exporters of so-called nonessential domestic products[6] were given the right to use 1 to 10 percent (average 5 percent) of export earnings for importing about 40 different popular items not normally approved for import. The system was reinforced in 1953 and early in 1955 by increasing the proportion of export earnings that could be used for importing popular items. The system was abolished in late 1955.

After 1955, the multiple exchange rate system was maintained by sales of dollar-denominated deposits held by exporters in the Bank of Korea. With the dollar deposit system, exporters were insured against exchange risk, since their foreign exchange earnings took the form of dollar-denominated deposits at the Bank of Korea. Deposits could be sold to importers at a market price, generally higher than the official exchange rate. The deposit system was abandoned in 1961 when attempts were made to unify the exchange rate.

In addition to the multiple exchange rate system, exports were favored through tariff exemptions on imports of raw materials (as of 1959), direct subsidies for some exports, and preferential credit. On January 20, 1955, the Ministry of Commerce and Industry announced the provision of 3.9 million won for export subsidies in that year. Export subsidies were paid on five items:

50 won per ton of kaolin exports, 42.5 won per ton of agalmatolite, 100 won per ton of flourite, 1,500 won per ton of dried anchovy, and 700 won per ton of dried fish. In 1956, export subsidies were suspended when the government failed to provide for them in the budget. The export subsidy regulation was not implemented until 1961 when an allowance was made in the budget.

Exporters also received preferential credit terms on trade credits (credits which enable exporters to receive payment in local currency before delivery to final users in importing countries), foreign exchange loans for importing capital goods and raw materials, and production loans in local currency. Trade credits for exports were given preference in the allocation of domestic loans and were managed outside the quarterly loan ceilings which were part of the price stabilization efforts of the late 1950s. Export credits were made at preferential interest rates, and in assessing the collateral value of export letters of credit (L/Cs) or shipping documents, the market exchange rate rather than the official rate was used.

In addition to the export credit system, a series of arrangements gave exporters preferential access to foreign exchange loans. Beginning in June 1950, foreign exchange loans were granted to exporters on the basis of export L/Cs. These loans made it possible for an exporter to import even before his export proceeds became available. The system was abolished after the adoption of the special foreign exchange loans in December 1952.

The first special foreign exchange loan fund, which operated from December 1952 to July 1954, gave preference to exporters. Initially, more than half of the funds were allocated on the basis of past export performance. Foreign exchange loans allocated to exporters could be used for importing consumer goods. The export incentive effect of the special foreign loan system, however, declined in the later stage because of the continuous increase in the proportion of the first special loan fund allocated to industrial end-users rather than to exporters.

Beginning in September 1959, credit was made available for up to 75 percent of production costs of exporters through an export operating loan fund of 200 million won financed by counterpart funds. The interest rate was 10 percent with a term of less than a year.

Another method of encouraging exports is implicit in the system under which traders are licensed. Under the Trade Transactions Law of 1957, all exporters and importers were required to register at the Ministry of Commerce and Industry. A prerequisite for registration was a minimum export of $3,000 for exporters and a minimum export of $10,000 for importers in 1958. This form of trading system is unusual in that the importer's registration was granted according to his export performance. Minimum exports for registration were raised in 1959 to $5,000 for exporters and $20,000 for importers. To *maintain* the status of exporters and importers, traders had to sustain an annual export

TABLE 3–3

Major Export Incentives

Description	Dates Applicable
Tariff exemptions on imports of raw materials and spare parts	1959–72
Domestic indirect and direct tax exemptions	1961–72
Accelerated depreciation	1966–72
Tariff and tax exemptions granted to domestic suppliers of exporting firms	1965–72
Wastage allowance subsidies	1965–72
Import entitlement linked to exports	1951–55, 1963–65, and 1966–71
Reduced rates on public utilities	1967–71
Registration as an importer conditional on export performance[a]	1957–72
Dollar-denominated deposits held in Bank of Korea by private traders[b]	1950–61
Korean Trade Promotion Corporation	1964–72
Monopoly rights granted in new export markets[c]	1967–71
Direct export subsidies	1955–56 and 1961–64
Export targets by industry	1962–72
Credit subsidies	
Export credits[d]	1950–72
Foreign exchange loans	1950–54 and 1971–72
Production loans	1959–72
Bank of Korea discount of export bills	1950–72
Import credits	1964–72
Capital loans by medium industry bank	1964–72
Offshore procurement loans	1964–72
Credits for overseas marketing activities	1965–72

NOTE: Though many of these incentives applied after 1972, this table is up to date only until 1972.

a. Minimum export by trader wishing to register as an importer increased from $10,000 in 1958 to $300,000 in 1970.

b. From December 1957 to 1961, these deposits could be sold legally. Black markets, however, were well developed long before 1957.

c. Authority existed from 1962, but was not widely used until 1967.

d. The rate on export credits was gradually lowered over the whole period.

performance exceeding a certain standard. Minimum exports were $10,000 for export business and $50,000 for import business in 1958. A year later minimum requirements for registration were raised by 100 percent.

Table 3–3 lists the major export incentives that were offered Korean firms from 1950 to 1972. Though most of them were not applied until after 1960, some had already appeared by that date.

END OF AN ERA

By 1960, foreign trade and economic institutions had progressed from the complete disarray of the early 1950s. However, the bureaucratic mechanisms that governed trade and payments were complex and cumbersome. Despite full recovery from the Korean War, the South Korean economy began to stagnate in the early 1960s for reasons given in Chapter 2. As political repression led to deepening disenchantment with the Rhee regime, the stage was set for the student revolution of April 1960 and the economic changes that followed.

NOTES

1. Allocating U.S. aid dollars to private importers was no problem until after the Korean War. During the war U.S. aid mainly took the form of civil relief goods imported and distributed directly by the U.S. military authorities.

2. Fifteen won in currency used at that time. There have been two currency reforms since 1945: a 100:1 revaluation in February 1953 and a 10:1 revaluation in June 1961. All won figures in this volume are converted to current denominations.

3. These peaks reflect the period in which the official exchange rate was adjusted upward on the basis of an average black market exchange rate or a weighted average price of dollars derived from Bank of Korea dollar auctions. These auctions, held in 1949 and early 1950, were not a major allocation mechanism; rather, they were a means of testing the market price of foreign exchange so that the official rate could be adjusted.

4. Because of this delay, the South Korean government suspended won advances beginning December 15, 1952, and advised the UNC to redeem the accumulated advances and to procure won currency from the Bank of Korea. In return, the UNC stopped the supply of petroleum products for civilian use.

5. Missionary transactions included remittances by foreign religious organizations for charities in Korea. Service dollars were those earned by providing services to UNC. These dollars could be transferred to the import account with the approval of the government.

6. The total of 57 items included starfish, dolls, lacquerwares, and nuts.

Chapter 4

Two Liberalization Episodes and Their Short-Term Consequences, 1961 to 1966

Both the Chang Myon civilian government that came to power after the student revolution of April 1960 and the military government that supplanted it following the coup of May 1961 were basically reformist. On the domestic front, the military government reformed the budget process, the taxation machinery, and the currency system. Just prior to the coup, the civilian government had attempted to unify the exchange rate system and had devalued the won in January 1961 from 65 to 100 won to the dollar and again in February from 100 to 130. The military government continued the pursuit of exchange rate reform and achieved complete unification of the system by June 1961. Other innovations included the institution in 1961 of a system of special tariffs to help soak up margins on restricted imports, a currency reform in 1961, and an easing of import restrictions in 1962.

The reforms of 1961–62, however, were not successfully carried out. The currency reform was largely a mistaken attempt to sterilize what were thought to be currency hoards. Each family was permitted to exchange old currency for new up to a limited amount. The reform was expensive, caused massive confusion and did not accomplish the stated objectives. The multiple exchange rate was reinstituted in 1963 and import controls were strengthened. By 1963, the exchange rate system had reverted to a Bhagwati-Krueger Phase II regime.

After the general election in early 1964, the nominally elected civilian government instituted a substantial set of reforms in 1964 and 1965 that were to be accompanied by a phenomenal economic performance. In May 1964, the won was devalued by almost 50 percent from 130 to 257 won to the dollar. This move was a prelude to the adoption of the unitary fluctuating ex-

42

change rate system that was introduced in March 1965. The exchange rate gradually stabilized at about 270 won per dollar in August the same year that the Exchange Bank intervened in the market. Quantitative restrictions were also eased. Between late 1964 and early 1965, importable items were increased from about 500 to 1,500 and the number of prohibited items was reduced. Special tariffs were raised to help soak up margins on restricted imports and import predeposit requirements were strengthened.

A second major effort was devoted to interest rate reform. In September 1965, the ceiling on commercial bank lending rates was raised from 16 to 26 percent with the result that the domestic supply of loanable funds available through the banking system increased rapidly, and additional investment demand spilled over into demand for foreign loans. This led to a great increase in private capital imports.

A third element of the liberalization package was an effective stabilization program. Collection of direct taxes was improved, rates were adjusted upward, and expansion of the money supply was strictly limited. Beginning in 1964, the government eliminated all deficits from the general budget and constrained itself to limited, sporadic short-term borrowing.

A fourth element of the reform was an intensification of the degree and number of subsidization programs for exports. Subsidized credit for exports became particularly attractive in contrast to the new and higher interest rates which had been raised by the interest rate reform.

By 1966, South Korea had moved from Phase III into Phase IV. The continuation of this new phase is discussed in the next chapter. In this chapter we discuss in detail the foreign exchange and trade policies that accompanied the two liberalization episodes (1961–62, 1964–65) and their consequences.

DEVALUATION AND EXCHANGE RATE UNIFICATION

The Chang Myon government attempted to unify the exchange rate in 1961 by changing the foreign exchange deposit system, in use since 1950, to the foreign exchange buying system in which all foreign exchange earnings were sold to the central bank at the official exchange rate. Foreign exchange deposits by residents were not authorized except for international airlines and shipping companies. Those who surrendered foreign exchange earnings to the central bank were given nontransferable exchange certificates valid for 90 days. (Although not legally transferable, the certificates were sold on the curb market.) Holders of exchange certificates were entitled to buy from the central bank at the official rate an amount of foreign exchange equal to the certificates' value. Concomitant with the unification of rates, the official exchange rate was raised twice—from 65 won to the dollar to 100 won on January 1, 1961 and to 130 won on February 2, 1961.

Although exchange rate reform of 1961 made the multiple exchange rate system illegal, multiple rates remained in use for a while afterward through sales of certificates on the curb market. The fixed single official exchange rate of 130 won to the dollar was only slightly higher than the most frequently quoted rates on United States aid and KFX import dollars in late 1960 and was lower than the market exchange rate on export dollars. As Table 3–1 reveals, the free market rates on Japan and other export dollars were 156.3 won and 141.6 won to the dollar in January 1961. Beginning in February 1961, the export dollar certificates were traded on the curb market at declining rates but at rates higher than the official exchange rate. The free market for export dollar certificates ceased to function after June as a result of intensified control by the military government followed by the abolition of the certificate system on July 20, 1961.

CHANGES IN TRADE POLICY, 1961 TO 1963

With the adoption of a unitary fixed exchange rate in June 1961, the differential between the import price and the domestic price became greater for some items restricted by import quota. Thus in July 1961, a Temporary Special Customs Law was enacted to capture the windfall profits that would otherwise accrue to importers receiving import licenses for restricted items. Under the law, about 700 items subject to import quotas were classified into four categories, I to IV, in order based on the ratio between the domestic price and the c.i.f. import price and the estimated degree of nonessentiality. A temporary special tariff was imposed on these classified import items in addition to regular tariffs. The special rates were 100 percent of import value on category I, 50 percent on category II, 30 percent on category III, and 10 percent on category IV. Adjustments were made periodically in the classification of items.

Import controls were revised twice in 1961. In the first half of 1961, the commodities proposed for import were listed in four classes: (1) automatic approval (AA) items that could be financed by any foreign exchange source without prior approval of the Ministry of Commerce and Industry; (2) AA special items that could be financed only by export earnings without prior approval of the Ministry; (3) restricted import items linked to specific commodity exports that required approval for imports; and (4) prohibited imports. The total number of importable items listed was 1,581, including 35 restricted items as shown in Table 4–1. Commodities not listed could not be imported without MCI approval.

TABLE 4-1

**Number of Importable Items in Semiannual Trade Programs,
1961 to 1967 (First Half)**

	Automatic Approval	Restricted	Semi-restricted	Total Importable	Prohibited
First half 1961	1,546[a]	35[b]	—	1,581	305
Second half 1961	1,015	17	—	1,132	355
First half 1962	1,195	119	—	1,314	366
Second half 1962	1,377	121	—	1,498	433
First half 1963	776	713	—	1,489	442
Second half 1963	109	924	—	1,033	414
First half 1964	na	na	na	1,124	617
Second half 1964	na	na	na	496	631
First half 1965	1,447	92	19	1,558	624
Second half 1965	1,495	124	4	1,623	620
First half 1966	2,104	125	11	2,240	583
Second half 1966	2,307	127	12	2,446	386
First half 1967	2,950	132	—	3,082	362

NOTE: The numbers of importable and prohibited items for 1961 to 1963 and the first half of 1967 were based on the original semiannual trade programs while breakdowns for all other periods are based on final revised programs.

SOURCE: Bank of Korea, *Monthly Statistical Review,* June and December, 1961 to 1963; Bank of Korea, *Review of the Korean Economy,* 1964 to 1966; and Ministry of Commerce and Industry, *A Ten-Year History of Trade and Industrial Policy, 1960–1969.*

a. Includes 309 special items that could be imported only by export earnings.

b. Indicates import items linked to specific exports.

In the trade program for the second half of 1961, prepared for the first time by the military government, commodities were grouped in three categories: (1) AA items that could be imported without prior approval of the Ministry of Commerce and Industry; (2) restricted items that could be imported with official approval; and (3) prohibited items. The total number of importable items (restricted and AA items) was significantly reduced in the second half of 1961 compared with the first half, while the number of prohibited items increased.

In order to promote procurement from the United States, the trade program for the second half of 1961 differentiated aid-financed imports from KFX (foreign exchange held by the Bank of Korea) imports. The program stipulated that AID commodities could not be imported with KFX but only with AID funds. The differentiation continued, in principle, until 1970.

Throughout 1962, both the number of AA items and the total number of importable items were increased over the quotas of late 1961. In the first half of 1963, however, the number of AA items was sharply reduced, while the number of restricted items was increased. These stronger restrictions reflected the sharp decline in KFX holdings that year.

The Law Prohibiting Sales of Special Foreign Products, enacted by the military government in 1961, was represented as an attempt to restrict the import or smuggling of luxuries. The law banned domestic sales of a number of foreign items such as foreign-made cigarettes, coffee, cosmetics, and high-quality cloth.

Various efforts were made to increase export incentives during this period. A new system of subsidies, adopted in September 1961, classified export commodities into four categories for payment of subsidies; 25 won per dollar for special category exports (new commodity exports and net exports by bonded processing), 20 won for Category I, 15 won for Category II, and 10 won for Category III. Subsidy payments in 1961 totaled approximately 307 million won. In 1962 the number of exports supported by subsidies was expanded, and total payments reached 566 million won. Though the next year a higher rate was paid on manufactured exports, other rates were cut, and the list of items eligible for subsidy was shortened. The net result was a reduction in total subsidies paid to 354 million won. As a percent of the value of exports at the official exchange rate, subsidies came to about 6 percent in 1961, 8 percent in 1962, and 3 percent in 1963.

The preferential interest rate on export credits was gradually reduced from 13.87 percent per annum in 1960 to 8 percent in 1963, thus increasing the implicit export subsidy. This rate was well below the commercial bank loan rate of 16 to 17.5 percent.

Tax relief for exporters was instituted in 1961 by removing the domestic commodity tax from exports and by exempting exporters from the business activity tax. Income tax incentives included a 30 percent reduction of tax on income from exports and a 20 percent reduction on income from sales of goods and services to the United Nations Command and tourist services. The tax reductions on income from exports and other foreign exchange earning activities were raised to a uniform rate of 50 percent effective January 1, 1962.

Another facet of the military government's export strategy was the institution of full-scale export targets in 1962. Before the beginning of each year, the Ministry of Commerce and Industry was to set the new year's targets on the basis of past export performance and new export forecasts for separate commodities. Annual export targets were usually classified by commodity, region, and country of destination. Commodity targets were assigned to industrial associations and firms, and the regional and country targets to South Korean trade and diplomatic missions abroad. The Ministry maintained an "export situation room" to check actual performance during the year against the annual targets. In addition, an Expanded Export Conference, which was chaired by the President and attended by ministers, government officials, bankers, and exporters, usually met several times during the year to deliberate on the annual targets.

RETURN TO MULTIPLE EXCHANGE RATES, 1963

In 1961 and early 1962, the military government followed very expansionary fiscal and monetary policies which led to inflation in 1962 and 1963. The economic situation was exacerbated by a bad harvest in 1962 and a consequent upsurge in imports of grain. The resulting decline in foreign exchange holdings brought a return to a multiple exchange rate system in 1963 through the institution of a full-scale export-import link and the emergence of an import-rights premium market. The trade program for imports was made much more restrictive in the first half of 1963 when automatic approval items were cut 50 percent. In the second half of 1963 automatic approval items were nearly eliminated, restricted items increased eightfold, and total importable items reduced by almost one-third (Table 4–1).

Under the link system, exporters were given the right to use 100 percent of their export earnings for imports. In early 1963, raw materials for exports and for five-year plan projects, as well as scrap iron and cement, could be imported without import entitlement obtained through export. Once the import of these items increased sharply, however, the government removed all exceptions on July 31, 1963. The free market premium rate on import rights gradually rose from 32 won per dollar in January 1963 to 65 won in April 1964. The rise in this premium prompted the government to enact the Temporary Special Excess Profits Tax Law to levy 50 won per dollar on sales of dollars acquired by the government through U.S. supporting assistance and PL 480 aid after December 1963. The effective exchange rates on both exports and imports became, therefore, much higher than the official exchange rate.

EXCHANGE RATE REFORM, 1964 TO 1965

The exchange rate reform, announced on May 3, 1964, began with a large devaluation from 130 won to 257 won. For a while thereafter, foreign exchange certificates (which were earned by exports and carried an import entitlement) continued to sell at a premium above the official exchange rate of about 255 won to the dollar.

On March 22, 1965, the government announced the actual implementation of the unitary fluctuating exchange rate system. The government felt confident that the rate would not fluctuate widely since relative price stability had been attained by the second half of 1964. As an extra precaution, standby credits of $9.3 million were made available by the IMF for a foreign exchange stabilization fund. The unitary fluctuating exchange rate system worked in the following way:

(1) Residents who earned foreign exchange by exports or sales to the United Nations Command were required to surrender their exchange earnings for exchange certificates which were valid for a month from date of issue. They could be freely traded on the exchange market, but on expiration they had to be sold to exchange banks for won currency.

(2) Those who required foreign exchange had to present foreign exchange certificates when import licenses were issued by the Bank of Korea.

(3) The official exchange rate was announced every day by the Bank of Korea on the basis of exchange certificate prices quoted in the free exchange market.

(4) The foreign departments of commercial banks were authorized to act as brokers for transactions of certificates.

(5) The Bank of Korea had authority to intervene in the certificate market when the market price of certificates fluctuated sharply owing to seasonal or speculative factors.

Immediately after the announcement of the new foreign exchange rate system, the first market exchange rate on certificates was formed at 270 won to the dollar. The exchange rate on certificates, however, declined gradually to 256 won to the dollar at the end of April 1965. The rate began to rise again in May, and by the end of the month the market exchange rate was quoted at 280 won per dollar.

On June 22, 1965, the Bank of Korea first intervened in the market by increasing the supply of exchange certificates. In the beginning, intervention could not completely remove fluctuations in the market exchange rate since the Bank supplied only a limited amount of additional certificates from KFX holdings. But from August 22, 1965 through 1967, the exchange rate was completely pegged at around 271 won to the dollar by sales of certificates by the Bank.

LIBERALIZATION OF IMPORT RESTRICTIONS, 1964 TO 1966

After the May 1964 devaluation, the balance of payments situation improved markedly and trade restrictions were gradually liberalized. As shown in Table 4–1, between the last half of 1964 and the first half of 1965, the number of items eligible for importation increased substantially from about 500 to 1,500. Thereafter, the list continued to increase rapidly as did the number of automatic approval items. The number of prohibited items showed a marked decline from the second half of 1965 to the first half of 1967.

Also after the May 1964 devaluation, a new Temporary Special Tariff Law was enacted to soak up margins between c.i.f. import prices and domestic prices of restricted import items. About 2,200 import commodities, for which the "foreign exchange ratio"[1] exceeded 30 percent, were classified in categories I and II. The special tariff was imposed on the difference between the domestic wholesale price of an imported good and the landed price of that import plus regular tariff, commodity tax, incidental expenses, and normal profit. A tariff rate of 90 percent was applied to category I and 70 percent to category II.

To administer the special tariff, the Bank of Korea and the Ministry of Finance made a monthly survey of domestic wholesale prices of import commodities. On the basis of this price survey, the list of items for the special tariff was expanded from about 2,200 in 1964 to about 2,700 after 1965. Those items to which a regular tariff did not apply were, however, exempted from the special tariff.

In 1964 an import prepayment deposit requirement was introduced. The requirement was revised from 100 to 255 won per dollar, or to 100 percent of import value, with the exchange rate change in 1964. After March 1965 the import prepayment deposit system was transformed into a system under which all commercial importers were required to deposit foreign exchange certificates equivalent to the value of imports at the time of the opening of the L/C.

INTENSIFICATION OF EXPORT INCENTIVES

Along with the exchange reform and import liberalization, the period 1964–66 saw marked intensification of export incentives (Table 3–3). Direct export subsidies were abolished in 1964, but other incentives grew in number and importance. Particular emphasis was placed on an expansion of credit incentives. The preferential rate on export credits was reduced from 8 percent in 1963 to 6.5 percent in February 1965, and to 6.0 percent in June 1967, further increasing the implicit export subsidy. The Bank of Korea lowered the discount rate on export bills from 4.5 percent to 3.5 percent in 1966. This rediscount of bills was enormously profitable for commercial banks which financed nearly all export credits through rediscounting bills.

In 1964, the number of types and the volume of preferential loans for export increased substantially. In addition to export credits and operating loans from counterpart funds, the following preferential loan arrangements existed:

(1) loans for suppliers of U.S. offshore procurement (mainly for Viet Nam);

(2) credits for importers of raw materials and equipment for export industries;

(3) export usance (credits to exporters who ship without L/Cs but receive payment after shipment);

(4) export industry promotion loans;

(5) Medium Industry Bank equipment loans for conversion of factories to export production; and

(6) Medium Industry Bank equipment loans for specialized export industries.

In addition to the preferential loans listed in Table 4–2, a standby credit system was instituted in 1965 for supporting the overseas marketing activities of export firms. The standby credit, which was a type of L/C for service transactions, could be opened by the Bank of Korea for (1) guaranteeing the opening of an export L/C by an overseas branch to its domestic head firm and the settlement of the export L/C, (2) guarantee money for international bidding and contracts, and (3) other financial guarantees for foreign exchange earning activities of overseas branches. The domestic firms were required to submit foreign exchange certificates or a foreign exchange payment guarantee issued by a foreign exchange bank for opening the standby credit.

In 1964, government support for foreign market development was gradually intensified. The Korea Trade Promotion Corporation (KOTRA) was founded and quickly expanded its overseas branch network to increase the sales of Korean products in foreign markets. In addition, the government sent special trade missions to many foreign countries and concluded trade agreements with a number of them from 1964 to 1966, including India, Burma, Cambodia, Italy, Austria, West Germany, Japan, and Mexico. The government also authorized the Korean Trader's Association to collect 1 percent of the value of all c.i.f. imports from importers for use in export promotion.

In 1965, the long-established practice of giving preference to exporters in the granting of import licenses was expanded and formalized. Exporters were given automatic right to import raw materials duty free up to certain limits. The limits established for each export commodity were based on a technically determined ratio of required raw materials to output plus an additional factor called a wastage allowance. The wastage allowance is administratively determined and is varied from time to time. Since it applies to raw materials which are generally limited by import controls or subject to high duties, the markups between import price and domestic price are quite large. That portion of the wastage allowance not used in production could be sold locally (since, unlike in other countries, these imports could be sold legally), sometimes at great profit to export industries.

In order to increase the domestic value-added content of exports, export incentives were extended to producers of intermediate goods used in the production of exports through a system of local letters of credit (L/Cs). The local L/C system came into effect in the second quarter of 1965 as the result of a revision of the Foreign Exchange Control Regulation. The local L/C system enabled exporters to issue local L/Cs to domestic producers of export goods and intermediates for export products on the basis of export L/Cs received by the exporters. The local L/Cs issued by exporters could be settled in foreign exchange certificates when export shipment was made. Domestic producers with local L/Cs could get the same treatment as exporters in obtaining preferential bank loans, import licenses for necessary raw materials, and exemption from import duties and the business activity tax.

In the latter part of 1966, an export-import link system was reintroduced. The main purpose of the system was to increase exports with low profit margins and to develop new export markets by linking export performance with the import rights either for popular consumer items or for imports of inputs for exported commodities. For instance, the exporters of woolen yarn and fabrics, sweaters, and clothing were given the rights to import raw wool and mohair at a rate of 25.5 to 85 percent of their export earnings (depending on the export commodity). Exporters of radios and electronic products were given the import rights to television accessories, exporters of chinaware the import rights to porcelain, exporters of domestically assembled watches and exporters to Switzerland the import rights to Swiss watches.

Finally, an additional tax incentive granted to exporters in 1966 was a special method of accelerated depreciation.

EFFECTS OF THE LIBERALIZATION EFFORTS

The attempt to unify exchange rates in 1961 and to effect other reforms failed because the policies of the newly established military government, which were at first inflationary, became more restrictive and complex as a result of a very bad harvest in 1962. The reforms of 1964–65 were accompanied by very successful economic performance across the board. Consider the exceptional nature of the changes that took place between 1964 and 1966:

(1) an average annual growth rate of real GNP of 9.6 percent;

(2) a decline in the rate of inflation from 35 percent in 1964 to 10 percent in 1965 and 9 percent in 1966 (wholesale price index);

(3) the ratio of domestic saving increased from 5.7 to 11.7 percent of GNP;

(4) exports increased by more than 40 percent per year;

(5) mining and manufacturing output increased at about 14 percent per year;

TABLE 4–2
Preferential Bank Loans for Exports, 1964 to 1966
(millions of won)

	Outstanding Credit (December 31)			Annual Interest Rate	Term	Other Conditions
	1964	1965	1966			
Export credit	1,857	3,866	3,628	6.5	90 days	150 won through Feb. '65 and 200 won thereafter per dollar to exporter or export goods producers on the basis of export L/Cs or supply contracts.
Loans for suppliers of U.S. offshore procurement	526	655	1,192	6.5	90 days	200 won per dollar to suppliers to Korean troops in Viet Nam and 150 won per dollar for other suppliers on the basis of supply contracts.
Credit for import of raw materials for exports	6,684	6,325	9,975			
(Payment guarantee)	(4,101)	(4,005)	(5,417)	3.0	60 days	Commercial bank guarantee at the time of L/C opening, up to ¼ of annual export earnings.
(Domestic usance-foreign exchange)	(2,588)	(2,320)	(4,558)	6.0	90–135 days	Export industries with export L/C or contracts.

Export usance	690	456	431	6.5	90–120 days	120 won per dollar to exporters on D/P and D/A basis and exporters with consignment sales arrangement.
Export industry promotion loans	77	63	41	26	90 days	120 won per dollar to export goods producers (Net export earning should exceed 30%).
Export industry operating loans (counterpart funds)	190	170	186	18[a]	1 year	A maximum of 10 million won to each exporter or export goods producer.
Equipment loans for conversion into export industry	—	603	1,014	13	5 years	A maximum of 10 million won to each small and medium industrialist specified by Ministry of Commerce and Industry
Loans for export specializing industry	—	—	93	13	5 years	
Total	10,024	12,138	16,560			

SOURCE: Bank of Korea.

a. Includes 2 percent credit guarantee charges.

(6) bank time and savings deposits increased about 4 times in 1965 constant prices; and

(7) government revenue increased from 7.3 percent of GNP to 10.8 percent.

It would be a mistake to attribute all of these achievements directly to liberalization. Industrial growth was actually very rapid in 1962 and 1963, before the successful liberalization began. In 1964, in fact, growth of manufacturing and mining slowed to 6.9 percent, down from 15.7 percent the year before. Social overheads and services grew at 3.0 percent in 1964 compared with 7.4 percent in 1963 and 8.9 percent in 1962. GNP growth in 1964 was a healthy 8.3 percent, only because of a particularly good harvest; value added in agriculture grew by 15.5 percent.

The liberalization episode was impressive because it was accompanied by such a rapid decline in the rate of inflation. The May 1964 devaluation of about 50 percent (from 130 won to 257 won to the dollar) was not inflationary largely because of the monetary and fiscal stabilization program. Another fact is important here also: the devaluation was more de jure than de facto, at least with respect to exports. The multiple exchange rate system and the various taxes and subsidies on exports resulted in an effective exchange rate for exports which was little changed after the 1964–65 devaluation. Consolidation of exchange rates since the 1964–65 liberalization eliminated the multiple exchange rate premia and was accompanied by suspension of payments of direct export subsidies (for statistical details, see the next chapter). Since the devaluation was not really de facto, there was relatively little upward pressure on prices of export goods.

The sharp rise in the bank deposit rate in 1965 also helped to curb inflationary pressures. The great rise in savings and bank deposits substantially reduced the velocity of circulation of the money supply.

The rapid growth of exports certainly cannot be attributed entirely to liberalization, since the trend dates from 1959. In 1960 exports increased from $20 to $33 million and have not ceased to grow to the present time. Various export incentives were intensified and the effective exchange rate on exports increased by about 11 percent, but this did not spur a noticeable increase in the rate of growth of exports. The most that can be said is that liberalization probably laid the groundwork for continued rapid growth of exports over the following decade and that without those efforts, such phenomenally rapid export growth could not have continued. Likewise, the exchange liberalization, the interest rate reform, and the fiscal reforms probably laid the basis for a decade of rapid growth in GNP which would not have been possible otherwise.

These hypotheses are reexamined at the end of this book after a discussion of other statistical evidence. Unfortunately, no clear answers emerge; the evidence is more suggestive than definitive. Nevertheless, much of the evidence, however imperfect, seems to indicate that the trade and exchange rate policies of the Korean government throughout the decade following the first attempts at liberalization, rather than the liberalization package by itself, were important contributors to the rapid growth of the South Korean economy.

NOTES

1. Foreign exchange ratio = (domestic wholesale price of imported goods) minus (regular tariff + commodity tax + normal expenses) divided by (normal foreign exchange price of the import on c.i.f basis). This formula was basically an estimate of the premium which could be obtained by an importer licensed to import a restricted item.

Chapter 5

Further Efforts at Liberalization: 1967 to Early 1973

From 1967 to 1972 the growth of GNP, exports, and imports continued at a very rapid pace. While foreign private capital imports replaced foreign assistance as the major source of foreign savings, the exchange rate, which had been pegged at 270 won to the dollar by the Bank of Korea since August 1965, was allowed to devalue gradually beginning in 1968. The rate reached 326 in June 1971 and then 370 following a further devaluation of 13 percent. Later in 1971, gradual devaluation was allowed to resume and it continued until June 1972 when the rate was pegged at about 400 won to the dollar.

A follow-up trade liberalization program, launched in 1967, switched the positive-list approach to trade controls to a negative-list approach and revised the tariff structure so as to eliminate some of the very high rates. Another tariff reform, discussed throughout much of 1972, was instituted in early 1973.

In August 1972, a new set of economic policy reforms was announced. These reforms included a set of regulations to govern the so-called unorganized money market, reductions in bank interest rates, price stabilization efforts, continued stabilization of the exchange rate, reduction in export incentives, and liberalization of import controls.

Despite these and other attempts at further liberalization and reform, resort to the old price-distorting policies and controls was common. A number of factors were involved. First, any adverse trends in the balance of payments prompted a return to the old methods. For example, when import demand increased sharply in late 1968, the government placed additional import items on the restricted list and increased export incentives.

56

Secondly, as debt service payments began to rise, even though foreign exchange holdings seemed quite adequate in the late 1960s and early 1970s, concern over future debt repayments increased along with a fear for the vulnerability of the basic balance of payments. Restrictions on capital movements were strengthened in 1970.

Finally, and probably most important, certain vested interests in the business community had much to lose from further liberalization and favored a return to price-distorting mechanisms. Since these interests wielded considerable political power, the tariff reform of 1967 brought few real changes although the initial proposals of the Ministry of Finance would have substantially simplified the tariff structure. The business interests, many of them exporters who benefited greatly from tariff exemptions and wastage allowances, exerted pressure through the Ministry of Commerce and Industry, and thus fostered a bureaucratic struggle between the two ministries. For good measure, related business groups staged a sit-down protest against the tariff change in the offices of the Ministry of Finance.

In another demonstration of their influence, the vested interests exerted strong pressure on the Ministry of Finance just prior to the June 1971 devaluation. The pressure came mainly from large firms with heavy foreign debts because devaluation would greatly increase the burden of repaying their foreign loans, which were denominated in dollars. The holders of foreign debt were compensated by increased availability of local loans. The government also felt it had to peg the exchange rate at its new value rather than continue with a gliding peg.

From 1967 to 1972, pressure to extend export subsidies increased while monopoly rights for new export markets and products were granted in 1967 and 1968. Exporters were ranked according to performance and the more successful were given better administrative treatment. Freight and power rate discounts were given to large exporters, wastage allowances were expanded, and interest rate subsidies on loans to exporters grew very rapidly. In early 1973, however, some of the subsidies were reduced or eliminated.

The period from 1967 to early 1973 can be characterized as a prolongation of Phase IV while attempts to consolidate reforms continued. But South Korea did not quite achieve a completely liberalized Phase IV regime because reforms were periodically retarded by adverse economic developments and by increasingly effective political resistance from certain business interests opposed to further reform.

EFFORTS TO LIBERALIZE TRADE, 1967 TO EARLY 1973

Trade liberalization was attempted in 1967 through a change from the positive-list system of import controls to the negative list,[1] and through tariff reform. The first of these measures was much more successful than the second. The basic impetus for the attempted liberalization was the marked increase in foreign exchange holdings in 1966 brought about by a rapid expansion of commodity exports, increased service earnings expatriated by South Korean nationals in Viet Nam and West Germany, and a larger inflow of foreign loans (including cash loans).

As shown in Table 5-1, the new negative-list program greatly enlarged the number of Automatic Approval (AA) items for import. More than half of the 30,000 commodities specified in the SITC (Standard International Trade Classification) manual became AA items since they were excluded from the negative list. Prohibited or restricted items numbered 336 under the old system and 12,872 under the new. This discrepancy, however, is misleading since items omitted from the positive list had to be treated ad hoc and often were, in fact, prohibited or restricted. If these additional items are taken into account (see figures in parentheses in Table 5-1) the total number prohibited and restricted under the positive-list system comes to 26,484. The increase in imports resulting directly from liberalization was approximately $27 million in the final five months of 1967 and $68 million or 20 percent of total imports in 1968 according to estimates by the Ministry of Commerce and Industry.

TABLE 5-1

Total Importable Subitems before and after Adoption of the
Negative-List Trade Program

	Program Ended July 24, 1967	New Program[a] Effective from July 25, 1967
Prohibited import items	244 (26,148)[b]	2,617
Restricted import items	92	10,255
Automatic Approval import items	3,760	17,128
Total	4,096	30,000

SOURCE: Ministry of Commerce and Industry.

a. The classification of commodities was based on the SITC Manual published by the United Nations. It was roughly equivalent to the classification in the old program.

b. Total number of prohibited items, i.e., those explicitly prohibited plus those prohibited because they were not listed in any category.

Although the government originally announced that it would gradually expand trade liberalization from the start made in the second half of 1967, the semiannual trade programs adopted in 1968 and afterwards showed a gradual increase in the number of restricted items (Table 5–2). The increase in the number of restricted items became more prominent beginning the second half of 1968 as import demand expanded greatly during 1968 and 1969.

Even under the negative-list system, imports of machinery from countries with which South Korea showed a trade deficit (Japan, for example) required prior approval of the Ministry of Commerce and Industry, regardless of the specifications in the trade program. The negative-list system applied only to new, not used, commodities. Used commodities were subject to a more restrictive set of rules.

The tariff reform announced on November 29, 1967 effective the first of the year was presumably intended to simplify the system along lines suggested by Ronald McKinnon. In his consultant's report (1967), Professor McKinnon proposed a low uniform tariff rate of about 20 percent for most imports and a higher rate (maximum 90 percent) on a selected group of industries that South Korea really wanted to protect. He also proposed that high tariffs on finished goods should be replaced with commodity taxes applicable to both domestic and imported goods.

In the end, however, the basic idea of a low, uniform tariff combined with modestly higher rates for the protection of a selected, small number of industries was not implemented with the result that the new customs law was much the same as the old. The basic rates in the new law are compared with

TABLE 5–2
Import Program for Basic Items, 1967 to 1970

	Prohibited	Restricted	Automatic Approval	Total
Second half 1967 (final)	118	402	792	1,312
First half 1968 (original)	116	386	810	1,312
First half 1968 (final)	71	479	756	1,312
Second half 1968 (final)	76	508	728	1,312
First half 1969 (final)	75	514	723	1,312
Second half 1969 (final)	74	530	708	1,312
First half 1970 (final)	73	526	713	1,312
Second half 1970 (original)	73	524	715	1,312

NOTE: The classification of import items is based on the United Nations' SITC Manual. The total shown in the table is an aggregation of 30,000 subitems.
SOURCE: Ministry of Commerce and Industry.

the old rates by major section of the BTN (Brussels Tariff Nomenclature) classification in Table 5–3. The total number of basic commodities subject to duties was increased from 2,044 to 3,019. The new rates were slightly higher than the old in all major sections of the BTN classification, except for sections 14, 18, and 19. The highest tariff rate in the old law, 250 percent, was now reduced to 150 percent.

TABLE 5–3

Changes in Legal Tariff Rates before and after Tariff Reform, 1967

(simple average rate)

BTN Section	Old Rate (percent)	New Rate (percent)
1. Live animals and animal products	32.5	38.4
2. Vegetable products	38.5	36.8
3. Animal & vegetable fats and oils	39.6	42.3
4. Prepared foodstuffs, beverages, spirits, vinegar, and tobacco	84.3	95.1
5. Mineral products	15.9	25.2
6. Products of the chemical and allied industries	27.6	29.7
7. Artificial resins and plastic materials	32.4	34.5
8. Raw hides and skins, leather, fur skins and articles thereof	55.2	58.1
9. Wood and articles of wood	40.1	44.2
10. Paper making material, paper and paperboard and articles thereof	43.0	54.2
11. Textiles and textile articles	59.0	71.0
12. Footwear, headgear, umbrellas, sunshades, whips, riding-crops, etc.	74.3	82.9
13. Articles of stone, plaster, cement, asbestos, mica, etc.	48.9	53.8
14. Real pearls, precious stones and metals	43.7	36.1
15. Base metals and articles thereof	32.9	35.6
16. Machinery and mechanical appliances	27.4	30.6
17. Vehicles, aircraft, vessels, etc.	39.6	36.2
18. Optical, photographic, cinematographic, measuring, checking and precision instruments and apparatus, etc.	44.4	40.4
19. Arms and ammunition	54.7	37.7
20. Miscellaneous manufactured articles	78.9	81.9
21. Works of art, collectors' pieces and antiques	0	0
Total number of items	(2,044)	(3,019)

NOTE: BTN—Brussels Tariff Nomenclature.
SOURCE: Official *Tariff Tables*, 1964 and 1968.

Weighted average tariff rates by major product groups in the old and new schedules are compared in Table 5–4. The table also compares the actual tariff rates (the ratio of all actual tariff collections to c.i.f. imports) by major product group. While statutory tariffs declined for most categories, actual tariff collections increased because of the pattern of exemptions. It should be noted, however, that the old and new tariff rates shown in Table 5–4 include both the regular tariff rates and the special rates levied to soak up margins on controlled imports, while the simple average tariff rates shown in Table 5–3 represent only the regular tariffs.

Although the legal rate structure remained basically the same, the new 1968 law allowed for greater administrative flexibility. Administrative duties could be levied on restricted commodities when imported in excess of quotas. Under certain conditions, emergency duties, countervailing duties, and so-called beneficial duties could be levied. The government had the authority to change statutory rates by as much as 50 percent by administrative decree.

TABLE 5–4

Weighted Average Tariff Rates Compared:
Major Product Groups, Old and New Schedules

(percent)

Product Group	Statutory Tariffs		Actual Tariff Collections per Unit of c.i.f. Value	
	1966	1968	1966	1968
Agriculture, forestry, and fishing	33.4	28.5	11.5	14.2
Processed foods	55.2	54.1	6.6	25.5
Tobacco and beverages	132.6	106.3	22.3	40.3
Mining and energy	11.8	13.5	6.2	7.7
Construction materials	34.5	25.0	8.1	12.7
Intermediate products I	31.9	40.7	6.8	12.7
Intermediate products II	51.8	44.7	10.6	14.4
Nondurable consumer goods	74.2	43.2	12.6	9.0
Consumer durables	74.5	73.7	20.4	34.4
Machinery	25.5	47.0	8.7	7.5
Transport equipment	12.8	19.8	1.4	1.6
Scraps and unclassifiable	25.4	33.1	8.3	18.2
Noncompetitive imports	21.9	16.9	21.9	9.2
Weighted Average	43.1	40.6	9.9	15.6

NOTE: Statutory and actual tariff rates include both the regular and special tariff rates. The average tariff rates were first obtained for 231 nonservice input-output sectors, weighted by actual imports and then aggregated into the major product groups using total supply weights for respective years.

Even after the adoption of the new regular tariff schedule, the special tariffs were still effective. The system of tariff exemptions under the new law remained almost the same as before. Imports of raw materials for the production of exports, capital goods for export production and other major industries, and capital goods imports by foreign-owned enterprises were exempt from custom duties. Since exemptions were substantial and growing, mainly because of increased exports and increased tariff exemptions related to exports, the legal tariff structure did not have the same significance as it might have had in other countries.

The government made some adjustments, however, to the list of tariff exemptions in the period following the tariff reform. For instance, in October 1968 the government removed 14 commodities from the customs-exempt list, including cement and petroleum. In addition, machinery and equipment for fertilizer and automobile plants and highway construction were transferred from the tariff-exempt list to the tariff-reduced list.

As import demand increased rapidly in late 1968, the government tightened import prepayment deposit requirements for some categories of imports, and further raised the amount of prepayment per dollar of import in 1969. Prepayment requirements for non-aid-financed imports on an L/C basis from "specified areas" (within 10 days shipping time, mainly Japan) were raised from 150 percent in the second half of 1968 to 200 percent in 1969 on items whose basic tariff rates were in the range of 30–49 percent, except for 13 items. In 1970, all prepayment requirements were set equal to the 1968 level regardless of source. The prepayment requirements for imports on a documents-against-payment (D/P) basis were raised from 30 to 50 percent in 1969 on imports from the "specified areas"; however, for imports from other areas the 5 percent prepayment requirement was maintained as before. In addition, items whose basic tariff rates exceeded 50 percent and nonessential and luxury commodities designated by the United Nations Economic Commission for Asia and the Far East were excluded from the list of items importable on a D/P basis.

For imports on documents-against-acceptance (D/A) and on a usance basis, an annual ceiling was established for each year. In 1969, the prepayment requirements were raised from 10 to 30 percent on D/A imports from the "specified areas," while a 30 percent prepayment requirement on usance imports was maintained. Prepayment requirements for D/A and usance imports from all areas were unified at 30 percent in 1970.

In late 1972 and early 1973, some additional liberalization measures were taken. The number of automatic approval items was increased by eliminating some of the previously restricted items from the negative list, and the number of quota items was also reduced, while quota amounts per restricted item tended to increase.

In early 1973, the special tariff, which had been used to tax large differences between international and domestic market prices for some imports, was completely abolished. There was also a general tariff reform, effective from February 5, 1973, which changed regular tariff protection to encourage new import substitution industries and reduce protection of old industries. Tariff rates on heavy industrial and chemical products and intermediate goods were raised, while the previous high rates on finished goods, particularly textile products, were generally reduced by about 10 to 50 percentage points. The Ministry of Finance announced that the reform brought about a reduction in the simple average tariff rate from 38.8 to 31.3 percent. The tariff reform, however, increased administrative authority to adjust the tariff rates within 100 percent of the legal rate. In fact, the tariff authorities established the administrative rates on some imported raw materials much lower than the legal rates, in order to minimize the domestic cost-push effect of increases in international prices of major industrial raw materials which took place in 1973. Domestic commodity tax rates on both imported and domestically produced commodities, particularly on electrical appliances and other household goods, were also reduced by about 10 to 15 percentage points.

GROWTH OF EXPORT SUBSIDIES ·

Export incentives continued to grow from 1967 to early 1973 (Table 3-3). Preferential loans became an increasingly powerful tool for export promotion after the interest rate reform of 1965. Since the reform raised ordinary bank loan rates to 26 percent per annum (at which rate the excess demand for loans was still positive) while leaving the rates on export loans unchanged, interest subsidies implicit in the preferential loans for export increased considerably after September 1965. Because of the increased differential between commercial bank interest rates and preferential export rates and the proliferation of various preferential loans for exports, the implicit interest subsidies for exports increased from approximately 1.3 billion to 15.3 billion won, or from 7.6 won per dollar of export to 17.3 won between 1965 and 1970.[2] As a percentage of total exports valued at the official exchange rate, interest rate subsidies increased from about 3 percent in 1965 to 6 percent in 1970.

Table 5-5 shows the growth of the various subsidized loan schemes for exports between 1967 and 1970. Loans for offshore procurement and credit for imports of capital equipment grew rapidly beginning in 1967. In 1968 and 1969, the export industry operating loans (financed from the Counterpart Fund) and export industry promotion loans were abolished. In their place, the government introduced loans for domestic production of raw materials used

TABLE 5-5
Preferential Loans for Exports, 1967 to 1970

	Outstanding Credit (million won as of December 31)				Annual Interest Rate (percent)	Term	Remarks
	1967	1968	1969	1970			
1. Export credit	6,618	8,072	11,866	19,129	6.0	90–135 days	200 won per dollar through '69, 220 won in '70 and 260 won in '71
2. Loans for suppliers of U.S. offshore procurement	3,399	3,567	5,291	4,510	6.0	90 days	150 won per dollar through '68, 180 won in '69 and 220 won in '70
3. Credit for imports of raw materials for export	17,835	20,239	31,868	49,981	1.5	60 days	Green card exporters exempted from guarantee fees
(Payment guarantee)	(11,292)	(8,859)	(14,201)	(21,244)			
(Domestic usance-foreign exchange)	(62)	(29)	—	—	6.0	90–135 days	Foreign exchange value of imports
(Import loans)	(6,481)	(11,351)	(17,666)	(28,737)	6.0[a]	90–135 days	Won equivalent of imports
4 Export usance	652	550	1,986	4,463	6.0	90–120 days	Won loan per dollar equivalent to export credit
5. Loans for export	—		35	154	6.0	90–120 days	Won loan per dollar equivalent to export credit

No. Item					Interest rate (percent)	Term	Remarks
6. Foreign exchange loans for import of capital goods for export industries	1,849	7,802	10,297	21,372	12.0	3–5 years	80 percent of import value through '68 and 90 percent in '69
7. Export industry promotion loans	61	368	28	7	26.0	90 days	Abolished in 1969
8. Export industry operating loans (Counterpart Fund)	193	—	—	—	18.0	1 year	Abolished after 1968
9. Equipment loans for conversion into export industry	1,531	2,237	2,536	2,826	12.0	5 years	A maximum of 10 million won to those industries specified by the Ministry of Commerce and Industry
10. Loans for export specializing industries	292	563	742	807	12.0	5 years	
11. Loans for production of raw materials	—	—	134	833	6.0 [a]	90–120 days	220 won per dollar in '69 and '70
12. Loans for preparing agricultural and fishery products for export	—	—	3,413	4,001	12.0	90–180 days	70 percent of required funds
Total	32,430	43,398	68,196	108,083			

SOURCE: Bank of Korea; Medium Industry Bank.

a. Raised to 9.0 percent per annum, June 1971.

in producing exports and for processing of agricultural and fishery products for export in May and September 1969 (rows 11 and 12, Table 5–5).

The flexible wastage allowance grew in importance as an incentive to export during the late 1960s as the proportions of wastage allowed gradually increased for many industries. The Korean Traders Association (1969) estimated that the implicit subsidies arising from the wastage allowances on imported raw materials averaged 12.7 won per dollar export, or about 4.6 percent of the official exchange rate in 1968. The amount of subsidies per dollar, however, showed a wide variation by type of export commodity. For instance, the subsidies implicit in wastage allowances were as high as 48 to 59 won per dollar of export (about 17 to 21 percent of the official exchange rate) for woolen fabrics, rayon fabrics, and footwear. Business firms and trade associations have lobbied persistently for increased wastage allowance.

The total amount of tax concessions for export grew rapidly from 1965 to 1970 (Table 5–6). Relief per dollar of export more than doubled in those six years.

As mentioned in Chapter 3, importer's licenses were granted only to firms whose export performance met minimum standards. The minimum exports required for a license, which were set at $30,000 in 1964, were raised to $100,000 in 1966, $200,000 in 1969, and $300,000 in 1970. In addition, in 1969, traders were graded in four classes (blue-, white-, yellow-, and red-card holders) on the basis of annual export performance. High performance traders were given a number of special benefits, including exemption of col-

TABLE 5–6
Tax Concessions for Exports, 1965 to 1970

	1965	1966	1967	1968	1969	1970
Internal tax (millions of won)	2,838	5,021	7,724	11,127	17,207	26,330
Regular and special tariff (millions of won)	2,962	5,333	8,224	19,261	22,551	34,700[a]
Total tax relief (millions of won)	5,530	10,354	15,952	30,388	39,758	61,030
Total exports[b] (millions of dollars)	175.1	250.3	334.8	486.2	658.3	882.2
Tax relief per dollar of export (won)	31.6	41.4	47.6	62.5	60.4	69.1

SOURCE: National Tax Administration.
a. Preliminary figures.
b. Includes military goods sales abroad.

lateral for regular and special tariffs, relaxation of tax surveillance, and preferential treatment in foreign exchange allocations for overseas activities.

Certain exporters were given monopoly rights in new export markets or for the export of new commodities. The system originated in 1962 but was not applied to many commodities until 1967. Monopoly rights were given, among others, for the following commodities: arrowroot wallpaper (all countries), processed brassware (Japan), apples and pears (Taiwan), silk for sashes (Japan), artificial eyelashes (EEC), oak leaves (Japan), and rice cake (Japan).

Finally, railway freight rates on export minerals were given a 30 percent discount beginning in 1967. Export industries with power-receiving capacity of less than 200 KWH whose electric power costs amounted to more than 20 percent of total manufacturing costs were granted a 30 percent discount on electricity charges.

As a follow-up on the August 1972 reforms, many export incentives were reduced. The 50 percent reduction in tax on corporation and individual business income earned from export business was abolished. The government also announced a gradual adoption of a tariff-rebate system under which tariffs are collected at first on all imports but collections for imported raw materials for exports are refunded later when actual exports occur. Until 1973, imports of raw materials for exports were granted tariff exemptions at the time of customs clearance, and tariffs plus some penalty were imposed later when importers did not fulfill export obligations. Finally, the preferential interest rate on export credit was raised from 6 to 7 percent. This slight increase, combined with the general reduction in ordinary bank loan rates, reduced the implicit subsidies from preferential loans to the export sector.

EXCHANGE RATES

From August 1965 through 1967, the exchange rate was pegged by the Bank of Korea at about 271 won to the dollar. Beginning in 1968, the won was allowed to devalue gradually, at a rate believed to be sufficient to maintain purchasing power parity. The rate had reached 326 by June 1971, an annual rate of increase close to 9 percent, when an abrupt devaluation of 13 percent brought the rate to 370. Until the end of the year, the rate remained at this value and then after further gradual devaluation, the won was pegged at about 400 to the dollar in June 1972.

The U.S. dollar, meanwhile, underwent two devaluations. The first, of about 10 percent in early 1972, resulted from the Smithsonian Agreement of December 1971. The second, also 10 percent, stemmed from a parity change for the dollar in February 1973 and from the subsequent flotation of other currencies against the dollar in the spring of 1973. These changes had the effect of devaluing the won with respect to currencies other than the dollar. Since most of South Korea's foreign trade is carried on with countries other than the United States, these changes in the value of the dollar made a great difference in the cost of Korea's imports and the prices of her exports.

Table 5–7 lists exchange rates on a purchasing-power-parity basis taking into account the changes in the value of the won with respect to major currencies other than the dollar. Thus for 1972, the official rate averaged, over the year, 391.8 won to the dollar. The purchasing-power-parity rate was 254.1, and the purchasing-power-parity rate adjusted for changes in the value of other currencies was 271.9 won to the dollar.

In 1972 and early 1973, the Korean currency was very strong. Previously 1965 had been regarded as the year when the exchange value of the

TABLE 5–7

Official Exchange Rate at Purchasing Power Parity, 1965 to 1973

(1965 prices)

	1965	1970	1971	1972	1973 (April)
1. Official exchange rate (won per dollar)	265.4	310.7	347.7	391.8	398.9
2. Trade-weighted average WPI of major trading partners (1965=100)	100.0	112.8	114.2	117.2	128.9
3. Korea's WPI (1965=100)	100.0	146.0	158.4	180.7	187.7
4. Purchasing-power-parity exchange rate 1 × 2 ÷ 3	265.4	240.0	250.7	254.1	273.9
5. Trade-weighted effective[a] devaluation due to foreign currency realignments (percent)	—	—	—	7.0	10.0
6. Purchasing-power-parity exchange rate including foreign currency realignments	265.4	240.0	250.7	271.9	301.3
7. Annual increase (percent)	—	2.4	4.5	8.5	10.8

SOURCE: Table 5–8; Bank of Korea, *Monthly Statistics*, April 1973; Economic Planning Board, "Monthly Report on Economic Trends" (Briefing material for the President, in Korean), June 11, 1973; U.S. Department of Commerce, *Commerce Today*, April 2, 1973, p. 4.

a. Exchange rates of the won vis-à-vis other major currencies were expressed in terms of dollars using the dollar rate for major currencies prevailing in the base period, 1965. These rates in terms of dollars were averaged using trading shares as weights in a weighted-average calculation.

won placed Korea in its strongest competitive position ever. Yet compared with 1965, the purchasing-power-parity exchange rate in April 1973 was 13 percent higher. It was particularly favorable for exports, not only because of the various devaluations both of the won and the dollar, but also because of relative rates of inflation. Wholesale prices in Korea's major trading partners increased about 10 percent by April 1973 compared with the average for 1972, while the South Korean index showed an increase of only 4.6 percent during the same period.

Between 1970 and April 1973, the purchasing-power-parity rate adjusted for currency realignments increased significantly (see line 7 of Table 5–7). By 1972, the rate was 13 percent higher than it had been in 1970 and by April 1973 it was 26 percent higher.

QUANTITATIVE ESTIMATES OF THE RESTRICTIVENESS OF THE TRADE AND PAYMENTS REGIME, 1958 TO 1970

Tables 5–8 and 5–9 show how the trade and payments regime has varied in degree of restrictiveness, both for exports and imports, and how various measures of effective exchange rates have changed over time.

Table 5–8 analyzes the effective exchange rate for exports. To obtain these figures, the average export dollar premium and total subsidies per dollar of export are added to the official exchange rate. For the period 1958–61, an excess of the average free market price of export dollar certificates over the official exchange rate was taken as export premium per dollar. In 1963 and 1964 a premium emerged because of the export-import link and the free market sale of import entitlements attached to export dollars.

The won value of total export subsidies increased greatly over the decade of the 1960s from 1.2 to 86.5 won per dollar of export. Direct subsidies were important briefly from 1961 to 1964, but internal tax exemptions, customs duties exemptions, and interest rate subsidies were all important throughout most of the decade. Subsidies on freight and power rates, monopoly rights, and administrative incentives are not quantified in Table 5–8 because they are relatively small.[3]

Table 5–9 lists the components of the effective exchange rate on imports. Two separate effective rates are determined, one based on legal tariff rates, and the other including an adjustment for exemptions from the legal tariff rates. In addition to an adjustment for tariffs, the foreign exchange tax and total premia on export dollars per dollar of imports are added to the average official exchange rate. The total adjustment based on actual tariffs, labelled total actual tariffs and tariff equivalents per dollar of import in row B8 of

TABLE 5-8

Price-Level-Deflated and Purchasing-Power-Parity Effective Exchange Rates on Exports, 1958 to 1970

	1958	1959	1960	1961
A. Official exchange rate (won per dollar)	50.0	50.0	62.5	127.5
B. Average export dollar premium (won per dollar)	64.0	84.7	83.9	14.6
C. Export subsidies				
1. Direct subsidy payments (mil. won)	—	—	—	307
2. Internal tax exemptions (mil. won)	na	na	na	na
3. Customs duties exemptions (mil. won)	na	na	na	na
4. Interest rate subsidies (mil. won)[a]	19	25	38	39
5. Total export subsidies (1–4) (mil. won)	19	25	38	346
6. Total exports (mil. dollars)[b]	16.5	19.8	32.8	40.9
7. Won subsidies per dollar export (5÷6) (won)	1.2	1.3	1.2	8.5
D. Effective exchange rate on exports (A+B+C7)	115.2	136.0	147.6	150.6
E. Korea's wholesale price index (1965=100)	39.9	40.8	45.2	51.2
F. Price-level-deflated effective exchange rate on exports (D÷E)	288.7	333.3	326.5	294.1
G. Average wholesale price index of major trade partners (1965=100)[d]	97.2	97.7	97.9	98.3
H. Purchasing-power-parity effective exchange rate on exports (F×G)	280.6	325.6	319.6	289.1

Table 5–9, fluctuated between 1958 and 1965 from 14 to 38 won to the dollar. Between 1965 and 1970, however, it remained remarkably steady at about 25 won to the dollar. Legal average tariffs and tariff equivalents on imports increased markedly, from 23.3 won per dollar of import in 1962 to 72.0 won in 1970. The increasing level of customs duty exemptions, however, kept actual tariff collections per dollar of imports almost constant. The adjustments for obtaining effective rates of exchange do not make allowance for price premia resulting from quantitative restrictions, although these are taken into account in the effective rates of protection calculated in Chapter 10. This omission should not, however, be very important, since the special tariffs, originally instituted in July 1961, tend to soak up such premia because of the way they are administered.

The effective exchange rates for both exports and imports are deflated by two price indexes: the South Korean wholesale price index and a purchasing-power-parity index. The latter is the ratio of the South Korean wholesale

1962	1963	1964	1965	1966	1967	1968	1969	1970
130.0	130.0	214.3	265.4	271.3	270.7	276.6	288.2	310.7
—	39.8	39.7	—	—	—	—	—	—
566	354	350	—	—	—	—	—	—
310	527	992	2,838	5,021	7,724	11,127	17,207	26,330
255	571	1,197	2,692	5,333	8,224	19,261	22,551	34,700ᶜ
47	248	719	1,330	2,571	4,935	7,395	9,690	15,280
1,178	1,700	3,258	6,860	12,925	20,883	37,783	49,448	76,310
54.8	86.8	119.1	175.1	250.3	334.8	486.2	658.3	882.2
21.5	19.6	27.4	39.2	51.6	62.4	77.7	75.1	86.5
151.5	189.4	281.4	304.6	322.9	333.1	354.3	363.3	397.2
56.0	67.5	90.9	100.0	108.8	115.8	125.2	133.7	145.9
270.5	280.6	309.6	304.6	296.8	287.6	283.0	271.7	272.3
97.6	98.3	98.5	100.0	102.8	104.0	105.6	108.8	112.8
264.0	275.8	305.0	304.6	305.1	299.1	298.8	295.6	307.2

NOTE: na—not available.
SOURCES: Bank of Korea; Ministry of Finance; USAID, Korea Mission.

a. Interest rate subsidies were calculated by estimating the average interest rate on all outstanding loans to business firms at about 26 percent. This was taken as an estimate of the equilibrium interest rate, and interest rate subsidies were taken as the subsidy element of all loans at less than 26 percent. The estimate of the average interest rate on loans was derived from Kim Mahn Je (1970).

b. Includes military goods sales abroad.

c. Estimated by applying the average rate of tariff exemptions on imports of raw materials and capital goods for export in 1968–69 to the value of c.i.f. imports for exports in 1970, because actual exemption figures not available.

d. An average of wholesale price indexes in the United States and Japan, weighted by Korea's annual trade volume with the respective countries. It is noted that Korea's imports from and exports to the United States and Japan generally increased from about 43 percent of Korea's total trade volume in 1958 to 83 percent in 1970.

TABLE 5-9

Price-Level-Deflated and Purchasing-Power-Parity Effective Exchange Rates on Imports, 1958 to 1970

	1958	1959	1960	1961
A. Official exchange rate (won per dollar)	50.0	50.0	62.5	127.5
B. Tariff & tariff equivalents				
1. Actual tariff collections (mil. won)	2,969	3,559	5,150	5,306
2. Tariff exemptions (mil. won)	na	na	na	na
3. Foreign exchange tax (mil. won)	1,425	4,722	5,046	251
4. Premiums for total exports (mil. won)[a]	1,056	1,677	2,752	597
5. Total actual tariffs and tariff equivalents (1+3+4) (mil. won)	5,450	9,958	12,948	6,154
6. Total legal tariffs and tariff equivalents (1+2+3+4) (mil. won)	na	na	na	na
7. Total c.i.f. imports (mil. dollars)	378.2	303.8	343.5	316.1
8. Actual tariffs and tariff equivalents per dollar import (5÷7) (won)	14.4	32.8	37.7	19.5
9. Legal tariffs and tariff equivalents per dollar import (6÷7) (won)	na	na	na	na
C. Effective exchange rate on imports				
1. Official exchange rate plus actual tariffs per dollar of import	64.0	82.8	100.2	147.0
2. Official exchange rate plus legal tariffs per dollar of import	na	na	na	na
D. Price-level-deflated effective exchange rate on imports (deflated by line E in Table 5-8)				
1. C1÷E from Table 5-8 (actual basis)	160.4	202.9	221.6	287.1
2. C2÷E from Table 5-8 (legal basis)	na	na	na	na
E. Purchasing-power-parity effective exchange rate on imports				
1. D1 × G from Table 5-8 (actual basis)	155.9	198.2	216.9	282.2
2. D2 × G from Table 5-8 (legal basis)	na	na	na	na

price index to a weighted average wholesale price index of major trading partners (the United States and Japan). The effective exchange rate deflated by the South Korean wholesale price index is called the price-level-deflated effective exchange rate while the effective exchange rate deflated by the purchasing-power-parity index is denoted the purchasing-power-parity effective exchange rate. As an indicator of the incentive effect for exports and the relative price of imports, the purchasing-power-parity effective exchange rates are the most meaningful.

1962	1963	1964	1965	1966	1967	1968	1969	1970
130.0	130.0	214.3	265.4	271.3	270.7	276.6	288.2	310.7
6,847	6,708	8,509	12,847	18,003	25,413	37,881	44,724	50,924
2,919	5,464	7,236	9,682	20,295	32,374	66,411	86,240	92,000[b]
79	—	—	—	—	—	—	—	—
—	3,455	4,728	—	—	—	—	—	—
6,926	10,163	13,237	12,847	18,003	25,413	37,881	44,724	50,924
9,845	15,627	20,473	22,529	38,298	57,787	104,292	130,964	142,924
421.8	560.3	404.4	463.4	716.4	996.2	1,462.9	1,823.6	1,985.0
16.4	18.1	32.7	27.7	25.1	25.5	25.9	24.5	25.7
23.3	27.9	50.6	48.6	53.5	58.0	71.3	71.8	72.0
146.4	148.1	247.0	293.1	296.4	296.2	302.5	312.7	336.4
153.3	157.9	264.9	314.0	324.8	328.7	347.9	360.0	382.7
261.4	219.4	271.7	293.1	272.4	255.8	241.6	233.9	230.6
273.8	233.9	291.4	314.0	298.5	283.9	277.8	269.3	262.3
255.1	215.7	267.6	293.1	280.0	266.0	255.1	254.5	260.1
276.2	229.9	287.0	314.0	306.9	295.3	293.4	293.0	295.9

NOTE: na—not available.
SOURCE: Table 5–8.
   a. Average premium per dollar export given in Table 5–8 multiplied by total value of exports for each year.
   b. Estimated by applying the average ratio of tariff reductions and exemptions to the value of c.i.f. imports in 1968–69 to the value of imports for 1970.

The bias toward export promotion in the trade and payments regime is clearly revealed by a comparison of purchasing-power-parity effective exchange rates for exports and imports (Table 5–10). The effective exchange rate for exports exceeded the effective exchange rate for imports by a wide margin in every year except for 1961–62 and 1965. In the periods 1958 to 1960 and 1963 to 1964, the major difference in effective rates for exports and imports was caused by the export dollar premium. The devaluations of January and February 1961 were soon followed by exchange rate unification. The net effect on the export side was that the price-deflated effective exchange rates declined rather than rose between 1960 and 1961. Thus, the devaluation was more than offset by the elimination of premiums as far as exports were concerned. On the import side, the price-deflated effective exchange rate of won to the dollar increased sharply as the result of the devaluation. Thus, the effective rates for exports and imports were brought closely into line in 1961 and 1962.

In 1963 and 1964, export dollar premia emerged again through the market for import entitlements, and the effective exchange rates for exports and imports again diverged sharply. The devaluation of May 1964, from 130 to 257 won to the dollar, the float in the spring of 1965 to 271 won to the dollar, and the 1964 unification of rates again brought the effective rates for exports and imports into line. Despite the enormous nominal devaluation between 1963 and 1965 (about a 115 percent increase in the won/dollar rate) the purchasing-power-parity effective won/dollar rate for exports rose only about 11 percent. On the import side, however, the devaluation was more effective.

After 1965, the export and import rates moved increasingly out of line because of rapidly growing export subsidies. Export subsidies as a percent of the effective exchange rate are compared with actual tariffs and tariff equivalents as a percentage of the effective exchange rate in Table 5–10. By 1970, about one-fifth of the effective exchange rate for exports represented subsidies of one form or another.

The quantitative estimates, outlined in tables 5–8 through 5–10, confirm the impressions of our analysis of individual trade and exchange rate policies —liberalization efforts in 1961–62 and 1964–65, followed by rapid backsliding in 1963 and gradual backsliding from 1967 to 1971. This pattern emerges most clearly in looking at columns D and E of Table 5–10. The premia and subsidies as a percentage of the effective exchange rate on exports follow the pattern of the liberalization efforts. Column G shows, however, that tariffs and tariff equivalents declined steadily as a percentage of the effective exchange rate on imports from 1959 to 1970 (except for a slight increase in 1967). The major reasons are the elimination of the foreign exchange tax in 1962, the gradual shift of imports toward capital goods with low or zero tariffs, and the increasing tariff-exempt importation of raw materials for export industries.

Comparison of Purchasing-Power-Parity Effective Exchange Rates for Exports and Imports, 1958 to 1970

	Purchasing-Power-Parity Effective Exchange Rate on Exports[a] (A)	Purchasing-Power-Parity Effective Exchange Rate on Imports[b] (B)	Ratio (A÷B) (C)	Percentage Components of Effective Exchange Rate on Exports			Percentage Components of Effective Exchange Rate on Imports	
				Premia[c] (D)	Subsidies[d] (E)	Official Exchange Rate[e] (F)	Tariff and Tariff Equivalents[f] (G)	Official Exchange Rate[g] (H)
1958	280.6	155.9	1.80	55.5	1.0	43.5	22.5	77.5
1959	325.3	198.2	1.64	62.2	1.0	36.8	39.6	60.4
1960	296.6	216.9	1.37	56.7	0.8	42.5	37.6	62.4
1961	289.1	282.2	1.02	9.7	5.6	84.7	13.2	86.8
1962	264.0	255.1	1.03	0.0	14.1	85.9	11.2	88.8
1963	275.8	215.7	1.28	21.3	10.3	68.7	12.2	87.8
1964	305.0	267.6	1.14	14.1	9.7	76.2	13.2	86.8
1965	304.6	293.1	1.04	0.0	12.8	87.2	9.4	90.6
1966	305.1	280.0	1.09	0.0	15.9	84.1	8.4	91.6
1967	297.4	266.0	1.12	0.0	18.2	81.8	8.6	91.4
1968	298.8	255.1	1.17	0.0	21.9	78.1	8.5	91.5
1969	295.6	254.5	1.16	0.0	20.6	79.4	7.8	92.2
1970	307.2	260.1	1.18	0.0	21.8	78.2	7.6	92.4

a. Based on row H, Table 5–8.
b. Based on row E1, Table 5–9.
c. Row B, Table 5–8, as percent of row D.
d. Row C7, Table 5–8, as percent of row D.
e. Row A, Table 5–8, as percent of row D.
f. Row B8, Table 5–9, as percent of row C1.
g. Row A, Table 5–9, as percent of row C1.

SUMMARY AND CONCLUSIONS

From 1967 until June 1971, the effective exchange rate for exports was maintained by gradually increasing export subsidies. Attempts were made to liberalize import controls and tariffs but these foundered. A devaluation of the won
in June 1971, two dollar devaluations in 1972 and 1973, and a yen revaluation caused the balance of payments to improve markedly and export subsidies
were partly dismantled in early 1973.

Under increasing pressure from business interests the government in late
1972 adopted a basically different strategy—one in which price inflation and
interest rates would be reduced and the exchange rate held stable. Though the
short-run response of the economy and the balance of payments has been satisfactory, prior devaluations and a worldwide economic boom have been more
important factors than the reforms in producing the desired result. It remains
to be seen whether these policies will succeed in the long run. The strength of
the won may be eroded by continuing high costs of petroleum, grains, and
other natural resources that Korea imports in large quantities. It may be impossible to keep prices in check and further devaluations may be required to
keep the economy growing at a rapid pace.

NOTES

1. Under the positive-list system, only those items listed in the trade program could
be imported or exported, subject to specifications made in the program. But under the
negative-list system, the trade program lists only those items whose imports or exports
are either prohibited or restricted. Therefore, unlisted items in the negative-list program
represent Automatic Approval items, whereas the unlisted items in the positive-list
program are either prohibited or restricted.

2. See Table 5–8 for details on interest rate subsidies.

3. Subsidies by the wastage allowance on imported raw materials are considered
to be included in internal tax and customs duties exemptions, since the tax and customs
duties exemptions include exemptions for the proportion of wastage allowance (both
technological wastage loss and additional allowances).

Chapter 6

Exports and the Growth
and Structure of the Economy

Very rapid growth of exports has been the outstanding feature of South Korea's economic performance over the 1960s and early '70s and has been a significant determinant of the growth and structure of the South Korean economy as a whole.

PATTERN OF EXPORT GROWTH

Table 6–1, which gives exports and export growth rates from 1953 until 1972, shows that rapid growth began in 1959 and averaged 38.5 percent between 1958 and 1972. Exports in 1973 reached $3.2 billion, almost a doubling over the previous year.

Table 6–1 demonstrates the relative unimportance of U.S. procurement for Viet Nam which only began in 1967. The growth rate of exports exclusive of exports to South Viet Nam was even more rapid than growth in total exports, except in 1967 and 1968. Nevertheless, exports, net of sales to Viet Nam, grew at rates of 28 and 42 percent, respectively in 1967 and 1968—a very creditable performance by any standard. In 1972, exports to Viet Nam accounted for less than 3 percent of the total.

As Table 6–2 shows, 78 percent of South Korean exports in 1961 were primary products—mainly tungsten, coal, dried laver (seaweed), and fish. By 1971, 86 percent were manufactured products and only 14 percent were primary products. Though total exports expanded more than 40 times between 1961 and 1972, manufactured exports expanded almost 170 times in those

77

TABLE 6–1
Export Growth, 1953 to 1973

Year	Total Exports ($ million)	Growth Rate (percent)	Year	Total Exports ($ million)	Growth Rate (percent)	Exports Net of Sales to Viet Nam ($ million)	Growth Rate (percent)
1953	40	—	1963	87	58	87	58
1954	24	−40	1964	119	37	119	37
1955	18	−25	1965	175	47	175	47
1956	25	39	1966	250	43	250	43
1957	19	−24	1967	335	34	320	28
1958	17	−11	1968	486	45	455	42
1959	20	18	1969	658	35	622	37
1960	33	65	1970	882	34	835	34
1961	41	24	1971	1,132	28	1,068	28
1962	55	34	1972	1,676	48	1,624	52
			1973	3,271	95	3,225	99

SOURCE: Bank of Korea, *Economic Statistics Yearbook,* various issues.

years, a rate of growth averaging more than 60 percent per annum. Admittedly, the growth started from a very small base, but it continued even after exports had reached a substantial percentage of GNP. From 1967—when exports were almost 9 percent of GNP—to 1972, the growth rate of total exports averaged 38.2 percent and manufactured exports 44.5 percent.

Table 6–3 lists the major manufactured exports of the period 1961–72. In 1961, they were plywood, cotton fabrics, and plates and sheets of iron and steel. The growth of exports of these products was rapid over the next decade and they remained important in 1972. Electrical machinery and apparatus, clothing, footwear, and wigs were not exported at all in 1961, but by 1972 they accounted for 39 percent of total exports and 45 percent of manufactured exports.

The largest market for Korean exports in the early 1960s was Japan, and from 1965 onwards the most important has been the United States (Table 6–4). Though of very little significance as an export market in the 1950s and very early '60s, the United States absorbed more than 50 percent of Korea's exports in 1968, but has become a somewhat less important customer in recent years. Since 1965, Japan has taken about one-quarter, and the remaining quarter has been split between other Asian countries and Europe. In 1973, exports to Japan were expected to increase substantially. The several revalua-

TABLE 6–2
Structure and Growth Rates of Exports, 1961 to 1973

Year	Total Export Transactions[a]		Primary Product Exports			Manufactured Exports		
	Amount ($ million)	Annual Growth Rate (percent)	Amount ($ million)	Percent of Total	Annual Growth Rate (percent)	Amount ($ million)	Percent of Total	Annual Growth Rate (percent)
1961	42.9	32.5	33.5	78.0	—	9.4	22.0	60.8
1962	56.7	32.2	41.4	73.0	23.6	15.3	27.0	62.2
1963	84.4	48.8	40.8	48.3	−1.4	43.6	51.7	184.8
1964	120.9	43.2	58.6	48.4	43.6	62.3	51.6	42.9
1965	180.5	49.3	68.1	37.7	16.2	112.4	62.3	80.3
1966	225.8	41.7	96.1	37.6	26.4	159.7	62.4	42.1
1967	358.6	40.2	107.4	29.9	11.8	251.2	70.1	55.4
1968	500.4	39.5	113.5	22.7	5.7	386.9	77.3	54.1
1969	702.8	40.4	147.7	21.0	30.1	555.1	79.0	43.4
1970	1,003.8	42.8	164.4	16.4	11.3	839.4	83.6	51.2
1971	1,352.0	34.7	189.1	14.0	15.0	1,162.9	86.0	38.5
1972	1,807.0	33.7	222.7	12.3	14.1	1,584.3	87.7	36.2
1973	3,254.2	80.2	381.0	11.8	71.1	2,872.8	88.2	81.3

SOURCE: Economic Planning Board, *Major Economic Indicators*, various issues.

a. These figures are based on records of settlements of export transactions kept by the Ministry of Commerce and Industry. They usually exceed other export figures cited in this volume (e.g., tables 2–7 and 6–1), which are determined on a customs clearance basis.

TABLE 6–3
Major Manufactured Exports, 1961 to 1973
(amounts in millions of dollars)

Year	Plywood		Cotton Fabrics, Woven		Plates & Sheets of Iron & Steel		Electrical Machinery & Apparatus		Clothing		Footwear		Wigs & Human Hair	
	Amount	Percent of Total Exports	Amount	Percent of Total Exports	Amount	Percent of Total Exports	Amount	Percent of Total Exports	Amount	Percent of Total Exports	Amount	Percent of Total Exports	Amount	Percent of Total Exports
1961	1.2	2.8	0.9	2.1	0.5	0.1	0.0	0.0	0.0	0.0	0.0	0.0	0.0	0.0
1962	2.3	4.1	1.8	3.2	0.5	0.0	0.1	0.2	1.1	2.0	0.2	0.4	0.0	0.0
1963	6.3	7.5	4.3	5.1	8.3	9.8	0.9	1.1	4.6	5.5	0.7	0.8	0.0	0.0
1964	11.4	9.4	11.1	9.2	2.1	1.7	1.6	1.3	6.6	5.5	0.9	0.7	0.2	0.2
1965	18.0	10.0	10.5	5.8	10.2	5.7	3.3	1.8	20.7	11.5	4.2	2.3	2.3	1.3
1966	29.9	11.7	10.1	3.9	7.1	2.8	8.3	3.2	33.4	13.1	5.5	2.2	12.0	4.7
1967	36.4	10.2	12.6	3.5	0.9	0.3	9.3	2.6	59.2	16.5	8.1	2.3	22.7	6.3
1968	65.6	13.1	13.3	2.7	0.8	0.2	21.8	4.4	112.2	22.4	11.0	2.2	35.1	7.0
1969	79.2	11.3	18.6	2.6	3.6	0.5	42.3	6.0	160.8	22.9	10.5	1.5	60.2	8.6
1970	91.4	9.1	26.4	2.6	7.6	0.8	48.5	4.8	213.6	21.3	17.3	1.7	100.9	10.1
1971	124.3	9.2	31.0	2.3	20.1	1.5	74.3	5.5	304.3	22.5	37.4	2.8	69.9	5.2
1972	153.6	8.5	34.8	1.9	68.1	3.8	137.4	7.6	442.2	24.5	55.4	3.1	73.8	4.1
1973	270.8	8.3	56.5	1.7	129.3	4.0	345.3	10.6	749.9	23.0	106.4	3.3	81.5	2.5

SOURCE: Economic Planning Board, *Major Economic Indicators*, various issues.

TABLE 6-4
Exports by Country, 1960 to 1973
(percent of total exports)

	United States	Japan	Other Asia	Europe	Rest of World
1960	6.7	63.4	11.6	14.1	4.3
1961	9.4	50.2	23.3	8.4	8.6
1962	21.8	42.8	22.3	11.5	1.5
1963	28.0	28.6	33.3	9.1	1.0
1964	29.7	31.9	23.3	13.1	2.0
1965	35.2	25.1	23.9	12.2	3.6
1966	38.3	26.5	15.4	13.6	6.2
1967	42.9	26.5	13.9	10.4	6.4
1968	51.7	21.9	11.5	8.0	7.0
1969	50.1	21.4	13.0	8.9	6.5
1970	47.3	28.0	9.8	9.1	5.7
1971	49.8	24.5	10.4	8.2	7.0
1972	46.7	25.1	11.3	10.1	6.7
1973	31.7	38.5	10.3	11.8	7.8

SOURCE: *Economic and Statistics Yearbook, 1973*, pp. 184–185; *1970*, pp. 296–297; *1966*, p. 264; *1962*, p. 220.

tions of the yen vis-à-vis the dollar and the gradual devaluation of the won with respect to the dollar from December 1970 to June 1972 left the won in a very favorable position with respect to the yen in 1973. This has stimulated exports from Korea to Japan.

NET FOREIGN EXCHANGE CONTENT OF EXPORTS

Many of South Korea's exports have a particularly high import content—for example, cotton, woolen, and synthetic textiles; plywood; wigs; steel; and electronics. Some require more natural-resource-based raw materials than can be produced locally, except at very high cost, such as iron ore, cotton, wool, leather, round wood for plywood, and human hair (in sufficient quantities). Others require industrial raw materials that are not produced locally in adequate amounts despite attempts to produce import substitutes for petrochemicals, synthetic yarns, plastics, and sophisticated electronic components. Though the import content of silk textiles, fertilizers, cement, tiles, and a range of primary products is low, for most exports it is high.

It is difficult to determine the total import content (direct and indirect) of South Korea's exports. The Ministry of Finance publishes figures only on the direct import content of exports, including imports for bonded processing and an estimate of other private imports used directly in exports.[1] Import content is estimated for the years 1967 to 1973 as follows:

1967	1968	1969	1970	1971	1972	1973
40.0%	43.7%	43.9%	44.3%	46.3%	36.8%	42.3%

The Korea Productivity Center (1970) produced estimates of 32.2 percent and 41.7 percent for 1967 and 1969 for the direct import content, based on a survey of 45 commodities accounting for 85.4 percent of total exports. The Korea Trade Research Center of Seoul National University (1969) produced estimates of both the direct and indirect import content using the 1966 input-output matrix. They also computed an implicit "charge" for imported capital inputs. For 1966, they estimated the direct and indirect import content at 40.0 percent and for 1968 at 44.4 percent.

All observers apparently agree that the import content of Korea's exports increased during the late 1960s, despite the incentives given after 1965 to domestic suppliers of exporting firms, but did seem to fall off in the early '70s.

South Korean exports are import intensive largely because of the particular products in question rather than because of the processes used to produce them. Since manufactures tend to be more import intensive than primary products, and the former are more important relative to the latter, the import content of South Korea's exports is high. Another factor in the high import content of exports is the greater import intensity of manufactured exports relative to all manufactures. In the table below, we contrast the results from the 1970 input-output estimates of the direct import intensity of total production with the Korea Productivity Center results for direct import intensity in 1969:[2]

	1970 Input-Output Estimates of Direct Import Intensity of General Production (percent)	Korean Productivity Center Estimates of Direct Import Intensity for Exports in 1969 (percent)
Primary products	1.2	1.1
Food, beverages, and tobacco	10.9	0.2
Other manufacturing	25.0	53.8
All commodities	14.2	41.7

We see that exports are more import intensive than general production, but that the differences are far smaller when corrected for the type of products exported or produced. In fact, for primary products and processed foods, exports are less import intensive than general production.

Although the import intensity of Korean exports is higher than for production in general, it is not appropriate to characterize South Korean exports as resulting largely from bonded processing. Value added domestically is quite substantial. The degree of import content and its tendency to increase in the 1960s does take some of the bloom off of Korea's spectacular export performance. Yet even if allowance were made for this fact by adjusting South Korean exports and their growth downward, the performance would still be remarkable by any standard of international comparison.

RANGE OF EXPORT INCENTIVES

As we have mentioned before, the number and variety of export incentives used in South Korea is striking (Table 3–3). Although some of them predate the mid-1950s, most incentive programs have been introduced and gradually intensified since the end of the Korean War. Their net effect has been an effective exchange rate for exports that has exceeded that for imports.

Another means of encouraging exports is implicit in the government's method of administering the various export subsidies and targets. Rather than dealing with each individual exporter, the government has worked through exporters' associations composed of all the exporters in a particular industry. For example, wastage allowances, import entitlements, preferential loans, and export targets were often allocated to an association, which in turn devised methods of parceling the incentives and targets among its members. These associations, moreover, have tended to serve as informal cartels for allocating domestic sales and this arrangement has enabled firms to charge somewhat higher prices in local markets. In some instances these higher prices reflect the absence of tariff and internal tax exemptions and for some commodities (e.g. wigs), there is almost no domestic market. Nevertheless, the presumption remains that for a limited range of commodities there is an element of monopoly in domestic pricing. For these commodities, price discrimination between domestic and foreign sales potentially subsidizes exports. This problem is discussed in more detail in Chapter 10.

EXPORT SENSITIVITY TO SUBSIDIES
AND EXCHANGE RATES

The value of a number of subsidies to exports was calculated as part of the determination of the purchasing-power-parity effective exchange rates on exports and imports (tables 5–8 and 5–9). In Table 6–5, the purchasing-power-parity effective exchange rate on exports is divided into three components: (1) that due to the official exchange rate, (2) that due to premia resulting from the multiple exchange rate system, and (3) that due to a number of export subsidies. Subsidies include direct subsidies, tax rebates, utility rate rebates, and the value of subsidized credit for exports. In Table 6–5, the three components of the effective exchange rate are deflated separately, while only the aggregate series is deflated in Table 5–8, line H.

These data can be used to estimate the sensitivity of exports to exchange rates and export subsidies. Statistically, there are a number of problems, the

TABLE 6–5

Effective Exchange Rate on Exports, Purchasing-Power-Parity Basis, 1955 to 1970

(won per dollar)

Year	Official Exchange Rate	Premia Due to Multiple Exchange Rates	Export Subsidies per Dollar of Exports	Effective Exchange Rate on Exports
1955	99.7	159.9	0.0	259.6
1956	132.1	139.8	0.0	271.9
1957	118.1	139.1	0.0	257.2
1958	121.8	155.9	3.0	280.7
1959	119.7	202.8	3.1	325.6
1960	135.4	181.7	2.6	319.7
1961	244.8	28.0	16.4	289.2
1962	226.6	0.0	37.5	264.1
1963	189.3	58.0	28.4	275.7
1964	232.2	43.0	29.6	304.8
1965	265.4	0.0	39.2	304.6
1966	256.3	0.0	48.7	305.0
1967	243.1	0.0	56.0	299.1
1968	233.3	0.0	65.5	298.8
1969	234.5	0.0	61.2	295.7
1970	240.2	0.0	67.0	307.2

SOURCE: Same as Table 5–8.

main difficulty being that from 1955 to 1970 the effective exchange rate for exports remained remarkably steady. This was particularly true after 1964. Although the effective official exchange rate has varied dramatically from year to year, subsidies and export premia have also changed in such a way as to keep the effective exchange rate for exports relatively constant. Another factor affecting our estimate is that exports after the Korean War were very small for a country of South Korea's size and GNP per capita. Much of South Korea's export growth in the late 1950s and early '60s was a matter of catching up after the devastation of two major wars in little more than a decade. Since the extraordinarily rapid rate of growth indicates that exporting was extremely profitable at prevailing exchange rates, it is plausible to hypothesize that South Korean exports were constrained more by the capacity to produce goods than by the relative profitability of producing for export instead of for domestic markets.

The sensitivity of exports can be tested by using exports of manufactured goods (XGM) as the dependent variable, and nonagricultural output (YNA), the official exchange rate on a purchasing-power-parity basis (ORD), and all other export incentives (i.e., a combination of multiple exchange rate premia and subsidies denoted by $SUBX$) as explanatory variables. If the whole period 1955 to 1970 is included, the results are very poor. From 1957 to 1970, we obtain the following result:

$$XGM = -241.4847 + 0.3323YNA + 0.2629ORD + 0.1471SUBX \quad (6\text{--}1)$$
$$(-3.92) \quad (11.29) \qquad (1.70) \qquad (1.27)$$

Estimation Technique: Cochrane-Orcutt Iterative Technique

$R^2 = 0.9900$

$d = 1.3742$

$\rho = 0.8701$

The coefficient of YNA is highly significant, which indicates that general capacity in nonagriculture is the most significant factor explaining exports. That is, the general capacity of the economy to produce is probably an important determinant of exports. The elasticity of manufactured exports with respect to changes in the exchange rate (ORD) is 2.14 and with respect to export subsidies is 0.95. The coefficients of the official exchange rate ORD and the subsidy level for exports $SUBX,$ however, are not significant.

This result can be greatly modified, however, if the time span is changed from 1957–70 to 1963–70. The coefficient of ORD becomes 1.713 and the t ratio is over 13.8; the coefficient of $SUBX$ becomes 1.305 with a t ratio of 10.9.[3] With such a short period, however, the degrees of freedom are limited.

The exchange rate variable, *ORD,* and the subsidy variable, *SUBX,* are almost constant and show fairly limited variation from 1963 to 1970, making the results still more suspect. Finally, the implied elasticities for the exchange rate and subsidy variables from 1963 to 1970 are enormous, equal to 6.16 for *ORD* and 4.69 for *SUBX.* Any period beginning before 1963, however, gives insignificant results for the coefficients of *ORD* and *SUBX.*[4]

It seems reasonable to infer that the responsiveness of exports changed sharply after 1963, but the period is too short for accurate estimation of parameters. We may infer that before 1963 sensitivity to exchange rate policy was lacking because exports, particularly manufactures, were insignificant and because the system of multiple exchange rates then in use was very inefficient. After 1963, both government officials and private entrepreneurs were more export oriented. Multiple exchange rates gave way to a system that relied more heavily on high official exchange rates combined with export subsidies, particularly in the form of tax and tariff relief (Table 6–5). Exports became very much more sensitive to exchange rate policies and despite rapid inflation, the rate on exports was maintained at a high level after the reforms of 1964 by a combination of official devaluations and growing export subsidies.

Another factor that may have fostered the increased responsiveness of exports after 1963 was the reduced risk of exporting once the exchange rate for exports was stabilized after 1964. As the predictability of export earnings increased, it became more reasonable for individual entrepreneurs to concentrate on exports.

MEASURING STRUCTURAL CHANGE

In the remainder of this chapter, we shall discuss the use of input-output data and national accounts to evaluate the role of exports in the growth of the Korean economy, particularly in relation to the other sources of output growth, namely domestic demand expansion and import substitution. Our analysis extends from 1955 to 1968. We could not extend it beyond 1968 because at the time the research was done, 1968 was the last year for which an input-output table was available.

The analysis of structural change in South Korea is based on a series of five input-output tables. That for 1955 was prepared especially for this study and gives information at a 29-sector level of detail.[5] Those for the remaining observation years—1960, 1963, 1966, and 1968—provide the information in a 117-sector breakdown.[6] Because of this difference, it is not possible to present the same information for all five observation years.

The input-output tables distinguish between competing and noncompeting imports. The former are defined as items that are also produced domestically;

the latter as items not produced in Korea in the year for which the table was compiled. By virtue of this definition, the list of items classed as noncompeting changes from table to table. Failure to adjust the statistics year by year to a common list of noncompeting imports would lead to a severe understatement of the degree of import substitution practiced, for much of it has come through introducing the production of formerly noncompeting imports (e.g., petroleum products). We have adjusted the data so that virtually all imports are treated as competing. The original data with explanatory documentation are available from the authors. The tables provided here are confined to aggregated data and present most of this data in terms of shares and/or compositions within total figures; this mode of presentation seems of greater relevance to the general reader than the presentation of the raw statistics.

A study of structural change is most meaningfully conducted in terms of real, i.e., constant price, magnitudes: thus it was necessary to deflate the current price input-output statistics into constant price figures. A procedure often followed in other studies of this type is to deflate all magnitudes for a given observation year by the same index, say the GDP deflator. While this procedure does suffice to insure that, on average, changes over time are not misstated because of price level changes, it fails to take account of relative price changes. In our deflation procedure, output deflators at the 117-sector level were used to estimate inter-sectoral relative price changes, while independent time series on the general wholesale price level, the wholesale price level of imported commodities, the price level of exports, and the exchange rates on imports and exports were used to determine aggregate price level changes for imports, exports, and domestic sales. The resulting figures at constant domestic market prices incorporate, insofar as possible given the limitations of the price indexes, changes over time both in the average price level and in the structure of relative prices. These constant price statistics were further deflated by the nominal protection rates estimated for 1968 to yield a set of input-output statistics at constant world market prices.[7] Deflation to constant world market prices was carried out for commodities only; there are no estimates here of magnitudes for nontradables measured in some equivalent of constant world market prices.

For our basic indicators of structural change, we split the growth of production of a sector over time into three categories: domestic demand expansion (DE), export expansion (EE), and import substitution (IS). There are a number of ways to accomplish such a decomposition, depending upon whether one examines first differences or deviations from proportional growth and upon how one relates imports to other elements in the system.[8] Here we shall report on one set of estimates that uses a particular mode of decomposition. Though we have experimented with a variety of methods, they all lead to the same general conclusions reported here.[9]

The decomposition begins with the fundamental supply-demand balance equation of input-output analysis:

$$X_{j,t} = W_{j,t} + C_{j,t} + Z_{j,t} + E_{j,t} - M_{j,t} \qquad (6\text{-}2)$$

where $X_{j,t} =$ gross output in sector j in period t;

$W_{j,t} =$ intermediate demand for the output of sector j in period t;

$C_{j,t} =$ private plus government consumption demand for the output of sector j in period t;

$Z_{j,t} =$ investment demand (including net stock accumulation) for the output of sector j in period t;

$E_{j,t} =$ export demand for the output of sector j in period t; and

$M_{j,t} =$ imports of items classified in sector j in period t.

We shall define import substitution as a change in the ratio of imports to *domestic* demand. Let $m_{j,t}$ be defined as $M_{j,t}/D_{j,t}$, where

$$D_{j,t} = W_{j,t} + C_{j,t} + Z_{j,t} \qquad (6\text{-}3)$$

is total domestic demand for the output of sector j in period t. Letting $t = S$ denote the first period, from (6–2) and (6–3), we may write

$$X_{j,S} = (1 - m_{j,S})\, D_{j,S} + E_{j,S}. \qquad (6\text{-}4)$$

For the second period (T), from (6–2) and (6–3) we may write:

$$X_{j,T} = D_{j,T} + E_{j,T} - M_{j,T}. \qquad (6\text{-}5)$$

If we add $m_{j,S} \cdot D_{j,T}$ and subtract the same quantity on the right hand side of (6–5), we have

$$X_{j,T} = (1 - m_{j,S}) \cdot D_{j,T} + E_{j,T} + m_{j,S} \cdot D_{j,T} - M_{j,T}. \qquad (6\text{-}6)$$

Subtracting (6–4) from (6–6) yields

$$(X_{j,T} - X_{j,S}) = (1 - m_{j,S}) \cdot (D_{j,T} - D_{j,S}) + (E_{j,T} - E_{j,S}) \qquad (6\text{-}7)$$
$$+ (m_{j,S} - m_{j,T}) \cdot D_{j,T}$$

or

$$\Delta X_j = (1 - m_{j,S}) \cdot \Delta D_j + \Delta E_j - \Delta m_j \cdot D_{j,T} \qquad (6\text{-}8)$$

where Δ is the difference operator and

$(1 - m_{j,S}) \cdot \Delta D_j =$ contribution of domestic demand expansion (DE);

$\Delta E_j =$ contribution of export expansion (EE);

$- \Delta m_j \cdot D_{j,T} =$ contribution of import substitution (IS).

Equation (6–8) gives the breakdown of growth into that due to expansion of domestic demand, that due to export expansion, and that due to import substitution. The contribution of domestic demand is the domestic demand coefficient $(1 - m_{j,s})$ times the change in domestic demand (ΔD_j) for the sector j. The contribution of exports is merely the increase in exports, and the contribution of import substitution is minus the change in the import coefficient (Δm) times domestic demand $(D_{j,T})$ in period T for sector j.

We shall use equation (6–8) to decompose the change in output into its component parts. It is important to recognize, however, that any decomposition is essentially a descriptive device and involves some arbitrary choices. For example, the choice of the first period as the base for defining the import ratio is wholly arbitrary. Use of the second period's import ratio—an equally arbitrary choice—as the reference point would give

$$\Delta X_j = (1 - m_{j,T}) \cdot \Delta D_j + \Delta E_j - \Delta m_j \cdot D_{j,s}. \tag{6–9}$$

If the import ratio declined over time, then both measures of import substitution would be positive, but that based on the first period's import ratio would be greater if domestic demand has grown (i.e., $- \Delta m_j \cdot D_{j,T} > - \Delta m_j \cdot D_{j,s}$). Conversely, the contribution of domestic demand to growth will be smaller when the first period is taken as the base. The bias in either case results from using values for two discrete points in time, which means that we face an index number problem.[10]

There are several ways to circumvent this problem, a number of which were tried. The approach reported here is the use of "chained" measures. Rather than apply the decomposition simply to the data for 1955 and 1968, we have separately decomposed the change in output over each interval for which we have input-output data; the estimates for each interval are then summed to give the growth contribution estimates between 1955 and 1968. The same method was applied to decompose changes in output between 1960 and 1968.

As well as being sensitive to the index number problem, measures of import substitution are also sensitive to the level of aggregation employed. Estimates based on highly aggregated data reflect both changes in the conditions of supply within individual subsectors producing uniquely defined products and changes in the pattern of domestic demand. For example, there may be no import substitution in the sense defined above when one sums the estimates for individual sectors, and yet the ratio of aggregate imports to total domestic demand may have changed because of shifts in the composition of demand. In our study of trade policy, we are primarily interested in the import substitution stemming from changes in the conditions confronting suppliers. We have therefore estimated the growth contributions at the 117-sector level. The aggregate estimates presented below are thus aggregates of the growth contributions for individual sectors rather than growth contributions calculated from data aggregated over the sectors. While this removes the effect of changes in the composition of demand among the 117 sectors, the effects of demand shifts within individual sectors remain in the estimates.

The measures defined above give the direct contributions of import substitution and export expansion to the growth of a sector's output. However, part of the growth of *intermediate* demand for a sector's output may also be attributable to import substitution or to export expansion, albeit in other sectors which require the output of the particular sector as intermediate input. The total, direct plus indirect, effect of import substitution and export expansion can be calculated through the use of the inverse input-output matrix. Below we shall estimate both the direct and the total growth contributions. Only the former are relevant to assessing how producers within *individual* sectors have responded to incentives policies. The latter are, however, relevant to measuring the contributions of import substitution and export expansion to the economy's growth.

CONTRIBUTIONS TO SOUTH KOREA'S ECONOMIC GROWTH

Estimates of contributions to growth based on constant world prices are presented in Table 6–6. For the period 1955 to 1968 all sectors are grouped in five broad aggregates. These appear in Part 1 of the table. For the period 1960 to 1968 the tradable goods sectors were grouped according to the eleven categories shown in Part 2. The two intermediate product categories shown there indicate different stages of processing, I being at a lower stage than II.[11] The first two industries listed are primary and the remaining nine are manufacturing industries.

Tradable goods were also grouped according to the four trade categories shown in Part 3. This classification includes:

   (X) Export industries (exports greater than 10 percent of total production);
  (IC) Import-competing industries (imports greater than 10 percent of total domestic supply);
 (XIC) Export and import-competing industries (exports greater than 10 percent of total production and imports greater than 10 percent of total domestic supply); and
 (NIC) Non-import-competing industries (all other sectors).

The figures in Table 6–6 are the absolute growth contributions divided by the respective changes in output; thus they state the proportion of the change in output that is attributable to each cause.

TABLE 6-6

Direct and Indirect Contributions to Economic Growth

(percent of total growth of sector)

	Domestic Demand Expansion		Export Expansion		Import Substitution	
	Direct	Total	Direct	Total	Direct	Total
Part 1. 1955–68: Broad Sectors						
1. Primary	109.2	94.7	4.0	19.4	−13.2	−14.2
2. Manufacturing	80.0	72.5	13.7	22.0	6.3	5.5
3. Social overhead	91.4	86.7	8.8	12.3	−0.2	0.9
4. Services	96.4	86.7	5.0	14.9	−1.4	−1.6
5. Other	81.5	70.9	35.9	46.4	−17.4	−17.3
Total	89.0	80.3	11.2	20.2	−0.3	−0.6
Part 2. 1960–68: Industrial Groups						
1. Agriculture, forestry, and fishing	108.1	94.9	−0.1	15.9	−7.9	−10.8
2. Mining and energy	88.1	70.6	15.9	28.2	−3.9	1.2
Primary	106.5	92.9	1.2	16.9	−7.6	−9.8
3. Processed food	90.4	87.8	7.8	11.7	1.8	0.5
4. Beverages and tobacco	93.8	88.9	4.0	9.9	2.2	1.1
5. Construction materials	86.4	84.8	5.6	7.4	8.0	7.8
6. Intermediate products I	68.2	54.0	17.0	32.3	14.8	13.6
7. Intermediate products II	84.6	72.1	10.4	25.6	5.0	2.4
8. Nondurable consumer goods	57.1	53.0	36.2	40.2	6.8	6.8
9. Durable consumer goods	81.2	78.1	23.2	27.2	−4.4	−5.3
10. Machinery	141.1	139.5	8.0	12.2	−49.0	−51.8
11. Transport equipment	141.7	144.6	0.2	4.2	−41.9	−48.8
Manufacturing	81.7	74.0	15.1	24.3	3.2	1.7
Part 3. 1960–68: Trade Categories						
1. Export goods (X)	45.4	37.9	52.7	60.4	1.9	1.8
2. Import-competing goods (IC)	109.3	97.5	0.5	16.1	−9.8	−13.6
3. Non-import-competing goods (NIC)	93.5	85.3	1.4	10.9	5.1	3.9
4. Export and import-competing goods (XIC)	90.7	76.7	47.2	61.8	−37.9	−38.5
All commodities	88.2	79.0	11.4	22.4	0.3	−1.4

NOTE: All results are aggregated from 117-sector input-output data, except for 1955–60 which is from 29-sector data. Totals may not reconcile because of rounding. Figures for 1955 to 1968 are based on constant domestic market price data, and all other figures are based on constant world market prices.

The most striking result of this analysis is the predominance of export expansion over import substitution. From 1955 to 1968, 20.2 percent of total growth was attributable directly and indirectly to export expansion, while −0.6 percent was due to import substitution. Thus, on balance, there was negative import substitution but substantial export expansion. Naturally, expansion of domestic demand was the most important factor, accounting for more than 80 percent of total growth. From 1960 to 1968, export expansion was relatively even more important, and accounted for 22.4 percent of growth compared with −1.4 percent for import substitution.

Another striking conclusion to be drawn from Table 6–6 is that export expansion generated considerable domestic backward linkages while import substitution did not. The average contribution of export expansion for either the 1955–68 or 1960–68 period almost doubles when indirect effects are taken into account. That is, growth of exports generates substantial demand for domestically produced intermediate goods.

It is of interest to compare the relative importance of time periods with respect to export expansion and import substitution. The following figures show the *total* contribution of each to the growth of aggregate commodity output for each subinterval:

	1955–60	1960–63	1963–66	1966–68
Export expansion	12.9%	6.3%	31.4%	21.3%
Import substitution	10.2	−6.9	8.9	−6.6

Export expansion contributed more to the growth of commodity output in each subperiod than did import substitution. The combined contribution of export expansion and import substitution was greatest from 1963 to 1966, the same period in which the major policy reforms were carried out and rapid growth began. Growth of primary exports and import substitution in manufacturing had characterized the earlier period but after 1960 manufactures dominated the growth of exports and there was less import substitution than there had been in the late 1950s.

The figures below show the *direct* contributions of export expansion and import substitution to the growth of *manufactured* output alone:

	1955–60	1960–63	1963–66	1966–68
Export expansion	5.1%	6.2%	29.4%	13.0%
Import substitution	24.2	0.9	14.4	−0.1

The late 1950s is seen to have been a period of major import substitution in manufacturing when exports played a relatively minor role in Korea's industrialization. Export growth is again seen to have made its major relative contribution from 1963 to 1966. Both these and the preceding figures for import substitution clearly reflect the effect of the high capital inflow that financed large imports of capital goods in the late 1960s.

We turn now to the estimates of direct contribution by individual industries, an analysis that can only cover 1960 to 1968. Table 6–7 shows the share of direct trade effects (i.e., export expansion plus import substitution) in the output change of each of the eleven industrial groups listed in Part 2 of Table 6–6.

The importance of trade effects was greatest for intermediate products and consumer goods (groups 6, 7, 8, and 9). Along with agriculture and processed food (groups 1 and 3) these industries were also the major sources of the growth of total domestic demand and output. Because of rapid growth of investment, import substitution (a rise of import shares) in investment goods production (groups 10 and 11) was negative. Thus the growth of the investment goods industries was almost wholly due to domestic demand. Exports contributed more than import substitution to the growth of *every* group (except group 5, construction materials). It is also remarkable that for every group 1963–66 stands out as having been the period when exports contributed most.

While import substitution played a relatively modest role in each industry's growth over the eight years, it did predominate in some industries during shorter intervals. Furthermore, the relatively low share of import substitution from 1960 to 1968 in the aggregate for manufacturing need not imply that it was unimportant to the 92 individual sectors. Nonetheless, in only 12 out of the 80 manufacturing sectors was import substitution responsible for more than 20 percent of the sector's growth. Sectoral import shares actually increased, leading to negative import substitution, in 39 of the manufacturing sectors and in 8 of the 12 primary sectors. Export expansion, on the other hand, was the source of more than 20 percent of the growth of 20 manufacturing sectors. The contribution of domestic demand expansion was more than 80 percent of the individual sector's growth in well over half of the manufacturing sectors (53 out of 80); thus the importance of domestic demand growth observed in the aggregate carries through for the individual sectors as well.

COMPARISONS WITH "NORMAL" DEVELOPMENT PATTERNS

The contributions of the respective sources to Korea's growth may be compared with a set of norms developed by Chenery (1969). Chenery used a somewhat different, though similar, set of measurements, which will now be

TABLE 6-7
Direct Trade Effects by Industry, 1960 to 1968

Group[b]	Trade Effect	Absolute[a] Value of: Export Expansion	Absolute[a] Value of: Import Substitution	Period of Highest Contribution to Sector's Own Growth — Export Expansion Period	Share	Period of Highest Contribution to Sector's Own Growth — Import Substitution Period	Share
1	-8.0%	-0.3	-16.7	1963-66	2.8%	1963-66	17.0%
2	9.6	7.3	1.7	1963-66	37.1	1966-68	2.9
3	6.2	2.2	1.2	1963-66	11.4	1960-63	26.4
4	12.0	2.9	-0.7	1963-66	24.1	1963-66	12.4
5	13.6	1.4	2.1	1963-66	10.9	1963-66	20.1
6	31.8	27.7	24.1	1963-66	23.2	1963-66	49.8
7	15.4	13.3	6.3	1963-66	23.9	1966-68	7.1
8	43.0	39.3	7.3	1963-66	96.0	1960-63	27.9
9	18.8	3.8	-0.7	1963-66	27.0	1960-63	50.4
10	-41.0	1.5	-9.1	1963-66	47.4	1963-66	-16.9
11	-41.7	0.1	-12.5	1963-66	1.8	1966-68	-11.8

a. In billions of won at constant 1965 world prices.
b. These industrial groups are described in Table 6-6.

developed. Let $m'_{j,t} = M_{j,t}/(D_{j,t} + E_{j,t})$; that is, define import substitution in relation to the change in the ratio of imports to total demand including the sector's exports. Then for the first period, we may write:

$$X_{j,S} = (1 - m'_{j,S}) \cdot D_{j,S} + (1 - m'_{j,S}) \cdot E_{j,S}. \qquad (6\text{-}10)$$

For the second period, we write

$$X_{j,T} = (1 - m'_{j,S}) \cdot D_{j,T} + (1 - m'_{j,S}) \cdot E_{j,T} + m'_{j,S} \qquad (6\text{-}11)$$
$$\cdot (D_{j,T} + E_{j,T}) - M_{j,T}.$$

Chenery classifies growth by sector in terms of the deviation of its growth from that of overall income. Let λ be the ratio of total income in the second period to that in the first. Then multiply the first period's equation by λ and subtract from the second period's equation:

$$\delta X_{j,T} = \underbrace{(1 - m'_{j,S}) \cdot \delta D_{j,T}}_{\substack{\text{Domestic} \\ \text{demand} \\ \text{contribution}}} + \underbrace{(1 - m'_{j,S}) \cdot \delta E_{j,T}}_{\text{Export contribution}} \qquad (6\text{-}12)$$

$$+ \underbrace{(m'_{j,S} - m'_{j,T}) \cdot (D_{j,T} + E_{j,T})}_{\substack{\text{Import} \\ \text{substitution} \\ \text{contribution}}}$$

where δ is the "deviation" operator such that $\delta Y_T = Y_T - \lambda Y_S$ for any variable Y.

The figures shown below give the total, i.e., direct plus indirect, contribution of each source to the deviation from proportional growth of industrial output (as defined by Chenery) from 1955 to 1968, using the Chenery measure just developed. The norms are derived from cross-country and time series data for developing countries and they correspond to the growth of per capita income from $100 to $200.

	Domestic Demand Expansion	Export Expansion	Import Substitution
All country norm	50%	18%	32%
Large country norm	55	24	21
Korea (1960–68)	60	38	2

The industrialization of a "normal" country is considerably less dependent upon export expansion and considerably more dependent upon import substitution.

Another instructive comparison is that of structural changes in aggregate magnitudes for the South Korean economy with those observed in other countries at roughly the same level of per capita income. The most recent comparative study of changes in economic structure is that of Chenery (1970 a, b), where pooled cross-section and time series data are used to estimate regressions from which structural "norms" may be inferred.[12] In Chenery's classification, "industry" equals manufacturing plus construction plus other in our

TABLE 6–8

**Observed Structure in South Korea and Structural Norms
for Less Developed Countries**

Observed Structural Shares

	1955	1960	1966	1968	1972
1. Per capita GNP	$79	$86	$113	$133	$179
2. Capital inflow ratio to GDP	7.7%	8.5%	9.0%	11.8%	4.9%
3. Share of investment in GDP	12.0	10.9	21.9	27.1	20.8
4. Share of exports in GDP	1.7	3.4	10.5	13.3	21.0
5. Share of manufacturing exports in GDP	0.4	1.2	7.5	9.3	17.8
6. Imports as percent of GDP	10.0	12.7	20.4	26.5	26.1
7. Primary share of GDP	48.0	42.2	40.1	33.2	32.0
8. Industry share of GDP	13.0	15.6	21.6	24.1	26.0
9. Utilities share of GDP	3.5	5.3	6.1	7.7	7.5
10. Services share of GDP	35.5	36.9	32.2	35.0	34.5

Structural Norms According to Chenery Equations

	Actual Capital Inflow		Zero Capital Inflow	
Large Countries				
1. Per capita GNP	$79	$179	$79	$179
2. Share of investment in GDP	14.4%	20.2%	12.8%	19.2%
3. Share of exports in GDP	9.8	10.8	16.0	14.8
4. Share of manufacturing exports in GDP	1.4	2.9	0.5	2.3
5. Imports as percent of GDP	17.6	15.8	16.1	14.8
6. Primary share of GDP	52.8	33.5	55.4	35.3
7. Industry share of GDP	14.4	24.9	11.7	23.1
8. Utilities share of GDP	5.2	7.1	5.6	7.4
9. Services share of GDP	27.6	34.5	27.3	34.2

TABLE 6–8 (concluded)

Large Manufacturing Countries

	Actual Capital Inflow		Zero Capital Inflow	
1. Per capita GNP	$79	$179	$79	$179
2. Share of investment in GDP	10.3%	23.1%	12.2%	24.3%
3. Share of exports in GDP	8.1	10.9	9.9	12.0
4. Imports as percent of GDP	15.8	15.8	9.9	12.0
5. Primary share of GDP	51.7	33.5	51.1	33.1
6. Industry share of GDP	17.0	24.4	19.2	25.8
7. Utilities share of GDP	2.9	8.2	3.4	8.5
8. Services share of GDP	28.4	33.9	26.3	32.6

SOURCES (Observed Structural Shares):

Line 1. For 1955 through 1968, GNP in 1965 prices from Bank of Korea, *National Income Statistics Yearbook,* 1971; divided by midyear population estimates from Bank of Korea, *Economic Statistics Yearbook,* 1971, to get per capita GNP in 1965 won. An exchange rate of 278.7 won per dollar was used, equal to the legal exchange rate times our estimate of average nominal protection in 1965. The estimate for 1972 was derived from that for 1968, the ratio of 1972 GNP to 1968 GNP (both in 1970 prices), and the ratio of midyear population in 1972 to that in 1968. The sources for the latter were respectively the August, 1973 *Monthly Economic Statistics* published by the Bank of Korea and the *Economic Statistics Yearbook* for 1973.

Lines 2–4, 6. Bank of Korea, *Monthly Economic Statistics,* August, 1973, Table 91 (at current market prices). The capital inflow ratio equals imports minus exports divided by GNP plus imports minus exports.

Line 5. For 1955 through 1968, current price input-output data. For 1972, derived from trade statistics.

Lines 7–10. Bank of Korea, *Economic Statistics Yearbook, 1973,* Table 144 (Industrial Origin of GDP at Current Factor Cost).

classification, and "utilities" equals social overhead less construction. The data given in Table 6–8 for South Korea are consistent with his definitions; they are taken from the current price national income accounts.

The figures shown in Table 6–8 for structural norms at per capita incomes of $79 (corresponding to 1955) and $179 (corresponding to 1972) require some explanation. They have been estimated from the Chenery regressions in which the explanatory variables include: the log of per capita income and its value squared, the log of population and its value squared, the ratio of the foreign capital inflow to total domestic resources, and three dummy variables corresponding to three different time periods.[13] We have provided two sets of estimates. One is based on the Korean values of per capita income, population, and the observed capital inflow ratio. The other set was similarly obtained from the regressions except that the capital inflow ratio was fixed at zero. The difference between these sets of figures indicates the effects on the structural norms of foreign capital inflows at the rates observed in Korea. Both sets of estimates are derived using the appropriate values for the dummy variables based on the year from which the data were taken. With its population of 32.4 million in 1972, Korea falls in Chenery's large country (LC) and large manufacturing country (LMC) samples; thus estimates from the regressions over both samples are given. To summarize, the figures pertain to the "typical" structure of an economy of Korea's (then) per capita income and size, either based on the observed capital inflow rate or a zero capital inflow rate.

In Table 6–8, we see that Korea's structure in 1955 differed substantially from both the LC and LMC norms. This is understandable given the disruption caused by the Korean War. The most striking irregularity in Korea's structure in 1955 is the very low share of exports in Gross Domestic Product (GDP). The share of imports was also very low. Industrial production was below the norm and services output was exceptionally large as a share of GDP.

By 1972, Korea's exports as a percent of GDP were nearly double the norm for a country of her size, per capita income, and dependence on foreign capital. The ratio of imports to GDP was also unusually high, while the industry share was somewhat above the norm. Because 1972 was, in relative terms, a recession year, the investment rate in that year was nearly normal. However, from 1969 to 1971 it averaged 28.4 percent, well above the norm. Part of the reason for the exceptionally high 1972 export ratio relative to the norm is that Korea is being compared with other countries equally dependent on capital imports. However, even if we compute the norm by assuming that the trade deficit were zero, Korea's export ratio is still much higher than usual.

CONCLUSIONS

From these comparisons with the norm, it appears that (1) the share of primary production was probably lower than normal during the 1960s; that (2) the pace of industrialization was more rapid than in other countries; that (3) the growth of exports, especially of manufactures, was unusually fast; and that (4) the growth of investment was very large and far too quick to be attributed merely to high capital inflows. Exports were not retarded by capital inflows as much as the regressions that determine the norms might suggest; nor can the rapidity of their growth be explained away as simply the result of "catching up to the norm."

The foregoing discussion of exports has been largely descriptive. The rapid growth of exports, the ensuing alteration in the structure of the economy, and the responsiveness of exports to incentives are no proof of efficiency.

Likewise, the growing import content of South Korea's exports is no conclusive indication of inefficiency—it may merely demonstrate that Korea's comparative advantage lies in exporting commodities that happen to be import intensive. There is no reason to believe that more backward integration in exports would be any more efficient than a further expansion of existing types of exports or a venture into new export lines.

Efficiency in exports in particular and in trade and foreign exchange policy in general will be discussed in Chapter 10.

NOTES

1. See Ministry of Finance, *Foreign Trade of Korea,* various issues.
2. The 1970 input-output figures are given in Bank of Korea, *Economic Statistics Yearbook, 1973,* p. 359. The Korean Productivity Center data comes from p. 29 of Korean Productivity Center (1970).
3. The full equation, obtained by the Cochrane-Orcutt technique is:
$$XGM = -651.5 + 0.3357YNA + 1.713ORD + 1.305SUBX$$
$$(-17.0) \quad (61.7) \qquad (13.8) \qquad (10.9)$$
($R^2 = 0.9997$ and Durbin-Watson $= 2.3205$). If ordinary least-squares are used, the coefficients of *ORD* and *SUBX* become significant whenever the period is 1964–70. Before 1964, however, the data do not reveal any significant relationship.
4. Nak Kwan Kim has used quarterly data on exchange rates, export subsidies, relative prices in Korea and abroad, and demand in major export markets in an attempt to estimate export equations for specific commodities from 1965 to 1970. For electrical machinery, knitted outergarments, plywood, and wigs, exchange rate or export subsidy variables are significant and explanatory with high elasticities. For woven cotton fabrics, neither exchange rate nor subsidy variables are important, but exports of these products are controlled by quota. See Kim (1972).
5. The compilation of the 1955 input-output table was conducted under the supervision of Sae Min Oh, Chief, Input-Output Research Section, Bank of Korea, and was financed by grants from the University Committee on Research in the Humanities and Social Sciences and the Council on International and Regional Studies, Princeton University.
6. These were published in 1970 in mimeograph by the Bank of Korea in its *Korean Input-Output Tables for 1960, 1963, 1966 and 1968.*
7. An Annex describing the deflation procedure in detail is available from the authors on request. This Annex also explains how a number of independent statistical series (e.g., national income accounts, various price indexes, the index of manufacturing output) can be systematically "filtered" through a time series of input-output statistics to check the consistency of a large body of economic data for a particular country. Having performed this analysis, we have great confidence in our input-output estimates at constant prices at the 29-sector and higher levels of aggregation. The Annex also discusses the projection back in time of an index of nominal protection based on the 1968 nominal protection rates and observed changes in domestic prices relative to export and import prices.
8. Chenery (1960, 1962) was the first to employ this type of analysis. Our decomposition is closer to that employed by Lewis and Soligo (1965), however. They define

import substitution in relation to total demand, including exports. Their definition is appropriate if the level of aggregation is such that there is considerable reexport activity within broadly defined sectors. Since we are working with highly disaggregated data, the "reexport" specification is incorrect.

9. Details are available from the authors on request.

10. See Fane (1971).

11. These categories were employed in Balassa and Associates (1971).

12. Chenery has subsequently revised the regressions presented in the papers cited; the latest set of regressions, communicated privately to the authors, have been used here to estimate normal structural shares.

13. Total domestic resources are equal to GNP plus imports minus exports.

Chapter 7

Foreign Capital and the Exchange Rate Regime

Beginning in 1965, the South Korean economy became increasingly dependent on foreign borrowing. Foreign loan arrivals rose from $183.0 million to $787.4 million between 1966 and 1971, or close to 10 percent of GNP in 1971.[1] In 1965, a heavy proportion of the loans came from public sources overseas. Between 1968 and 1971 more than two-thirds of all foreign loan arrivals were commercial, mainly suppliers' credits for import of capital equipment from the United States, Japan, France, the United Kingdom, and West Germany (tables 7–1 and 7–2). The sources of public loans also shifted markedly, from a heavy reliance in the early 1960s on United States AID grants and development loans on very soft terms to greater reliance in the later '60s on Japanese, IBRD, and Asian Development Bank loans on relatively hard terms. The increasing emphasis on commercial loans and the shift of sources of public loans has greatly increased the cost of foreign capital imports. All loans greater than one year are denominated in foreign currency, the dollar, the mark, the yen, the franc, or the pound.

OFFICIAL ENCOURAGEMENT OF FOREIGN CAPITAL IMPORTS

The rapid increase in foreign commercial loans and the shift to more expensive sources of public loans has recently become a matter of concern to Korean officials. Throughout most of the 1960s, however, the government had strongly encouraged the import of private foreign capital as a major policy tool in

101

TABLE 7–1

Arrivals of Foreign Capital and Official Grants, 1966 to 1971

(millions of dollars)

	1966	1967	1968	1969	1970	1971
A. Foreign capital arrivals[a]	197.3	296.0	562.1	697.4	709.8	830.3
1. Three years and longer	197.3	239.3	355.5	640.3	653.7	691.5
a. Govt. and multilateral						
institutions-loans	72.8	105.6	70.2	220.9	217.0	317.0
b. Private loans	110.2	124.0	268.4	403.5	371.5	331.6
c. Equity	14.3	9.7	16.9	15.9	65.2	42.9
2. One to three years	—	56.7	206.6	57.1	56.1	138.8
a. Trade credits	—	54.7	166.6	27.1	31.1	49.3
b. Bank loans	—	—	40.0	30.0	25.0	89.5
c. Cash loans	—	2.0	—	—	—	—
B. Official grants	164.9	157.4	150.7	178.7	121.2	103.9
1. AID supporting assistance	61.6	47.1	43.4	28.6	17.0	12.4
2. PL 480	68.3	56.7	63.8	100.7	55.6	47.7
3. Japan P.A.C.[b]	29.3	37.4	30.0	32.1	28.2	16.6
4. Technical assistance	3.7	5.5	7.5	3.9	3.9	5.2
5. Other	2.0	10.8	6.0	13.4	16.5	22.0
Total	362.2	453.4	712.8	876.1	831.0	934.2

NOTE: Subitems may not add exactly to totals because of rounding.
SOURCE: Economic Planning Board; USAID.
a. Gross basis.
b. Property and claim fund as provided in the Korea-Japan Diplomatic Normalization Agreement of June 1965.

dealing with the balance of payments. The Foreign Capital Inducement Law was promulgated in January 1960 at a time when the Development Loan Fund (DLF) of USAID was the only source of foreign loans to Korea.

In early 1962, the government selected 9 major five-year plan projects (involving 19 businesses) that required foreign capital. The government then sent an economic mission to the United States, West Germany, and other industrialized countries in Europe to negotiate financing for the selected projects.

In July 1962, the government enacted two supplements to the Foreign Capital Inducement Law. One provided procedures for imports of capital goods by using long-term export credits of capital exporting countries and the other established procedures for granting repayment guarantees on foreign loans. As a safeguard, all foreign loans, investment proposals, and repayment guarantees had to be approved by the Foreign Capital Inducement Delibera-

TABLE 7-2

Foreign Loan and Investment Agreements, 1959 to 1971

(millions of dollars)

	1959–62	1963	1964	1965	1966	1967	1968	1969	1970	1971
A. Public loans	73.5	9.1	35.4	76.7	153.5	73.8	61.9	233.2	159.2	398.8
1. U.S.A.	49.9	9.1	29.8	71.5	95.0	32.0	28.0	114.9	59.4	120.7
2. Japan	—	—	—	—	44.9	29.9	18.6	11.3	8.9	87.0
3. West Germany	9.6	—	4.4	5.2	13.6	—	—	—	13.3	18.2
4. IBRD, ADB	—	—	—	—	—	—	11.8	89.5	60.0	165.9
5. Others	14.0	—	1.2	—	—	11.9	3.5	17.5	17.4	7.0
B. Commercial loans	1.9	55.3	63.3	78.1	105.1	155.4	483.9	622.8	325.8	347.9
1. U.S.A.	—	33.8	6.3	3.3	3.4	21.0	153.5	217.3	179.7	143.5
2. Japan	—	—	0.4	70.8	67.1	36.2	110.0	71.9	56.2	126.9
3. West Germany	1.4	16.6	16.4	—	22.7	39.5	48.6	48.1	3.7	15.7
4. France	—	2.5	20.5	—	11.2	12.5	29.3	129.0	4.9	6.3
5. U.K.	0.5	—	—	—	0.7	1.8	53.5	56.2	68.2	22.0
6. Others	—	2.4	19.7	4.0	—	44.4	89.0	100.3	13.2	33.3
C. Direct Investment	2.1	5.4	0.8	21.8	2.0	20.9	32.0	48.7	86.3	55.9
1. U.S.A.	2.1	5.4	0.4	21.0	1.9	18.5	17.0	15.1	50.1	23.1
2. Japan	—	—	—	—	—	1.7	8.5	26.7	22.2	28.2
3. Others	—	—	0.4	0.7	0.1	0.7	6.5	6.9	14.0	4.6
Total	77.5	69.8	99.5	176.6	260.7	250.1	577.8	904.6	571.3	802.6

NOTE: IBRD—International Bank for Reconstruction and Development; ADB—Asian Development Bank. Loans are for terms of three years or more. Subitems may not add exactly to totals because of rounding.

SOURCE: Economic Planning Board, *Major Economic Indicators*.

tion Committee, which was chaired by the Minister of the Economic Planning Board.

Tax concessions were also granted to stimulate foreign loans and technology imports, including full and partial exemptions from individual income or corporation income tax on the foreign lender's interest income accruing from approved foreign loans and from income tax on payments made to foreigners who provided technical services. Direct foreign investment was encouraged by full exemption from individual or corporation income tax of the foreign investor's income for the first 3 years, a 50 percent reduction in tax for the next 5 years, full exemption from customs duties on imported capital goods for approved foreign investment projects, and no capital gains taxes on foreign investment.

Because of the positive measures of the government to attract foreign capital, foreign loans and investments "finalized" increased sharply after 1962 and amounted to $222.7 million at the end of 1963 as shown in Table 7–3.[2] As already mentioned, foreign loans finalized at the end of 1960 were only about $18.8 million. At the end of 1963, commercial loans finalized amounted to $127.5 million, larger than the $84.4 million of finalized foreign public loans. Actual "arrivals" of the foreign loans and equity investment were, however, relatively small in 1961–63 as shown in Table 7–3, since finalized foreign loans and investment generally required a year or more before the goods and services financed by the foreign capital actually arrived.

In 1966 a new Foreign Capital Inducement Law revised and streamlined various past laws. The major changes were as follows:

(1) Restrictions on foreign direct investment were removed. First, foreign investors could invest without any floor on the amount; the old law had specified that domestic investors must own at least 25 percent of the equity in a given enterprise. Secondly, the maximum limit on annual profit repatriation of 20 percent of invested capital was removed completely.

(2) If foreign-financed firms threatened default on repayment of loans, the government was authorized to supervise their management and property and to take any measures necessary to achieve solvency.

(3) Enterprises benefiting from government-guaranteed loans were required to float authorized stock within 5 years from the date of approval of the government repayment guarantee.

(4) Government repayment guarantees were limited so that the annual debt service arising from such loans was not to exceed 9 percent of total annual foreign exchange receipts.

(5) Priority and special tax benefits were to be given to loan project applicants who used domestic capital goods for more than 50 percent of the loan amount contracted.

(6) Tax concessions given to enterprises with foreign equity were also

TABLE 7–3

Status of Foreign Capital Inducement, 1961 to 1963

(millions of dollars)

	Loans Finalized through 1963	Loan Arrivals			
		Before 1961	1962	1963	Cumulative through 1963
Public loans—Total (12 cases)	84.4	4.7	3.0	42.8	50.5
AID	61.6	4.7	3.0	27.8	35.5
IDA	14.0	—	—	12.4	12.4
West Germany	8.8	—	—	2.6	2.6
Commercial loans (24 cases)	127.5	—	3.5	18.0	21.5
West Germany	20.9	—	—	10.6	10.6
Italy & France	38.3	—	—	—	—
United States	17.3	—	3.5	6.6	10.1
Japan	38.7	—	—	—	—
Britain	0.6	—	—	0.6	0.6
Switzerland	9.3	—	—	0.3	0.3
Sweden	9.3	—	—	—	—
The Netherlands	2.1	—	—	—	—
Direct & joint investment (7 cases)	10.5	—	0.6	4.8	5.4
United States	6.6	—	0.6	4.8	5.4
West Germany	3.0	—	—	—	—
Japan	0.6	—	—	—.	—
Hong Kong	0.3	—	—	—	—
Grand total	222.7	4.7	7.1	65.6	77.4

SOURCE: Bank of Korea, *Annual Report for 1963*, p. 132.

slightly changed in the new law. Foreign enterprises were fully exempted from the individual income tax, the corporation tax, and the property tax for the first 5 years, and given a 50 percent exemption for the next 3 years. Tariff and commodity tax exemptions on the import of capital goods by foreign investors remained unchanged.

The main rationale for the new Foreign Capital Inducement Law was to give more favorable treatment to foreign direct investment. The new law made no substantial changes affecting foreign loans. However, the inflow of foreign loans was greatly accelerated after 1965. The interest rate reform of 1965 increased incentives to borrow from abroad and the system of commercial bank guarantees on repayments of foreign loans authorized in 1966 stimulated foreign lending. Since the interest rate reform of 1965 caused the rate on ordinary commercial bank loans to jump from 16 to 26 percent per annum, it greatly widened the interest rate gap between domestic bank and foreign loans.

The Korea-Japan Diplomatic Normalization Agreement of June 1965 was also important in increasing foreign capital inflows. According to the Agreement, South Korea was to receive the Property and Claims Fund from Japan, totalling $500 million ($300 million in grants and $200 million in public loans) over the next 10 years. In addition, the Japanese Government was to make available $300 million for commercial loans to South Korea. Initial grants and loans were received in 1966.

FOREIGN CAPITAL IN SOUTH KOREA'S ECONOMIC GROWTH

The inflow of foreign capital of all types (total foreign savings) was substantial between 1960 and 1972 (Table 7–4). In 1960, foreign saving accounted for almost 80 percent of total investment and 8.5 percent of GNP. Foreign

TABLE 7–4

Foreign Capital and Gross Investment, 1960 to 1972

(billion won, current prices)

Year	Foreign Transfers	Foreign Borrowing	Total Foreign Savings	Foreign Saving as Percent of Gross Investment	Foreign Saving as Percent of GNP
1960	22.06	−1.07	20.99	78.3	8.5
1961	29.51	−4.22	25.29	65.2	8.5
1962	30.73	7.22	37.95	83.4	10.9
1963	33.73	18.63	52.36	58.0	10.7
1964	44.03	5.10	49.13	48.1	7.0
1965	53.95	−2.42	51.53	42.2	6.4
1966	59.58	28.05	87.63	39.0	8.5
1967	60.94	51.92	112.86	40.2	9.2
1968	62.54	121.79	184.33	43.1	11.5
1969	70.86	158.16	229.02	36.9	11.0
1970	55.96	193.35	249.31	35.4	9.6
1971	59.32	294.68	354.00	44.0	11.2
1972[a]	66.71	148.32	215.03	26.7	5.6

SOURCE: Bank of Korea, *Economic Statistics Yearbook, 1973*, pp. 298–299.
a. Preliminary

saving as a percent of total investment declined substantially over the decade so that by 1972 it accounted for less than 35 percent of total investment. As a percentage of GNP, however, foreign savings had not shown any downward trend until 1972; previously they had fluctuated year-to-year around an average of about 10 percent of current price GNP. The average gross capital-output ratio from 1960 to 1970 was 2.5. Given this ratio, the average contribution to growth has been about 4 percentage points a year during the 1960s. Since the average rate of growth was about 10 percent over the decade, without foreign savings the growth rate might have been closer to 6 percent and total output in 1970 about 30 percent less than it actually was.

Rough estimates of the contribution of foreign capital to Korea's growth were also made by another method. We assumed that the increment in output each year due to foreign capital was the same as the estimated increment in output due to total investment in that year. The incremental capital-output ratio in this method was not assumed to be constant, but an increasing function of total investment. The contribution of foreign capital is expressed by the difference in 1971 GNP had there been no foreign capital imports from 1966 to 1970. The calculations were made for total foreign savings, total foreign borrowing (foreign savings less transfers from the rest of the world), and total foreign commercial borrowing (excluding borrowing from public sources). The results are (in billions of current won) as follows:

Actual 1971 GNP	3,151.55
Estimated 1971 GNP without foreign savings, 1966 to 1970	2,759.99
Estimated 1971 GNP without foreign borrowing, 1966 to 1970	2,924.65
Estimated 1971 GNP without foreign commercial borrowing, 1966 to 1970	3,023.01

These calculations assumed that the relationship between output growth in the nonagricultural sectors of the economy and investment in those sectors could be estimated by an ordinary least squares regression of real GNP in nonagricultural sectors on previous year's GNP and the previous year's real gross investment (equation 8–2 in Chapter 8). The results show that without foreign savings (which include foreign aid in the form of transfers and loans) between 1966 and 1970, total output in 1971 would have been about 12.4 percent less than it actually was.[3] Without foreign commercial borrowing (which includes no foreign aid flows), the level of output would have been only about 4.1 percent less. The contributions of foreign capital in the late 1960s were relatively modest because the incremental capital-output ratio rose in those years. The marginal contributions of investment to output declined. However, if one measures the contribution of foreign savings during the entire decade of the '60s, the difference in output is quite large. Output in 1971 would have been about a third less. That is, almost one-third of 1971 output can be attributed to foreign savings during the previous decade. Foreign borrowing, however, has not made nearly so substantial a contribution. Most foreign savings in the early 1960s took the form of aid transfers, while foreign borrowing only became large a few years later when capital productivity was considerably reduced.

COST OF CAPITAL IMPORTS

Although the contribution of foreign borrowing to South Korea's economic growth was modest, the costs of these capital imports incurred during the 1960s are making themselves felt a decade later in the form of debt service payments. As foreign debt accumulates, with more than $2 billion outstanding at the beginning of 1971 (including all debt with a maturity greater than one year), debt service payments have grown very rapidly, reaching $326.6 million in 1971 or about 28 percent of total export earnings.[4]

The expected high level of debt service payments in the remainder of the 1970s will introduce a good deal of inflexibility into Korea's balance of payments. With so much foreign exchange required to service loans, imports must bear a greater share of the burden of adjustment if foreign exchange earnings do not grow as rapidly as they have in the past.

Given the rapid rise in debt service and the experience of other countries burdened with large debt service payments, South Korea may find it necessary to renegotiate its outstanding debt. Projections by the Economic Planning Board and the aid donors show that by 1976 debt service including interest on contemplated borrowings should total about $650 million. However, exports have grown so rapidly since these projections were calculated that by 1976 the debt service ratio should be well below 20 percent. Although the costs of imported fuel and international loans have increased, they have been more than offset by the extremely rapid growth of South Korea's export earnings. Nevertheless, heavy debt service obligations may pose future difficulties. For according to the formula in Frank and Cline (1971), the critical ratio of debt service to export earnings in 1976 will be about 17.8 percent. If this figure should be exceeded by the actual debt service ratio, a rescheduling of the debt will be quite likely.[5]

REAL AND NOMINAL RATES OF INTEREST ON FOREIGN CAPITAL

We have seen how South Korea's rapidly increased borrowing from abroad and her shift to more costly sources of capital may make balance of payments adjustment more difficult and costly in the 1970s unless the foreign trade deficit is reduced. According to classical marginal economic analysis, however, the more relevant question is whether the rate of return on foreign financed investment has exceeded the rate of interest on foreign borrowing. If it has, then in theory foreign borrowing is profitable and should be encouraged.

But this approach ignores a number of macroeconomic factors that might determine the cost of foreign borrowing. First, there is the problem of reducing the trade deficit and of generating the trade surpluses eventually required to pay back principal and interest on foreign borrowing. Second, savings must increase rapidly enough not only to repay foreign loans, but also to finance sufficient domestic investment to maintain satisfactory rates of growth. Third, to the extent that foreign loans are the debts of government or defaulted by private investors under government guarantee, the government must have sufficient command over resources through taxation or local borrowing to pay its debts and finance its own domestic expenditures. Fourth, local firms that borrow large amounts abroad may be particularly vulnerable to credit squeezes and large devaluations. Finally, dependence on foreign borrowing and the debt servicing obligations that follow make balance of payments adjustment to short-run cyclic factors more costly and difficult.[6]

Even if these other factors are ignored, the classical view of foreign borrowing begs a number of questions in a world in which monetary, fiscal, and exchange rate policy can affect real rates of interest which do not necessarily reflect relative factor scarcities in different countries.[7] Under conditions of differential rates of inflation and differing degrees of monetary restraint among countries, social and private real rates of interest may diverge and lead to too much or too little foreign borrowing.

Our argument assumes that the U.S. dollar is *the* international reserve currency and that the world economy is one in which a Fisherian "real interest" analysis applies, i.e., one in which rates of inflation may vary from country to country but remain fairly steady within each country where expectations adjust to steady rates. In this theoretical framework, we argue that the real social cost of foreign borrowing in a country like Korea is the nominal rate of interest on foreign-currency-denominated foreign loans *less* the rate of inflation of prices of internationally traded goods. The nominal rate of interest must be so adjusted because repayment of a loan represents a future cost, either as foregone imports, or as additional exports to save or earn the necessary foreign exchange. If the prices of internationally traded goods go up, then the cost of servicing the loan is reduced by the amount of the price inflation. Symbolically, we write for the real social cost of foreign borrowing (r_s):

$$r_s = r_n - r_{ip} \qquad (7\text{-}1)$$

where r_n is the nominal rate of interest on foreign loans and r_{ip} is the rate of price inflation of internationally traded goods.

The private real interest cost to the local borrower, however, may be quite different. The nominal rate of interest on foreign borrowing must be adjusted by the *local* rate of price inflation *and* the rate at which the local currency devalues. The local borrower repays the loan in terms of local currency which must be converted into dollars at the future rate of exchange. As such, the real cost of repayment declines when the local price level increases and increases when the local currency is devalued. The formula, then, for the real private interest cost of the loan r_p is

$$r_p = r_n - r_{dp} + r_e \qquad (7\text{-}2)$$

where r_{dp} is the rate of domestic price inflation and r_e is the rate of local currency devaluation.

If the real private cost of foreign borrowing is less than the real social cost, then foreign borrowing will be excessive if local borrowers incur debt up to the level at which the real rate of return equals the real private cost of foreign borrowing. This is illustrated by the marginal efficiency of investment schedule as shown in Figure 7–1. The optimal level of foreign borrowing is F_1 at which point the real social cost of foreign borrowing equals the rate of return on investment. The actual level of foreign borrowing will tend toward F_2, the level at which the rate of return equals the private cost of foreign borrowing and which exceeds the optimal level. The social and private costs of foreign borrowing will thus only be equal if

$$r_e = r_{dp} - r_{ip} \qquad (7\text{-}3)$$

or if the rate of local currency devaluation equals the rate of domestic price inflation less the rate of inflation of prices of internationally traded goods.

EFFICIENCY OF FOREIGN BORROWING

The effect of a divergence between the real social and real private interest costs of a foreign loan on efficiency of investment can be shown in terms of a Fisherian analysis of consumption, investment and interest rates. For purposes of this analysis, we assume a single commodity world and two discrete time periods. The analysis may be generalized to multiple time periods, but the basic results should remain the same.

FIGURE 7–1

Marginal Efficiency of Investment Schedule

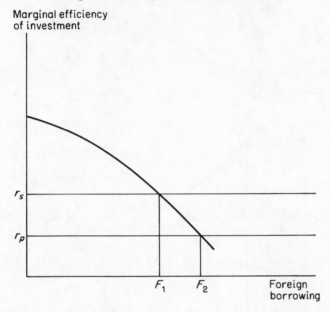

Figure 7–2 shows a Fisherian diagram with consumption in period t on the horizontal axis and consumption in period $t + 1$ on the vertical axis. If there is no saving and no investment, output in period t is OG, and output in period $t + 1$ is OE. Output in both periods is equal ($OG = OE$), and consumption in both periods is the same and equal to output.

The curve ABC is a transformation curve, the slope of which is one plus the single period rate of return on capital. The curve HI is a social indifference curve, the slope of which is the marginal rate of substitution between consumption in period t and period $t + 1$ or one plus the rate of time preference. The optimal distribution of consumption between period t and period $t + 1$ is shown by the point B. The optimal level of savings and investment in period t is given by the distance FG. Total output in period $t + 1$ is the same as total consumption in period $t + 1$ and equal to OD. The equilibrium or optimal interest rate is the same as the optimal rate of return on capital and the optimal rate of time preference. All are equal to the slope of the transformation curve ABC at B minus unity (or the slope of the indifference curve HI at B minus unity).

The analysis so far assumes that there is no foreign borrowing. If foreign capital is available *at a rate of interest less than the equilibrium interest rate* as shown in Figure 7–2, foreign borrowing can increase consumption in *both*

FIGURE 7–2

Optimal Consumption Allocation over Time: No Foreign Borrowing

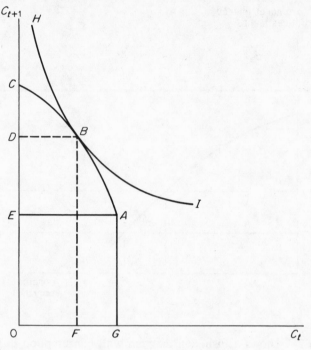

periods t and $t + 1$ and increase the level of social welfare. The possibility is depicted in Figure 7–3.

In Figure 7–3, the slope of the line MN is one plus the rate of interest on a foreign loan (i.e., foreign capital import). The availability of foreign loans allows for any combination of consumption in periods t and $t + 1$ along the line MN which is tangent to the transformation curve ABC. The optimal combination of consumption in periods t and $t + 1$ is represented by point B' which lies above and to the right of B, indicating that it is possible to achieve greater consumption in both periods when foreign borrowing is permitted.

Total foreign borrowing in period t is given by the distance KF' while domestic saving is $F'G$. Total income in period t is OG and consumption OF'. In period $t + 1$, total product (domestic) is OD', and LD' represents domestic savings. Foreign savings is negative and also equal to LD' which represents payments of principal and interest on the original loan KF'. The foreign borrowing is efficient when the rate of interest on the foreign borrowing is less than the domestic equilibrium rate without foreign borrowing.

FIGURE 7–3
Optimal Consumption Allocation over Time with Foreign Borrowing

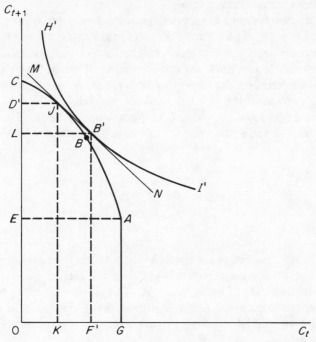

Suppose, however, we complicate our analysis by allowing a local money supply and price inflation. We assume a simple quantity theory. The government through its central bank determines a money supply and this in turn determines the price level for our single commodity. The foreign price of the commodity is assumed to be the *numeraire* so that the foreign price of one unit of the good is always unity. Suppose the existence of an exchange bank that exchanges local currency for foreign currency and vice versa at a rate determined by the government. To keep matters simple, suppose also that the exchange bank acts as an export and import agent. When it receives local currency, it purchases the domestic good and sells it abroad to obtain foreign currency to make payments abroad. When it receives foreign currency, it imports goods from abroad and sells them domestically to obtain local currency.

We assume that the exchange bank carries no reserves from period to period. Therefore, payments and receipts of foreign currency must balance. If local currency proceeds are not sufficient to make payments equal receipts, the government taxes local entrepreneurs in kind and turns the proceeds over to the exchange bank which then exports the commodities to obtain foreign currency to make payments. If payments are less than receipts, the exchange bank imports commodities with the excess receipts and the goods are distributed as subsidies to private individuals.

Given this simple model, suppose the price level rises from period t to period $t + 1$. Let p_{t+1}/p_t be the ratio of prices in the two periods. On the other hand, suppose the exchange rate between the foreign and domestic currency remains the same. If foreign loans are denominated in the foreign currency and the rate of interest on the foreign loans is r, the *real* value of the loan receipt in terms of local currency is L/p_t and the *real* value of the *local* currency repayments is $L(1 + r)/p_{t+1}$ where L is the amount of the loan in terms of local currency. The ratio of payments to the original amount of the loan in real terms is

$$(1 + r) \frac{p_t}{p_{t+1}} = (1 + r - \frac{\Delta p}{p_t}) + (\Delta p/p_{t+1}) (\Delta p/p_{t+1} - r) \quad (7\text{–}4)$$

$$\approx (1 + r - \frac{\Delta p}{p_t})$$

where $\Delta p = p_{t+1} - p_t$. The approximation indicates that the *real* rate of interest to the domestic borrower is nearly equal to the rate of interest r on the foreign loan less the rate of inflation $\Delta p/p_t$. This situation is depicted in Figure 7–4 where the slope of the line MN is the ratio of repayment in real terms to the original amount of the loan in real terms or approximately equal to $(1 + r - \Delta p/p_t)$.

Private entrepreneurs, acting on the basis of the private real rate of interest (assuming that they anticipate the inflation), borrow an amount KF' from abroad, expecting to reach the consumption point B'. The actual interest rate in terms of the *good* (the rate which the exchange bank must pay abroad), however, is represented by the slope $(1 + r)$ of the line $M'N'$. The local currency proceeds of the exchange bank are not enough to purchase the amounts of goods required to pay the foreign loan. The local currency proceeds are $D'P$ in terms of goods. In order to repay the loan, the government taxes local borrowers by an amount PL to meet the full repayment represented by $D'L$. The actual consumption point is B'' rather than B'. The actual consumption point B'' represents less consumption in both periods than could be achieved if private entrepreneurs acted on the basis of the real foreign rate of interest. For example, the point B which lies above and to the right of B'' could be achieved if the entrepreneurs acted under the correct assumption as to the interest rate.

The only way to reach the optimal point B, given the rate of price inflation, is to devalue the local currency at a rate equal to the rate of inflation. The real value of the local currency receipts of the loan are $L \cdot e_t/p_t$ and the real value of the local currency repayments is $L(1 + r) \cdot e_{t+1}/p_{t+1}$ where

FIGURE 7–4
Inefficiency in Consumption over Time

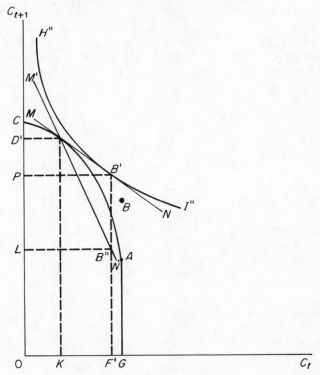

e_t is the exchange rate. The ratio of the two is equal to $(1 + r)$ if and only if $e_t/p_t = e_{t+1}/p_{t+1}$ or $1 + \Delta p/p_t$ is equal to $1 + \Delta e/e_t$.

In this model, when the rate of devaluation equals the rate of inflation, an efficient investment pattern is achieved. The analysis assumes that the international price is the *numeraire* and it can easily be generalized to a situation in which international prices increase. In that case, efficient investment occurs only when the local currency devalues at a rate equal to the difference between the rate of domestic inflation and the rate of inflation of international prices— that is, when the real private and social interest rates are equal.

REAL PRIVATE AND SOCIAL COSTS
OF FOREIGN BORROWING

In Table 7–5, we have estimated the private and social real interest costs for Korea from 1965 to 1970. They indicate that, if the appropriate domestic

TABLE 7–5
Private and Social Real Interest Costs, 1965 to 1970

	1965	1966	1967	1968	1969	1970
Nominal interest rate on foreign loans[a]	5.6	5.7	6.1	5.9	7.1	7.0
Less: rate of inflation of prices of internationally traded goods[b]	−2.3	−2.3	−2.3	−2.3	−2.3	−2.3
Equals: estimated real social interest cost of foreign loans	3.3	3.4	3.8	3.6	4.8	4.7
Nominal interest rate on foreign loans	5.6	5.7	6.1	5.9	7.1	7.0
Less: rate of domestic price inflation[c]	−11.3	−11.3	−11.3	−11.3	−11.3	−11.3
	(−8.5)	(−8.5)	(−8.5)	(−8.5)	(−8.5)	(−8.5)
Plus: rate of devaluation[d]	3.2	3.2	3.2	3.2	3.2	3.2
Equals: estimated real private cost of foreign loans	−2.5	−2.4	−2.0	−2.2	−1.0	−1.1
	(0.3)	(0.4)	(0.8)	(0.6)	(1.8)	(1.7)

a. Weighted annual average rate of interest on foreign loan agreements.

b. Rate of inflation from 1965 to 1970 of wholesale prices of major trading partners, using wholesale price indexes weighted by trade volume.

c. Rate of inflation of GNP deflator of Korea, 1965 to 1970. Figures in parentheses are rate of inflation of wholesale price index over the same period.

d. Average rate of devaluation exchange rate, 1965 to 1970.

price index is the GNP deflator, the private real interest cost has been 5.8 percentage points lower than the social real interest cost and that there has been a powerful incentive to import foreign capital at an excessive rate. In fact, the real private interest cost of foreign loans has been substantially negative. If the wholesale price index is used, however, the divergence between private and social costs is smaller, but still 3 percentage points.

The price index used for prices of internationally traded goods was a weighted average of U.S. and Japanese wholesale prices. This is probably a slight overestimate of the rate of price increase for South Korea's traded goods. Japanese export prices have tended to increase less rapidly than the wholesale price index while U.S. export prices have probably increased slightly more rapidly than wholesale prices. The difference, however, between growth in Japanese export prices and wholesale prices has probably been somewhat greater than the difference in growth of U.S. export prices and wholesale prices.[8] If South Korean export and import prices indexes were available, they would probably show somewhat more divergence between private and social real interest costs than those shown in Table 7–5 and thus somewhat more of an incentive to borrow abroad beyond the optimal level.

The rate of devaluation used in the computations in Table 7–5 was the average rate of devaluation between 1965 and 1970. This includes a period from August 1965 to the end of 1967 when the exchange rate was pegged at about 270 won to the dollar and rapid growth of foreign commercial borrowing began. Interviews with businessmen suggest that at that time, there was no expectation that the exchange rate would change as much as it did during the late 1960s. If this is true, the large influx of foreign capital may have been due in part to an underestimate of the real private costs because of an expectation of a stable exchange rate. The value of the won, however, gradually fell between the beginning of 1968 and mid-1971, at which time there was a sharp devaluation. Nevertheless, during 1968 and 1969, foreign commercial borrowing continued to grow rapidly. In 1970, however, the demand for foreign loans was reduced sharply. Perhaps by 1970, it had become clear to businessmen that movement in the value of the won was not temporary and that the true cost of foreign borrowing was likely to be greater than they had originally expected, although government ceilings on foreign borrowing may have been chiefly responsible for the slow growth of foreign borrowing in 1970.

In 1971 and 1972 also, the demand for foreign commercial borrowing seems to have slackened. According to businessmen interviewed, their desire for foreign loans was curbed by the devaluation of June 1971 and by the reintroduction of the rapidly gliding peg in early 1972.

FOREIGN BORROWING AND SECTORAL RESOURCE ALLOCATION

We have shown how a failure to devalue at a sufficient rate, given domestic price inflation, is likely to lead to excessive foreign borrowing and investment. We now note also that, because of the institutional nature of capital markets, low real private interest rates on foreign loans may distort the sectoral allocation of resources.

In particular, foreign commercial loans are often most easily available in the form of supplier credits. Thus, loans are often tied to purchases of capital equipment abroad. Of course, this is often true for public loans as well. This has two effects: First, low-cost foreign loans favor those sectors that are relatively heavy users of foreign capital equipment. Second, low-cost foreign loans relative to local commercial loans may be a form of negative protection to the local capital goods industries.

TABLE 7–6

**Comparative Real Interest Costs of Domestic and Foreign Loans,
1965 to 1970**

	1965	1966	1967	1968	1969	1970
Nominal local interest rates:						
Commercial bank prime rate	18.5	26.0	26.0	25.8	24.0	24.0
Korea Development Bank rate on equipment loans	9.5	11.0	11.0	11.0	12.0	12.0
Real local interest rates equals nominal rate less rate of inflation of 8.5 percent for wholesale price index (11.3 percent for GNP deflator) for 1965–70						
Commercial bank prime rate	10.0	17.5	17.5	17.3	15.5	15.5
	(7.2)	(14.7)	(14.7)	(14.5)	(12.7)	(12.7)
Korea Development Bank equipment rate	1.0	2.5	2.5	2.5	3.5	3.5
	(−1.8)	(−0.3)	(−0.3)	(−0.3)	(0.7)	(0.7)
Real private interest cost of foreign loans	0.3	0.4	0.8	0.6	1.8	1.7
	(−2.3)	(−2.4)	(−2.0)	(−2.2)	(−1.0)	(−1.1)

NOTE: Figures in parentheses are based on use of the GNP deflator. All other real interest rates are based on the wholesale price index.
SOURCE: Bank of Korea, *Economic Statistics Yearbook, 1971*, pp. 133–135.

Table 7–6 compares local real interest rates with the real private interest costs of foreign borrowing. Local real interest rates tend to be much higher, particularly those on commercial bank loans. Local capital equipment suppliers are thus at a disadvantage in that available sources of financing carry higher real interest costs than financial sources for purchase of foreign equipment. This disadvantage can be viewed as an effective tax on local equipment producers. This effective tax can be quantitatively assessed by measuring the difference in present value of a stream of repayments required to service two types of loan, a loan to purchase foreign equipment and a loan to purchase domestic equipment. (See the appendix to this chapter for mathematical details.)

Table 7–7 gives the percentage subsidy implicit in the purchase of 1,000 won of foreign machinery financed by a foreign loan instead of 1,000 won of domestic equipment financed by a domestic loan. Both KDB equipment and commercial bank loans in two different years, 1965 and 1970, are considered.[9]

TABLE 7–7

Present Value of Repayments on 1,000 Won Loan

	1965	1970
Foreign loan	775.4	813.4
Commercial bank loan	917.4	1,009.9
KDB equipment loan	765.9	808.8

NOTE: Terms are 5 years repayment, 20 percent down. Discount rate is 15 percent.

For KDB equipment loans, the cost of financing capital goods purchases whether locally or by foreign loan is about the same. For bank loans, however, the difference in cost is very great. The cost (present value of repayments) of financing a 1,000 won loan was 917.4 for a commercial bank loan, or 18 percent greater than the cost of a foreign loan. In 1970, the difference had grown to 24 percent. This means that local sellers were subject to an implicit tax of 18 to 24 percent when competing against foreign capital goods financed abroad when commercial bank loans were the source of local finance.

These estimates do not take into account the government's special loan fund instituted in 1967 for financing purchases of domestic machinery. Very little credit was provided at first under this program, and there were administrative difficulties at the outset. After a couple of years, however, this special loan fund grew in importance and offset some of the interest rate distortions that had favored foreign-made machinery purchases.

DISCONTINUOUS DEVALUATION AND GLIDING PARITY

We have not yet distinguished between discontinuous devaluations and gradual changes in the exchange rate. In South Korea, discontinuous devaluations occurred in February 1960, January and February 1961, May 1964, and June 1971. The rate was allowed to float for a while in the spring of 1965, between 1968 and June 1971, and again beginning in early 1972 until June of that year. Thus, Korea has alternated between a policy of gradual devaluation and an adjustable exchange rate peg. Both policies have been aimed at maintaining the purchasing power parity of the won by adjusting for the effects of domestic and international price inflation.

Whatever the effects of the two policies on commodity exports and imports might be, the effect of pegged rates with discontinuous devaluations on the capital side of the balance of payments is likely to be destabilizing under conditions of rapid domestic inflation. First, if borrowers of foreign capital come to expect fixed rates accompanied by occasional large devaluations, they will set a very high premium on guessing when the next devaluation will take place. If no devaluation is expected for a few years, the demand for foreign capital will be very great. Borrowers will attempt to borrow as much capital as possible when the exchange risk is believed to be low and conversely the demand for foreign loans may fall off sharply when expectations of an imminent devaluation are high. Thus, the demand for foreign loans will be very unstable and will fluctuate in response to rumors of devaluation. This effect, of course, occurs on the commodity side, but to a much lesser degree. When domestic producers expect a devaluation in the near future, the current demand for imports will be high and the short-run supply of exports will fall off. But the extent to which imports can be accelerated and exports held back may be limited by transportation and storage facilities. The cost of investing in transport and storage facilities to handle large short-run fluctuations in stocks as a hedge against devaluation may be very high. There is no comparable cost on the capital side. Increasing one's portfolio of foreign loans involves only the interest charges on the loans.

Second, pegged exchange rates with discontinuous devaluations distort the term structure of foreign loans. There is an increased premium on short-term credits in preference to long term. When credits are denominated in foreign currency, short-term credits with frequent roll-over substantially reduce the exchange risk to the borrower when large devaluations may take place. On the other hand, if borrowers expect devaluations to be gradual, continuous, and in line with the divergence between domestic and international price inflation, they have no reason to shift foreign loan portfolios to short-term loans as a hedge against devaluation.

Finally, pegged rates with discontinuous devaluations cause large and discontinuous changes in the value of foreign loan liabilities. In other words, producers and traders who have guessed incorrectly and find themselves holding large foreign loan liabilities may suffer large losses in their *net* real asset positions. Whenever large amounts of foreign loans are outstanding, abrupt and large devaluations can substantially affect the asset positions of firms and individuals. Those who suffer such losses are likely to resist further devaluations, as they have in Korea, and thus devaluation becomes a politically dangerous and increasingly difficult measure to implement. As a result, domestic inflation quickly erodes the purchasing power parity of the exchange rate and corrective action becomes longer delayed and more problematical.

As an alternative to gradual devaluation or to pegged exchange rates with discontinuous devaluation, a flat surtax on imports could be imposed together with the same flat subsidy on exports. This would be equivalent to a devaluation for commodity transactions. Since capital transactions and transfer payments would continue to take place on the basis of the nondevalued official exchange rate, the political problem that would otherwise arise from deterioration of the net asset position of borrowers of foreign capital could be avoided. The objection, however, to this approach is that real interest rates in terms of won would remain low and the social opportunity cost of foreign loans would continue to be greater than the private real interest cost of foreign loans. While flat surcharges and subsidies on commodity transactions may help maintain a realistic exchange rate for exports and imports, the demand for foreign loans would continue to exceed equilibrium.

To achieve an efficient level of foreign capital inflow and efficient use of foreign loans, a gliding parity approach to exchange rate adjustment has in our view a good deal of merit. Since a gliding parity offers no excessive incentives to borrow abroad, capital movement stability is more likely to be achieved. Real domestic interest rates, however, may exceed the real rate on foreign loans even if purchasing power parity is maintained. Thus, if purchases of domestic equipment are usually financed through domestic loans and imported equipment through foreign loans, the domestic machinery industry may remain at a disadvantage. If, however, the same real domestic interest rate had been maintained during the 1960s, while the official exchange rate was adjusted to maintain parity, then at least the disincentive to domestic machinery purchase would have been reduced, since the divergence between real interest rates on foreign and domestic loans would have been narrowed.

ECONOMIC POLICY AND FOREIGN LOANS

Exchange rate policy in South Korea has facilitated the inflow of foreign loans, perhaps excessively, and has resulted in a net disincentive to local machinery producers. In fact, a local guarantee program favors imported machinery. Domestic borrowers of foreign loans can obtain Korea Development Bank or commercial bank guarantees on repayment (both amortization and interest payments) in accordance with the Foreign Capital Inducement Law. This system greatly facilitates the import of foreign loans since foreign lenders are guaranteed repayment regardless of the domestic borrower's credit standing.

Second best solutions in place of gliding parity include either an interest equalization tax or quantitative restrictions on capital flows. The main rationale for an interest equalization tax would not be the common notion that it would equalize domestic and foreign loan interest rates, but rather that it would equalize the real interest cost in terms of won and the real interest cost in terms of dollars. A differential between foreign and domestic interest rates may reflect real differences in opportunity costs of foreign and domestic capital. The differential between real dollar and real won interest cost of foreign loans, however, represents a divergency between social and private costs.

Controls on foreign borrowing have been in effect since 1962 when the Foreign Capital Inducement Deliberation Committee was set up in the Economic Planning Board. In practice, however, foreign loan applications were generally encouraged if they could meet minimal criteria and no strict limits on foreign borrowing were enforced. Recently, however, an IMF standby agreement has required the Korean government to issue letters of intent to strictly limit foreign capital movements by loan categories based on the term of the loan. The strictest limitations were placed on one- to three-year loans, while very long term loans were given liberal treatment. The effect of IMF pressure can be seen in the 1970 figures for loan arrivals and agreements (tables 7–1 and 7–2). After increasing more than three and a half times between 1966 and 1969, foreign capital arrivals increased by less than 2 percent in 1970. Foreign commercial loan agreements, which increased almost ten times between 1964 and 1969, actually decreased in 1970. These restrictions on foreign capital imports may not be applied in the most evenhanded or efficient way, but they have virtually stopped the extremely rapid growth in foreign capital imports.

As part of the revision of economic policies in August 1972, domestic interest rates were lowered. At the same time, foreign interest rates had begun to creep up with the net result that the incentive to borrow abroad has been reduced. Furthermore, since South Korea's exports continue to grow very rapidly, and since imports in the early 1970s have on the average grown much less rapidly, the need to borrow abroad to finance a trade deficit has abated. The domestic machinery industry has begun to develop and special government-sponsored credit programs have spurred sales. Thus, the need to finance capital goods purchases abroad has become relatively less important. The days of very heavy foreign borrowing, excessively encouraged by distortions in interest rates, will probably come to an end in this decade. During the 1960s, however, the high degree of reliance on capital imports made important contributions to South Korean growth.

APPENDIX: CALCULATION OF IMPLICIT SUBSIDIES ON FOREIGN LOANS

For the purchaser of foreign equipment, the present value per won of a loan can be expressed in the following way: Let

$A_o \equiv$ down payment required on the purchase of equipment, expressed as a fraction per dollar lent

$A_t \equiv$ amortization payment in year t, expressed as a fraction per dollar lent, for $t = 1, \ldots, T$, where T is the maturity of the loan.

If e_t is the exchange rate (won per dollar) and p_t is the domestic price index, then

$$A_o{}^* = \frac{A_o \cdot e_o}{p_o},\qquad (7\text{--}5)$$

and

$$A_t{}^* = \frac{A_t \cdot e_t}{p_t}\qquad (7\text{--}6)$$

are the down payment and amortization payment, respectively, in real won terms. The present value per won of a loan to purchase the foreign equipment is

$$PV_f = \sum_{t=0}^{T} A_t{}^* / (1+\rho)^t + r_p \sum_{t=1}^{T} (1 - \sum_{\tau=0}^{t-1} A_\tau{}^*) / (1+\rho)^t \qquad (7\text{--}7)$$

where r_p is the real private rate of interest given in equation (7–2). The discount rate ρ is the real opportunity cost of domestic capital.

The present value per won of a loan used to finance the purchase of domestic equipment is

$$PV_d = \sum_{t=0}^{T} B_t / (1+\rho)^t + r_d \sum_{t=1}^{T} (1 - \sum_{\tau=0}^{t-1} B_\tau) / (1+\rho)^t \qquad (7\text{--}8)$$

where B_o is the down payment ratio and B_t for $t = 1, \ldots, T$ the amortization rate, respectively, in real won terms. r_d is the real rate of interest on domestic loans.

The differential between the present value per won of a loan used to purchase domestic equipment (7–8) and a loan used to purchase foreign equipment (7–7) is the implicit subsidy rate to the purchases of the foreign equipment or the implicit tax rate on purchases of domestic equipment.

$$\begin{array}{c}\text{Implicit tax rate on domestic producers}\\ \text{of capital equipment} = PV_d - PV_f.\end{array}\qquad (7\text{--}9)$$

Even if the price of domestic equipment is lower than the price of foreign equipment and the domestic and foreign equipment are equal in quality, the effect of the real interest rate differential may make it profitable to purchase the foreign equipment. That is, the implicit tax rate in (7–9) could more than make up for the difference in price.

These implicit tax rates or subsidy rates can be incorporated into a sectoral analysis of effective protection in much the same way as other taxes and subsidies are (see the previous chapter).

NOTES

1. This includes arrivals of loans of maturity greater than one year. Foreign loan arrivals are shown in Table 7–1 and include all the items under row A except for equity (direct) investment which came to be important only in 1970. "Arrivals" indicates the amount of credit actually drawn by local importers as distinct from the amount of borrowing based on completed loan agreements. Separate statistics are kept for arrivals and for agreements.

2. A loan is "finalized" when an agreement is signed, while loan arrivals may be delayed for several years after finalization.

3. This estimate is smaller than it would be if we assumed a constant incremental capital-output ratio.

4. USAID, Korea Mission.

5. Among 145 observations taken elsewhere during the 1950s and '60s, the critical debt service indicator was correct more than 90 percent of the time in predicting rescheduling. See Frank and Cline (1971).

6. For a more detailed discussion of these and other factors see Frank (1970).

7. For references to the literature about differential rates of price inflation under fixed exchange rates and how they may stimulate capital movements which are not necessarily in the direction of higher marginal efficiency of capital, see Willet (1970).

8. See McKinnon (1971). The price indexes used by McKinnon are taken from unpublished estimates by the U.S. Department of Labor. Export and import price indexes are not generally available for the major world-trading economies. Unit-value indexes, which are sometimes used as price indexes of traded goods, are usually quite unreliable.

9. Present value of 1970 loan is in terms of 1965 present value, using 1970 relative interest rates.

Chapter 8

Macroeconomic Relationships and Commercial Policy Variables

In this chapter we use an econometric model to test a number of hypotheses about the effects of commercial policy variables on macroeconomic behavior. Some other relationships are investigated such as the interest rate elasticity of savings and foreign capital imports. The basic model derived in this chapter is used in the next chapter to determine by simulation techniques the effect of commercial policy variables on the growth of the economy.

THE BASIC MODEL

In matrix form, the basic model can be expressed as follows:

$$B \cdot \psi_t + \Delta \psi_{t-\tau} + \Gamma_1 \phi_{1t} + \Gamma_2 \phi_{2t} + \Gamma_3 \phi_{3t} + e_t = 0 \qquad (8\text{--}1)$$

where B is a square matrix, ψ_t is a column vector of endogenous variables, $\psi_{t-\tau}$ is a column vector of lagged endogenous variables, ϕ_{1t}, ϕ_{2t}, and ϕ_{3t} are each vectors of exogenous variables, e_t is a column vector of error terms, and Γ_1, Γ_2, Γ_3 and Δ are matrixes. The exogenous variables ϕ_{1t} are called *basic* commercial policy variables; ϕ_{2t} are *derived* commercial policy variables, and ϕ_{3t} are other exogenous variables.

The endogenous variables of the system are described in Table 8–1. All of them are measured in terms of constant 1965 won. The exogenous variables are shown in Table 8–2 and except for rates and ratios, population, and dummy variables, all are shown in terms of 1965 constant won. Tables 8–3 and 8–4 show the matrix structure of the basic model expressed in equation

125

TABLE 8-1

Endogenous Variables of the Model

$\psi_{1,t}$ $= YNA_t$:	Nonagricultural value added
$\psi_{2,t}$ $= Y_t$:	Gross national product
$\psi_{3,t}$ $= DTR_t$:	Direct tax revenues
$\psi_{4,t}$ $= INT_t$:	Indirect tax revenues, excluding customs duties
$\psi_{5,t}$ $= SG_t$:	Government savings
$\psi_{6,t}$ $= GC_t$:	Grain consumption
$\psi_{7,t}$ $= IVG_t$:	Investment in grain inventories
$\psi_{8,t}$ $= MG_t$:	Imports of grain
$\psi_{9,t}$ $= ILG_t$:	Level of grain inventories
$\psi_{10,t}$ $= SC_t$:	Corporate savings
$\psi_{11,t}$ $= YDP_t$:	Disposable income of households
$\psi_{12,t}$ $= SH_t$:	Household savings
$\psi_{13,t}$ $= INA_t$:	Nonagricultural gross fixed investment
$\psi_{14,t}$ $= I_t$:	Total gross fixed investment
$\psi_{15,t}$ $= CK_t$:	Foreign commercial loans
$\psi_{16,t}$ $= DC_t$:	Consumption expenditures
$\psi_{17,t}$ $= MC_t$:	Imports of consumption goods
$\psi_{18,t}$ $= MK_t$:	Imports of capital goods
$\psi_{19,t}$ $= XGM_t$:	Manufactured exports
$\psi_{20,t}$ $= X_t$:	Total export of goods
$\psi_{21,t}$ $= MI_t$:	Imports of intermediate goods
$\psi_{22,t}$ $= M_t$:	Total import of goods
$\psi_{23,t}$ $= SK_t$:	Short-term capital movements and changes in foreign reserves
$\psi_{24,t}$ $= IV_t$:	Inventory investment

(8–1). To facilitate discussion of the model the endogenous variables (and therefore equations of the model) are separated into six groups. Group 1 contains two equations, one of which determines nonagricultural output and an identity which involves the determination of total GNP. Group 2 contains three equations relating to direct and indirect tax revenues and government savings. Group 3 contains four equations relating to grain consumption, grain imports, and grain inventories. Group 4 involves equations for household savings, corporate savings, fixed investment, foreign loans, and domestic consumption. Group 5 contains five equations relating to exports, imports, and short-term capital movements. Group 6 contains two identities, one concerning the balance of payments and the other concerning savings and investment.

TABLE 8–2
Exogenous Variables of the Model

Basic commercial policy variables

$\phi_{1,1,t}$	$= ORD_t$	:	Official exchange rate on purchasing-power-parity basis
$\phi_{1,2,t}$	$= XPX_t$	:	Export premium per dollar of exports
$\phi_{1,3,t}$	$= SOX_t$	:	Subsidies per dollar of exports
$\phi_{1,4,t}$	$= TAM_t$	:	Tariffs and foreign exchange tax per dollar of imports

Derived commercial policy variables

$\phi_{2,1,t}$	$= XPM_t$	:	Export premia per dollar of imports
$\phi_{2,2,t}$	$= SUBM_t$	:	Tariffs and tariff equivalents per dollar of imports
$\phi_{2,3,t}$	$= SUBX_t$	:	Subsidies and subsidy equivalents per dollar of exports
$\phi_{2,4,t}$	$= SXDT_t$	:	Total subsidies on exports in the form of internal tax relief
$\phi_{2,5,t}$	$= TAR_t$	:	Total tariffs and foreign exchange taxes
$\phi_{2,6,t}$	$= MARDEV_t$:		Average rate of devaluation averaged over current year and the two previous years

Other exogenous variables

$\phi_{3,1,t}$	$= YA_t$	:	Agricultural value added
$\phi_{3,2,t}$	$= G_t$	:	Current government expenditures
$\phi_{3,3,t}$	$= IA_t$	:	Investment in agriculture
$\phi_{3,4,t}$	$= PK_t$	:	Government capital improvements
$\phi_{3,5,t}$	$= NFI_t$	:	Net factor incomes from abroad
$\phi_{3,6,t}$	$= MST_t$	:	Net service imports (including factor payments), and net transfer payments abroad
$\phi_{3,7,t}$	$= RPG_t$	:	Wholesale price of grains relative to overall wholesale price level
$\phi_{3,8,t}$	$= POP_t$	:	Population
$\phi_{3,9,t}$	$= GP_t$	:	Grain production
$\phi_{3,10,t}$	$= RD_t$	:	Rate of interest on domestic savings deposits
$\phi_{3,11,t}$	$= LR_t$	:	Rate of interest on domestic commercial bank loans
$\phi_{3,12,t}$	$= RF_t$	:	Rate of interest on foreign commercial loans
$\phi_{3,13,t}$	$= RINF_t$	:	Current rate of inflation (GNP deflator)
$\phi_{3,14,t}$	$= RINF_{t-1}$	:	Lagged rate of inflation (GNP deflator)
$\phi_{3,15,t}$	$= CKDM_t$	:	Dummy variable used in foreign commercial loan (CK) equation
$\phi_{3,16,t}$	$= MNC_t$	:	Imports of nonclassified goods
$\phi_{3,17,t}$	$= NTOSH_t$	:	Transfers from government and corporate sectors to households
$\phi_{3,18,t}$	$= XGP_t$	:	Exports of primary products
$\phi_{3,19,t}$	$= RT$	:	Current account transfers from abroad
$\phi_{3,20,t}$	$= 1$	:	Constant term

TABLE 8–3
B Matrix for Endogenous Variables

	1 YNA	2 Y	3 DTR	4 INT	5 SG	6 GC	7 IVG	8 MG	9 ILG	10 SC	11 YDP	12 SH	
1 YNA	1												Group 1
2 Y	−1	1											Group 1
3 DTR		β	1										Group 2
4 INT	β			1									Group 2
5 SG			−1	−1	1								Group 2
6 GC		β				1							Group 3
7 IVG							1		−1				Group 3
8 MG						−1	−1	1					Group 3
9 ILG								β	1				Group 3
10 SC	β									1			Group 4
11 YDP		−1	1	1						1	1		Group 4
12 SH											β	1	Group 4
13 INA		β			β					β		β	Group 4
14 I													Group 4
15 CK													Group 4
16 DC		−1			1		1			1		1	Group 4
17 MC													Group 5
18 MK													Group 5
19 XGM	β												Group 5
20 X													Group 5
21 MI		β											Group 5
22 M								−1					Group 5
23 SK													Group 6
24 IV				−1						−1		−1	Group 6

THE DATA

The data used to estimate the basic model and its variations are for the most part compiled by the Bank of Korea and published in their annual series, *Economic Statistics Yearbook*. The data for all variables were compiled for the period 1955 to 1970 or for 16 years. Some data date from 1953. Thus all equations, except those containing lagged variables, could be run on 16 annual observations or more.

TABLE 8–3 (concluded)

		13 INA	14 I	15 CK	16 DC	17 MC	18 MK	19 XGM	20 X	21 MI	22 M	23 SK	24 IV	
1	YNA													Group 1
2	Y													
3	DTR													Group 2
4	INT													
5	SG													
6	GC													Group 3
7	IVG													
8	MG													
9	ILG													
10	SC													Group 4
11	YDP													
12	SH													
13	INA	1												
14	I	−1	1											
15	CK		β	1										
16	DC				1									
17	MC				β	1								Group 5
18	MK		β	β			1							
19	XGM							1						
20	X							−1	1					
21	MI							β		1				
22	M					−1	−1			−1	1			
23	SK			1					1		−1	1		Group 6
24	IV		1						1		−1		1	

All of the endogenous variables and most of the exogenous variables are in terms of constant 1965 won. Since many of the variables used in the model (e.g. imports of goods by type, capital imports of various kinds, and tax variables) are not given by the Bank of Korea in constant 1965 won, we deflated the Bank constant price or dollar data in a variety of ways. Exchange rate variables were adjusted by a purchasing-power-parity index. Adjustments were made to other Bank data; for example, domestic savings was adjusted to exclude changes in grain inventories and include transfers from abroad. A

TABLE 8–4
Basic Matrices of the Macro-model

	Δ Matrix — Lagged Endogenous Variables					Γ₁ Matrix — Basic Commercial Policy Variables				Γ₂ Matrix — Derived Commercial Policy Variables						
	YNA_{-1} 1	YNA_{-2} 2	INA_{-1}* 3		ILG_{-1} 5	ORD 1	XPM 2	SOX 3	TAM 4	XPX 1	SUBM 2	SUBX 3	SXDT 4	TAR 5	MARDEV 6	
1 YNA	-1		δ													Group 1
2 Y																
3 DTR																Group 2
4 INT													1			
5 SG														-1		
6 GC																Group 3
7 IVG					1											
8 MG																
9 ILG																
10 SC																
11 YDP																
12 SH																
13 INA			δ													Group 4
14 I	δ															
15 CK															γ_2	
16 DC																
17 MC						γ_1					γ_2					Group 5
18 MK						γ_1										
19 XGM						γ_1										
20 X						γ_1						γ_2				
21 MI											γ_2					
22 M																
23 SK																Group 6
24 IV																

* Logarithm to base e of INA.

TABLE 8-4 (concluded)

Γ_3 Matrix

No.	Var	1 Y	2 AG	3 IA	4 PK	5 NFI	6 MST	7 RPG	8 POP	9 GP	10 RD	11 LR	12 RF	13 RINF	14 $RINF_{-1}$	15 CKDM	16 MNC	17 NTOSH	18 XGP	19 Constant	Error Terms e	
1	YNA																			γ_3	e_1	Group 1
2	Y	−1																				
3	DTR																			γ_3	e_3	Group 2
4	INT																			γ_3	e_4	
5	SG					1																
6	GC							γ_3	γ_3											γ_3	e_6	Group 3
7	IVG																					
8	MG									1												
9	ILG									γ_3										γ_3	e_9	
10	SC										γ_3									γ_3	e_{10}	Group 4
11	YDP										γ_3											
12	SH										γ_3			γ_3						γ_3	e_{12}	
13	INA													γ_3	γ_3			1		γ_3	e_{13}	
14	I				−1																	
15	CK											γ_3	γ_3			γ_3						
16	DC											γ_3	γ_3		γ_3					γ_3	e_{15}	
17	MC																			γ_3	e_{17}	Group 5
18	MK																			γ_3	e_{18}	
19	XGM																			γ_3	e_{19}	
20	X																		−1			
21	MI																			γ_3	e_{21}	
22	M																−1					
23	SK				1		−1															Group 6
24	IV						−1															

detailed description of the data sources and adjustments to the data is given in the appendix to this chapter.

BASIC HYPOTHESES AND TESTS

Hypotheses tested in fitting the basic model and its variations include the following general types:

(1) exchange rate variables affect savings and investment behavior directly as well as exports, imports, and capital flows;

(2) various types of tariff and tariff equivalents and export subsidies have differential effects on imports and exports;

(3) private savings are sensitive to both nominal interest rate changes and expected rates of inflation;

(4) foreign loans are sensitive to nominal interest rates, expected rates of inflation and expected rates of devaluation.

Hypotheses of these types are tested using the conventional tests of significance. The results are described below. In addition, we tested the general hypothesis that the basic structure of the economy changed after the 1964 devaluation and liberalization. For all equations for which there were enough degrees of freedom, we ran regressions over the sample period 1964 to 1970 as well as over the whole period for which data were available to determine whether the structure was changed. We also tested all our equations using eleven observations from 1960 to 1970 and fourteen observations from 1957 to 1970 when possible. The rationale for the 1960–70 period is that 1960 is the year Rhee was overthrown and the first year of attempted economic reform. The 1957 to 1970 period is used to determine whether the post-Korean-War years 1953 to 1956 were so significantly affected by reconstruction that data from these years bias the results. In choosing what we call our "best results," we chose the longest sample period for which the results seemed to be stable. If the regression coefficients changed markedly, however, when a shorter sample period was used, we chose the results from the shorter sample period.

All of the equations of the model were estimated initially using ordinary least squares or the Cochrane-Orcutt technique if there seemed to be significant autocorrelation of the error terms. Various types of simultaneous estimation were then used to determine whether the simultaneous nature of the model seriously biased the estimated coefficients.

FURTHER DESCRIPTION AND ESTIMATION RESULTS

Group 1: Determination of GNP.

The first two equations of the model concern output in agriculture and nonagriculture. Output in nonagriculture sectors YNA is assumed to be related to nonagricultural investment INA in previous years.[1] In the estimated relationship, there was strong evidence for decreasing returns to investment. That is, the higher the level of investment, the greater seems to be the net incremental capital-output ratio.[2] The best results among several functional forms tried seem to be for the following equation for nonagricultural output:

$$YNA = -281.8254 + 0.9413 \, YNA_{-1} \qquad (8\text{--}2)$$
$$(-2.96) \quad (10.02)$$
$$+80.0668 \log_e (INA_{-1})$$
$$(2.64)$$

Estimation Technique: Ordinary Least Squares

Sample: 1957 to 1971[3]

$R^2 = 0.9960$

$d \ = 2.2310$

The t statistics are given in parentheses under each of the coefficients of variables in the equations. R^2 is the coefficient of determination and d is the Durbin-Watson statistic. The strength of decreasing returns in nonagriculture can be indicated by comparing incremental capital-output ratios when nonagricultural investment runs about 50 billion won in constant 1965 prices, as it did in the late 1950s and early '60s, as opposed to investment of about 400 billion won in constant 1965 prices, as in 1970. The capital-output ratio is approximately 1.6 when investment is 50 billion won and about 2.0 when investment is 400 billion won.[4]

The second equation in Group 1 is an identity relating total output Y to agricultural output YA and nonagricultural output YNA.

$$Y = YNA + YA \qquad (8\text{--}3)$$

Group 2: Government Taxation and Savings Equations.

The regression equations for government direct and indirect tax revenues were very well behaved. They exhibited very high coefficients of determination and were generally stable, regardless of the sample period used.

The dependent variable in the direct tax regression was potential taxation. That is, direct tax exemptions for exporters $SXDT$ were added to actual direct tax revenues DTR to get potential direct taxes. The results were as follows:

$$DTR + SXDT = -63.6088 + 0.1104Y \qquad (8\text{--}4)$$
$$(-7.14) \quad (16.42)$$

Estimation Technique: Cochrane-Orcutt Iterative Technique

Sample: 1953 to 1970

$R^2 = 0.9946$

$d = 0.9741$

$\rho = 0.8808$[5]

For indirect taxes INT, excluding tariffs and foreign exchange taxes, the results were:

$$INT = -16.2991 + 0.1193YNA \qquad (8\text{--}5)$$
$$(-3.63) \quad (15.86)$$

Estimation Technique: Cochrane-Orcutt Iterative Technique

Sample: 1953 to 1970

$R^2 = 0.9787$

$d = 1.4114$

$\rho = 0.4968$

The regression results indicate a very high degree of elasticity of both direct and indirect tax revenues over the entire period 1953 to 1970. The average elasticity for direct tax revenues was 2.53 and for indirect tax revenues 1.40. Since direct tax exemptions grew rapidly, particularly in the last half of the 1960s, potential tax revenues (excluding exemptions) were even more elastic. The average for direct taxes was 2.79.[6]

Government expenditure G is assumed in our model to be exogenous, and government savings SG is specified as an identity.

$$SG = DTR + INT + TAR - G \qquad (8\text{--}6)$$

where TAR is tariffs and foreign exchange taxes.

Group 3: The Grain Sector.

Grain consumption was assumed to be dependent on income Y, the relative price of grains RPG, total population POP, and the split between rural and urban population. Since urban population has been growing quite steadily along with total population, any measure of the relative rural-urban population is highly correlated with total population and the usual problems associated with multicollinearity arise. The coefficients on the two correlated variables are extremely sensitive to the sample and the estimation technique used. We finally concluded that the best results could be obtained by using the population variable only. The results are:

$$GC = 6.5619 + 0.02696Y - 31.3328RPG + 7.8016POP \qquad (8\text{--}7)$$
$$(0.20) \quad (1.58) \qquad (-2.21) \qquad\quad (5.18)$$

Estimation Technique: Ordinary Least Squares

Sample: 1955 to 1970

$R^2 = 0.9582$

$d \ = 1.7957$

The income variable Y and the population variable POP are also quite collinear, and this probably accounts for the lack of significance of the coefficient of the Y variable. Nevertheless, we felt a priori that the income variable should be retained.

The implicit average income elasticity for grain consumption from 1955 to 1970 is 0.1031 and the price elasticity is -0.0422. As one would expect, grain consumption is relatively price and income inelastic. Population growth is the major factor in determining growth in consumption.

Korean domestic savings figures are very much affected by changes in grain inventories. The harvest comes in late in the year and most of the production is held in inventories at the end of the year. Fluctuations in the level of grain inventories are more a function of grain production than anything else. Grain imports also affect the levels of grain inventories, but, for the most part, changes in inventory do not represent conscious savings decisions but are more a function of the effect of weather on the size of the harvest.

Since changes in grain inventories are such an important component of savings, we estimated their level ILG as a function of grain production GP and grain imports MG. The best results are:

$$ILG = -77.9743 + 0.5782MG + 0.7196GP \qquad (8\text{--}8)$$
$$(-7.25) \quad (7.52) \qquad (12.07)$$

Estimation Technique: Ordinary Least Squares

Sample: 1955 to 1970

$R^2 = 0.9607$

$d = 1.9038$

Once the level of grain inventories is determined by the stochastic equation (8–8), investment in grain inventories IVG is determined by the identity

$$IVG = ILG - ILG_{-1} \tag{8–9}$$

Imports of grain are determined also as grain consumption GC plus inventory change IVG less production GP. Production of grain is assumed to be exogenous.

$$MG = IVG + GC - GP \tag{8–10}$$

Group 4: Savings and Investment Behavior.

Savings are classified as household and corporate. Household savings SH is expected to be a function of the expected real rate of interest on local savings deposits and disposable income of households YDP. The basic specification is:

$$SH = a_0 + a_1 YDP + a_2 RRD^* \tag{8–11}$$

Of course, the expected real rate of interest RRD^* is not an observable variable. We assume, however, that the expected real rate of interest is a function of the current *nominal* rate of interest RD less the expected rate of inflation. The expected rate of inflation is assumed to be a function of current and past rates of inflation $RINF$.[7]

$$RRD^* = RD - b_0 RINF - b_1 RINF_{-1} \tag{8–12}$$

If (8–12) is substituted back into (8–11), we obtain the following result:

$$SH = a_0 + a_1 YDP + a_2 RD - b_0 a_2 RINF - b_1 a_2 RINF_{-1} \tag{8–13}$$

This is the equation which was estimated with the following result:

$$SH = -71.5504 + 0.08578 YDP + 193.0218 RD \tag{8–14}$$
$$(-4.47) \quad (4.23) \quad (2.94)$$

$$- 44.7071 RINF - 35.0608 RINF_{-1}$$
$$(-2.48) \quad (-2.87)$$

Estimation Technique: Cochrane-Orcutt Iterative Technique

Sample: 1955 to 1970

$R^2 = 0.9550$

$d = 3.0033$

$\rho = 0.7070$

The results were only somewhat different for other sample periods, but all sample periods reveal a high degree of significance for the real interest rate. The average interest rate elasticity over the sample period is 1.82, a very high interest rate elasticity.

Corporate savings SC, which form the bulk of private savings in South Korea, were assumed to be a function of nonagricultural value added, the expected real rate of interest on savings deposits, the average rate of protection on imports, and the average rate of subsidy on exports.[8] The rationale for including rates of protection or subsidy was that high levels of protection and subsidy should increase profits and lead to higher savings. The level of tariffs and tariff equivalents and subsidies per dollar of export did not seem to affect savings in any consistent or significant fashion. Furthermore, rates of inflation did not seem to possess much explanatory power and frequently carried the wrong sign in the regression. The best results were obtained using only two variables, nonagricultural value added YNA and the rate of interest on savings deposits RD.

$$SC = -0.5689 + 0.0730YNA + 115.2640RD \qquad (8\text{--}15)$$
$$(-0.16) \quad (10.51) \qquad\qquad (4.13)$$

Estimation Technique: Ordinary Least Squares

Sample: 1960 to 1970

$R^2 = 0.9827$

$d = 1.6131$

Both nonagricultural value added and the rate of interest were highly significant for all sample periods and various specifications. For business savings, the average interest rate elasticity is 0.34 over the sample period. Household savings seem to be substantially more interest rate elastic, but the significance of deposit rates for corporate savings is nonetheless substantial (a t ratio of 4.13). The rate of inflation was not a significant explanatory variable. Thus it seems that in Korea, corporate savings depend on the nominal rate of interest rather than on the expected real rate of interest (in contrast to household savings). The reason may be that although inflation reduces real interest costs, it also may be associated with increased profit rates which have a positive effect on corporate savings and investment. The two effects tend to cancel each other so that corporate savings show little sensitivity to the rate of inflation.

Disposable income of households YDP is determined by the identity:

$$YDP = Y - SC - INT - TAR - DTR + NTOSH \qquad (8\text{--}16)$$

That is, disposable income of households is total income less retained earnings, less taxes, and plus net transfers from the government and corporate sectors to households.

Investment in South Korea is financed by four main sources, private savings channeled through the commercial banking system in the form of deposits, government savings channeled through both the commercial banks and a series of development finance institutions,[9] retained earnings, and borrowing from abroad.

The demand for loans from both commercial banks and development finance institutions far exceeds the available supply of loanable funds even at the relatively high interest rates that marginal borrowers must pay.[10] Loans are rationed since legal interest rate ceilings cannot clear the market. The result is that much investment is financed through the unorganized money market and by borrowing from abroad. Since interest rates are controlled and credit is rationed, we decided to include as an independent variable for the nonagricultural investment equation the total level of savings largely available to government or channeled through the banking system. This includes government savings SG, public capital imports PK, corporate savings SC, and household savings SH. It does not include other sources of savings such as foreign commercial loans, reductions in foreign exchange reserves, and inventory disinvestment. The other explanatory variables tried were current and lagged income growth, the real local commercial bank loan rate, the real rate of interest on foreign loans, average tariffs and tariff equivalents per dollar of imports, export subsidies per dollar of export, and effective exchange rates.

Of all these explanatory variables, current and lagged income growth and available savings $(SG + PK + SC + SH)$ seemed to give the only good results. Import tariffs and export subsidies did not seem to have a direct impact on investment demand. The loan rates, foreign and domestic, were not good explanatory variables although the domestic loan rate was nearly significant at the 5 percent level for some regressions. The lack of strong significance of the domestic loan rate is probably due to the wide variety of loan rates at different types of banks and for different purposes. With such a variety of subsidized rates and the prevalence of credit rationing, it is expected that official loan rates would not have substantial explanatory value. The equation which we felt best for purposes of simulation, however, did include the domestic loan rate and was as follows:

$$INA = -19.0111 + 0.5802(YNA - YNA_{-1}) + 0.7525(YNA_{-1} \quad (8\text{-}17)$$
$$(-1.39) \quad (2.97) \qquad\qquad (3.39)$$

$$- YNA_{-2}) + 0.7263(SG + PK + SC + SH) - 36.8952RLR$$
$$(4.44) \qquad\qquad\qquad (-1.08)$$

Estimation Technique: Cochrane-Orcutt Iterative Technique

Sample: 1957 to 1970

$R^2 = 0.9948$

$d\ = 1.7044$

$\rho\ = 0.5643$

where RLR is the expected real rate of interest for domestic loans. The expected real rate of interest is the nominal rate less the expected rate of inflation which is assumed to be approximated by last year's rate of inflation:

$$RLR = LR - RINF_{-1} \qquad (8\text{-}18)$$

Since a large component of nonagricultural investment is available savings, the problem of simultaneity (discussed later) is particularly acute for this equation and requires further investigation.

Total investment I equals nonagricultural investment INA plus investment in agriculture IA.

$$I = INA + IA \qquad (8\text{-}19)$$

The next equation in Group 4 is a demand equation for foreign loans. Although, in principle, foreign loans over three years require approval from the Economic Planning Board, the Board has encouraged investors to borrow abroad. Beginning about 1970, however, concern over the rising level of debt service payments led the IMF to insist on restriction of the flow of foreign capital, and the restrictions imposed seemed to be effective.

The demand for foreign loans is assumed to be a function of the level of total fixed investment I, the expected real rate of interest on domestic loans RLR, and the expected real rate of interest on foreign loans RRF. That is,

$$CK = \alpha_0 + \alpha_1 I + \alpha_2 RLR + \alpha_3 RRF + \alpha_4 CKDM \qquad (8\text{-}20)$$

where $CKDM$ is a dummy variable equal to unity for 1970 and zero for all other years. The expected rate of interest on foreign loans involves not only the expected rate of inflation but the expected rate of devaluation. We assume that the expected rate of devaluation is approximated by the average of the current and two previous years' rates of devaluation. Thus

$$RRF = RF - RINF_{-1} + (RDEV + RDEV_{-1} + RDEV_{-2})/3 \qquad (8\text{--}21)$$

Equation (8–19) was estimated as follows:

$$CK = -23.7637 + 0.2634I + 148.5346RLR \qquad (8\text{--}22)$$
$$(-7.06) \quad (7.86) \qquad (2.87)$$

$$-77.5319RRF - 27.8443CKDM$$
$$(-2.02) \qquad (-3.06)$$

Estimation Technique: Ordinary Least Squares

Sample: 1959 to 1970

$R^2 = 0.9847$

$d = 2.5668$

The demand for foreign loans is sensitive to both the domestic and foreign loan interest rate. The average elasticities are 0.326 and −0.477. The significance of the dummy variable indicates that the restrictions on foreign borrowing had a significant effect in 1970.

The final equation in Group 4 is an identity for domestic consumption expenditure,

$$DC = Y - SC - SH - SG - IVG + RT + NFI \qquad (8\text{--}23)$$

Consumption equals income less savings, both private and government, less inventory investment in grains, plus net transfers and net factor incomes from abroad.

Group 5: Import and Export Equations.

Group 5 contains three import equations, an export equation, and two identities. Imports of consumption goods are assumed to depend on various components of the effective exchange rate for imports and the level of domestic consumption. Initially, the effective exchange rate for imports was broken up into three components: (1) the official rate, (2) tariffs and tariff equivalents, and (3) the total value of export premia per dollar of import. The coefficients for parts 2 and 3 were not significant and were unstable with respect to the sample used for all of the import equations. Thus parts 2 and 3 were combined into a single variable called *SUBM*. For imports of consumption goods *MC,* the two parts *SUBM* and *ORD* were combined, since there was no significant difference between their coefficients. The best results are:

$$MC = -8.1035 + 0.0596DC - 0.1055(SUBM + ORD) \quad (8\text{--}24)$$
$$(-2.15) \quad (11.75) \quad\quad (-5.43)$$

Estimation Technique: Ordinary Least Squares

Sample: 1955 to 1970

$R^2 = 0.9163$

$d = 1.2058$

where *DC* is domestic consumption. This equation results in an average elasticity of -2.10 for the effective exchange rate of imports, $SUBM + ORD$.[11]

For capital goods imports, a somewhat different model must be used. Most capital goods enter duty free and by special channels such as foreign aid loans or loans from abroad. The official exchange rate is the most relevant exchange rate to use. Since most foreign loans are tied to capital goods imports, we would expect the level of foreign borrowing to be an important determinant of capital goods imports. The level of investment is also a determinant of the magnitude of capital goods imports. The best regression results for *MK,* imports of capital goods, are obtained with foreign commercial loans *CK,* investment *I,* and the official exchange rate *ORD* as explanatory variables.

$$MK = 3.881 + 0.3610CK + 0.3311I - 0.0853ORD \quad (8\text{--}25)$$
$$(0.61) \quad (2.22) \quad\quad (6.58) \quad (-2.44)$$

Estimation Technique: Ordinary Least Squares

Sample: 1955 to 1970

$R^2 = 0.9876$

$d = 1.6974$

The elasticity of capital goods imports with respect to *ORD* is -0.36.

For imports of intermediate goods, we used the official exchange rate *ORD* and total tariffs, tariff equivalents, and export premia per dollar of import *SUBM* as the commercial policy variables. Other explanatory variables are gross national product *Y* and exports *X*. Manufactured exports *XGM* is used as a separate explanatory variable, since we believe that in general exports of manufactures are more intensive in their use of imports than other elements of expenditure on GNP. The resulting equation is:

$$MI = 9.9287 + 0.1772Y + 0.3610XGM - 0.3714SUBM \quad (8\text{-}26)$$
$$(0.42) \quad (3.53) \quad\quad (1.67) \quad\quad\quad (-2.53)$$
$$- 0.2197ORD$$
$$(-2.68)$$

Estimation Technique: Cochrane-Orcutt Iterative Technique

Sample: 1955 to 1970

$R^2 = 0.9893$

$d = 1.5915$

$\rho = 0.2554$

The average elasticity is $-.46$ for the official exchange rate ORD and -0.80 for $SUBM$. One would expect a higher elasticity for $SUBM$ if tariffs and tariff equivalents are levied selectively on commodity items with higher than average elasticity.

As Chapter 6 indicated, the export equation was the most difficult to estimate. The estimation procedures and results were discussed at some length in that chapter and we merely repeat the best results here for sake of completeness.

$$XGM = -241.4847 + 0.3323YMA + 0.2629ORD \quad (8\text{-}27)$$
$$(-3.92) \quad (11.29) \quad\quad (1.70)$$
$$+ 0.1471SUBX$$
$$(1.27)$$

Estimation Technique: Cochrane-Orcutt Iterative Technique

Sample: 1957 to 1970

$R^2 = 0.9900$

$d = 1.3742$

$\rho = 0.8701$

where XGM is export of manufactured goods.

The last two equations of Group 5 are identities giving the value of total imports and exports:

$$M = MG + MC + MK + MI + MNC \quad (8\text{-}28)$$

$$X = XGM + XGP \quad (8\text{-}29)$$

Group 6: Demand and Supply Balance.

The final group of equations contains two identities. The first is the balance of payments identity relating movements of short term capital and changes in monetary assets SK to the demand and supply of foreign exchange.

$$SK = M + MST - X - CK - PK \qquad (8\text{-}30)$$

where MST is net service imports plus net transfer payments abroad. The second identity makes inventory change the equilibrating item for aggregate demand and supply or between savings and investment

$$IV = SG + SC + SH + M + MST - X - I \qquad (8\text{-}31)$$

SIMULTANEOUS ESTIMATION

So far we have only discussed the results of single equation estimation techniques and have not yet attempted simultaneous estimation. There is some heuristic justification for this. A glance at the B matrix in Table 8–3 reveals a structure that is very nearly triangular.[12] The system is triangular except for one block of equations, the IVG, MG, and ILG equations. (See the block with dotted lines in the B matrix of Table 8–3.) It is well-known that if a structure is triangular (i.e. recursive) and the errors across equations are uncorrelated, ordinary least squares estimation is a consistent estimation technique. A slight generalization of this theorem is easy to prove: if the system is block-triangular and the errors across blocks are uncorrelated, each block may be treated as a simultaneous system and consistent estimation of each block results in consistent estimation for the system as a whole.

With this in mind, we attempted to estimate the block of equations, IVG, MG, and ILG, as a simultaneous system. This system can be written as follows:

$$IVG = ILG - ILG_{-1} \qquad (8\text{-}32)$$

$$MG = IVG + GC - GP \qquad (8\text{-}33)$$

$$ILG = \beta MG + \gamma_1 GP + \gamma_0 + e \qquad (8\text{-}34)$$

where e is an error term. If we substitute (8–32) into (8–33) and (8–33) in turn into (8–34) and solve for ILG, we obtain the following result:

$$ILG = \frac{\beta}{(1-\beta)} (GC - ILG_{-1}) + \frac{(\gamma_1 - \beta)}{(1-\beta)} GP + \frac{\gamma_0}{(1-\beta)} \qquad (8\text{-}35)$$

$$+ \frac{1}{(1-\beta)} e$$

This equation can be estimated by regressing ILG on the combination variable $(GC - ILG_{-1})$ and on GP. The result is

$$ILG = -139.51 + 0.654(GC-ILG_{-1}) + 0.625GP \qquad (8\text{-}36)$$

Estimation Technique: Ordinary Least Squares

Sample: 1955 to 1970

$R^2 = 0.8460$

$d = 1.52$

The original structural coefficients, β, γ_0 and γ_1 can be estimated then by indirect least squares by solving the following equations:

$$\frac{\gamma_0}{(1-\beta)} = -139.51 \qquad (8\text{-}37)$$

$$\frac{\beta}{(1-\beta)} = 0.654 \qquad (8\text{-}38)$$

$$\frac{(\gamma_1-\beta)}{(1-\beta)} = 0.625 \qquad (8\text{-}39)$$

The solution gives the following estimate of the structural equation (8-34):

$$ILG = -79.17 + 0.395MG + 0.773GP \qquad (8\text{-}40)$$

Comparing this result with the ordinary least squares result in equation (8-8), we see that the constant term changes relatively little, the coefficient of MG is reduced and the coefficient of GP increases.

If all the equations are regarded together as one large system, estimation is impossible because observations are too few. For example, consider the problem with a two-stage least squares approach. There are 35 exogenous and lagged endogenous variables. There are, however, a maximum of 18 observations from 1953 to 1970. Thus it is impossible to regress any of the endogenous variables on all the exogenous and lagged endogenous variables. Some technique has to be found to reduce the number of instrumental variables (exogenous and lagged endogenous).

A method for choosing instruments has been proposed by Fisher (1965). Some exogenous variables of the system of equations may add little causal information to the equation and hence be of little value in reducing the bias in estimation. Thus Fisher suggests the use of a causal ordering system for the set of all predetermined variables.

Our ordering system is similar to Fisher's and works as follows:

(1) The predetermined variables in equation i are called zero-order causal variables for equation i.

(2) For each endogenous variable in an equation (other than the dependent variable), we may determine the set of predetermined variables in the equation explaining that endogenous variable. Each set of such predetermined variables are first-order causal variables.

(3) For each equation j explaining an endogenous variable in equation i, there are a set of endogenous variables. The predetermined variables in the equations explaining this set of endogenous variables are second-order causal variables. The predetermined variables in the equation for a lagged endogenous variable contained in equation i are also called second-order causal variables.

The causal ordering described here may be defined more precisely in a recursive fashion.

It is very difficult to choose a set of predetermined variables as instruments. If one chooses too few, the simultaneous equations' bias to the estimates is likely to be a problem. If one chooses too many instruments, the endogenous variables, when regressed on the instruments, are nearly predicted perfectly, a problem of lack of degrees of freedom. We decided to run two sets of two-stage least squares estimates, one with the Fisher instruments of zero- and first-order causal variables, and another with a larger set of instruments up to the second order of causality.

In addition to the Fisher instruments, Fair (1970) suggests that when the errors in an equation are serially correlated a consistent estimation procedure requires the addition of all lagged variables in the equation as instruments.

Table 8–5 lists the instruments which are used for each equation. Tables 8–6 and 8–7 give the results using the two different sets of Fisher instruments, the first set using zero- and first-order causal variables and the second set using variables through the second order of causality. Note that for the YNA equation, there are no other endogenous variables in the equation. Thus two-stage least squares and ordinary least squares are equivalent. Note also in Table 8–5 that for the INT, SC, and XGM equations, there are no second-order causal variables. Thus the two-stage least squares estimates are identical whether or not second-order causal variables are included. When only the Fisher first-order causal variables are included, the ILG equation does not have enough instruments so that the equation is underidentified. It is only possible to estimate with two-stage least squares when second-order instruments are included. Finally, when instruments through the second order of causality are used, it is not possible to estimate the INA equation. There are too many instruments and no degrees of freedom.

TABLE 8–5

Instrumental Variables on the Basis of Causal Orderings

Stochastic Equation	Zero- and First-Order Instruments	Second-Order Instruments	Additional Instruments Due to Autocorrelation
YNA	YNA_{-1}, INA_{-1}	INA_{-2}, PK	—
DTR	$SXDT, YA$	YNA_{-1}, INA_{-1}	$(DTR + SXDT)_{-1}, Y_{-1}$
INT	YNA_{-1}, INA_{-1}	—	INT_{-1}
GC	RPG, POP, YA	YNA_{-1}, INA_{-1}	—
ILG	GP	ILG_{-1}, RPG, POP	—
SC	RD, YNA_{-1}, INA_{-1}	—	—
SH	$RD, RINF, RINF_{-1}, NTOSH, TAR$	$YA, RPG, POP, SXDT$	$RINF_{-2}, RD_{-1}, SH_{-1}, YDP_{-1}$
INA	$PK, TAR, G, RD, RINF, RINF_{-1}, YNA_{-1}, INA_{-1}, YNA_{-2}$	$YNA_{-2}, INA_{-2}, SXDT, NTOSH$	$PK_{-1}, (SG + SC + SH)_{-1}, YNA_{-3}, RLR_{-1}$
CK	$RLR, RRF, CKDM, IA$	YNA_{-1}, YNA_{-2}, PK	—
MC	$(SUBM + ORD), NFI, RT$	$YA, RD, RINF, RINF_{-1}, TAR, G, ILG_{-1}$	—
MK	$ORD, RLF, RRF, CKDM, IA$	YNA_{-1}, YNA_{-2}, PK	—
MI	$SUBM, ORD, YA, SUBX$	YNA_{-1}, INA_{-1}	$SUBM_{-1}, ORD_{-1}, MI_{-1}, Y_{-1}, XGM$
XGM	$SUBX, ORD, YNA_{-1}, INA_{-1}$	—	$SUBX_{-1}, ORD_{-1}, XGM_{-1}$

The results using two-stage least squares with first-order instruments are almost identical to the ordinary least squares results except for the GC, CK, MK, and MI equations. When second-order instruments are used, only the coefficient of the CK variable in the MK equation is substantially different from the ordinary least squares result. Furthermore, all the equations listed in Table 8–7 still have large degrees of freedom except for the CK equation. We must conclude that the problem of simultaneity is not great for our Korean econometric model.

TABLE 8–6
Two-Stage Least Squares Estimates with Fisher's
First-Order Instrumental Variables

	R^2	d	Estimation Technique
$DTR = -61.5843 + 0.1092Y - SXDT$ $\quad\quad (-6.56)\quad (15.26)$	.9944	0.9381	TSCORC
$INT = -17.2787 + 0.1202YNA$ $\quad\quad (-3.76)\quad (15.84)$	.9792	1.4411	TSCORC
$GC = 111.8904 + 0.0964Y - 40.4563RPG$ $\quad\quad (1.30)\quad (1.81)\quad\quad (-1.78)$ $\quad\quad + 2.2082POP$ $\quad\quad (0.50)$	.9006	0.8621	TS
$SC = -0.5678 + 0.0725YNA + 116.5768RD$ $\quad\quad (-0.16)\quad (10.41)\quad\quad\quad (4.16)$	.9827	1.6273	TS
$SH = -69.6454 + 0.08412YDP + 192.2094RD$ $\quad\quad (-4.43)\quad (4.16)\quad\quad\quad (2.92)$ $\quad\quad -45.1081RINF - 34.9772RINF_{-1}$ $\quad\quad (-2.48)\quad\quad\quad (-2.85)$	.9549	3.0123	TSCORC
$INA = -19.0076 + 0.5802(YNA - YNA_{-1}) + 0.7525(YNA_{-1} - YNA_{-2})$ $\quad\quad (-1.39)\quad (2.97)$ $\quad\quad + 0.7263(SG + SC + SH) - 36.8973RLR$ $\quad\quad (4.44)\quad\quad\quad\quad\quad (-1.08)$	.9948	1.7044	TSCORC
$CK = -24.9579 + 0.2889I + 115.0503RLR$ $\quad\quad (-6.23)\quad (5.31)\quad\quad (1.50)$ $\quad\quad -52.8461RRF - 32.4248CKDM$ $\quad\quad (-0.93)\quad\quad (-2.69)$	.9834	2.7436	TS.
$MC = -7.3710 + 0.0548DC$ $\quad\quad (-1.84)\quad (7.44)$ $\quad\quad -0.09356(SUBM + ORD)$ $\quad\quad (-4.02)$	.9101	1.0454	TS
$MK = 0.7415 + 0.2091CK + 0.3637I$ $\quad\quad (0.11)\quad (1.00)\quad\quad (5.60)$ $\quad\quad - 0.0740ORD$ $\quad\quad (-1.94)$	.9861	1.6003	TS
$MI = 18.0854 + 0.1564Y + 0.4503XGM$ $\quad\quad (0.74)\quad (2.98)\quad\quad (1.99)$ $\quad\quad - 0.3586SUBM - 0.1975ORD$ $\quad\quad (-2.39)\quad\quad\quad (-2.39)$	.9890	1.6074	TSCORC
$XGM = -242.4649 + 0.3332YNA + 0.2642ORD$ $\quad\quad (-3.94)\quad (11.26)\quad\quad (1.71)$ $\quad\quad + 0.1480SUBX$ $\quad\quad (1.27)$	.9900	1.3756	TSCORC

NOTE: *TSCORC* stands for two-stage least squares with Cochrane-Orcutt iterations. *TS* stands for ordinary two-stage least squares.

TABLE 8–7
**Two-Stage Least Squares Estimates with Fisher's
Second-Order Instrumental Variables**

	R^2	d	Estimation Technique
$DTR = -66.2773 + 0.1119Y - SXDT$	.9944	0.9745	$TSCORC$
$\quad\quad\;\;(-6.46)\quad\;(15.24)$			
$GC\;\; = 17.5453 + 0.03193Y - 33.3742RPG$			
$\quad\quad\;\;(0.47)\quad\;\;(1.67)\quad\quad\;\;(-2.27)$			
$\quad\quad\;\;+ 7.3280POP$	.9577	1.7572	TS
$\quad\quad\;\;(4.28)$			
$ILG\;\; = -92.5178 + 0.6702MG + 0.7853GP$	.9477	1.6311	TS
$\quad\quad\;\;(-6.30)\quad\;\;(5.04)\quad\quad\;\;(10.15)$			
$SH\;\; = -72.2550 + 0.08657YDP + 192.7797RD$			
$\quad\quad\;\;(-4.49)\quad\;\;(4.26)\quad\quad\quad\;\;(2.93)$			
$\quad\quad\;\;-44.6751RINF - 35.0964RINF_{-1}$	.9550	2.9992	$TSCORC$
$\quad\quad\;\;(-2.50)\quad\quad\quad\;\;(-2.87)$			
$CK\;\; = -23.6744 + 0.2615I + 151.0420RLR$			
$\quad\quad\;\;(-7.02)\quad\;\;(7.73)\quad\quad\;\;(2.89)$			
$\quad\quad\;\;-79.3805RRF - 27.5013CKDM$	.9847	2.5466	TS
$\quad\quad\;\;(-2.05)\quad\quad\quad\;\;(-3.01)$			
$MC\;\; = -8.3930 + 0.0597DC$			
$\quad\quad\;\;(-2.25)\quad\;\;(11.67)$			
$\quad\quad\;\;-0.1049(SUBM + ORD)$	.9162	1.2160	TS
$\quad\quad\;\;(-5.41)$			
$MK\;\; = 1.5311 + 0.2117CK + 0.3717I$			
$\quad\quad\;\;(0.23)\quad\;\;(1.15)\quad\quad\;\;(6.63)$			
$\quad\quad\;\;-0.0846ORD$	.9866	1.6893	TS
$\quad\quad\;\;(-2.33)$			
$MI\;\; = 10.3928 + 0.1760Y + 0.3672XGM$			
$\quad\quad\;\;(0.44)\quad\;\;(3.50)\quad\quad\;\;(1.69)$			
$\quad\quad\;\;-0.3700SUBM - 0.2188ORD$	.9891	1.5930	TS
$\quad\quad\;\;(-2.51)\quad\quad\quad\;\;(-2.66)$			

NOTE: $TSCORC$ is two-stage least squares with Cochrane-Orcutt iterations and TS is ordinary two-stage least squares.

APPENDIX: DATA USED IN THE ECONOMETRIC MODEL

Most of the data used for the regressions in this chapter are compiled by the Bank of Korea and published in their *Economic Statistics Yearbook*. A description of the raw data and their sources is contained in Table 8–8.

TABLE 8-8

Description of Raw Data and Sources

Data in billions of constant 1965 won

RY	:	Gross national product; BOK, *ESY 1971*, pp. 10–11[a]
$RYNA$	:	Value-added in nonagricultural sectors, ibid., pp. 14–15
RI	:	Gross domestic fixed capital formation, ibid., pp. 10–11
RIA	:	Investment in agriculture, ibid., pp. 28–29
$RNFI$	:	Net factor income from abroad, ibid., pp. 10–11
$RGRC$	:	Grain consumption, BOK National Accounts Division
$RIVG$	:	Grain inventory investment, ibid.
$RILG$	:	Grain inventory level, ibid.
RMG	:	Imports of goods, including freight and insurance; BOK, *ESY 1971*, pp. 44–45
RXG	:	Exports of goods, including freight and insurance, ibid.
$RMOS$	:	Imports of services, other than freight and insurance, ibid.
$RXOS$	:	Exports of services, other than freight and insurance, ibid.
RT	:	Net transfer receipts from abroad on current account, ibid.

Data in billions of current won

CY	:	Gross national product, *ESY 1971*, pp. 8–9
$CYDP$	:	Personal disposable income, ibid., pp. 36–37
CSH	:	Savings by households and private nonprofit institutions, ibid., pp. 22–23
CSC	:	Gross savings (including capital consumption allowances) by corporations and unincorporated enterprises, ibid.
CGS	:	Gross savings by government, including government enterprises, ibid.
$CSTD$	:	Statistical discrepancy between savings and gross domestic capital formation, ibid.
$CDTR$	:	Direct tax revenues, ibid., pp. 38–39
$CITR$	:	Indirect taxes, ibid.
CGT	:	Government transfers to the private sector, ibid.

Data in current millions of dollars

$DMGS$	:	Imports of goods and services, *ESY 1971*, pp. 266–267
DMG	:	Imports of goods, including freight and insurance, ibid.
$DCKL$	:	Long-term private capital imports, ibid.
$DCKS$	:	Short-term capital imports, ibid.
DMA	:	Net reduction in foreign assets of monetary institutions, ibid.
DXG	:	Total exports of goods, Ministry of Finance, *Foreign Trade of Korea, MOF, FTOK* annual through 1971
$DMGR$	:	Imports of grain (SITC 04), ibid.

(continued)

TABLE 8–8 (concluded)

DMC	:	Imports of consumption goods (SITC 0, 1, 732.1,8; excluding 04), ibid.
DMK	:	Imports of capital goods (SITC 7, excluding 732.1), ibid.
DMI	:	Imports of intermediate goods (SITC 2, 3, 4, 5, 6), ibid.
DXGM	:	Exports of manufactured goods, ibid.

Exchange rate and export premia in won per dollar[b]

OR	:	Exchange rate
RXS	:	Export premium per dollar of export

Tariffs, tariff equivalents, export subsidies, and export premia
in billions of won, current prices[b]

TM	:	Tariffs and tariff equivalents
PX	:	Total export premiums
SX	:	Total export subsidies
SXTAXD	:	Export subsidies in form of direct tax relief
SXTAXI	:	Export subsidies in form of indirect tax exemption

Price indexes

WPI	:	Wholesale price index, *ESY 1971*, pp. 314–315
WPIG	:	Wholesale price index for grains, ibid.
WPIOG	:	Wholesale price index for commodities other than grains, ibid.
WPITP	:	Wholesale price index for major trading partners, International Monetary Fund, *International Financial Statistics*[c]

Other data

PR	:	Farm population in millions of persons, *ESY 1971*, p. 6
PU	:	Nonfarm population in millions of persons, ibid.
NRD	:	Nominal interest rate on time deposits one year and longer, *ESY 1971*, p. 135 and *ESY 1960*
NRF	:	Interest rate on business loans in United States, United States Department of Commerce, *Survey of Current Business*
NLR	:	Commercial bank lending rate, *ESY 1957–71*

NOTE: BOK—Bank of Korea; ESY—*Economic Statistics Yearbook,* published by BOK; SITC—*Standard International Trade Classification,* manual published by the United Nations.

a. Where series is not continuous to 1953 in *ESY 1971,* it was traced as far back as possible in earlier yearbooks. The revised figures for 1970 were obtained from BOK, *Monthly Economic Statistics,* August 1971.

b. Sources for these items are mainly primary, including files of the Ministry of Finance, BOK, and USAID, Korea Mission.

c. Wholesale price indexes for the United States and Japan were averaged by using weights derived from their respective shares in total trade.

Table 8–9 gives the transformations to the raw data which are required to obtain the values of the endogenous and exogenous variables for the model. Much of the raw data are current price data and must be deflated to obtain values in terms of constant won. Direct and indirect tax revenues, private savings, government savings, government transfers to private sector, and subsidies in the form of direct and indirect tax exemptions are all deflated by a *GNP* deflator (i.e., multiplied by RY/CY as in Table 8–9). Imports of goods of various types are deflated by the overall import price deflator used in determining real *GNP* (i.e., multiplied by RMG/DMG). Capital imports are de-

TABLE 8–9

Transformations of Raw Data

Endogenous variables

YNA	$= RYNA$
Y	$= RY$
DTR	$= (RY/CY) \cdot CDTR$
INT	$= (RY/CY) \cdot (CITR - TM)$
SG	$= (RY/CY) \cdot CGS$
GC	$= RGRC$
IVG	$= RIVG$
MG	$= (RMG/DMG) \cdot DMGR$
ILG	$= RILG$
SC	$= (RY/CY) \cdot CSC$
YDP	$= (RY/CY) \cdot CYDP$
SH	$= (RY/CY) \cdot (CSH + CSTD) - RIVG$
INA	$= RI - RIA$
I	$= RI$
CK	$= ((RMG + RMOS)/DMGS) \cdot DCKL$
DC	$= Y - SC - SH - IVG - SG + RNFI$
MC	$= (RMG/DMG) \cdot DMC$
MK	$= (RMG/DMG) \cdot DMK$
XGM	$= (RXG/DXG) \cdot DXGM$
X	$= RXG$
MI	$= (RMG/DMG) \cdot DMI$
M	$= RMG$
SK	$= ((RMG + RMOS)/DMGS) \cdot (DMA + DCKS)$
IV	$= SG + SC + SH - I + M + RMOS - RXOS - RT - X$

Basic commercial policy variables

ORD	$= OR \cdot (WPITP/WPI)$
XPX	$= RXS \cdot (WPITP/WPI)$
SOX	$= ((SX \cdot 1000)/DXG) \cdot (WPITP/WPI)$
TAM	$= ((RM \cdot 1000)/DMG) \cdot (WPITP/WPI)$

(continued)

TABLE 8–9 (concluded)

Derived commercial policy variables

$XPM = (PX \cdot 1000/DMG) \cdot (WPITP/WPI)$

$SUBM = XPM + TAM$

$SUBX = SOX + XPX$

$SXDT = (RY/CY) \cdot SXTAXD$

$TAR = (RY/CY) \cdot TM$

$MARDEV = (RDEV + RDEV_{-1} + RDEV_{-2})/3$

where

$RDEV = (R - R_{-1})/R_{-1}$

and

$R = ORD + (SUBM \cdot RMG + SUBX \cdot RXG)/(RMG + RXG)$

Other exogenous variables

$YA = RY - RYNA$

$G = INT + TAR + DTR - SG$

$IA = RIA$

$PK = M + RMOS - RXOS - RT - X - CK - SK$

$NFI = RNFI$

$MST = RMOS - RXOS - RT$

$RPG = WPIG/WPIOG$

$POP = PR + PU$

$GP = RGRC + RIVG - (RMG/DMG) \cdot DMGR$

$RD = NRD$

$LR = NLR$

$RF = NRF$

$RINF = (GNPD - GNPD_{-1})/GNPD_{-1}$

where

$GNPD = CY/RY$

$MNC = M - MC - MK - MI - MG$

$NTOSH = Y - INT - TAR - DTR - SC - YDP$

$XGP = (RXG/DXG) \cdot (DXG - DXGM)$

---

flated by the price deflator for imports of goods and services (i.e., multiplied by $(RMG + RMOS)/DMGS)$. Nonclassified imports MNC, consumption DC, inventory investment IV, government expenditure G, public capital imports PK, and net transfers of other sectors to households $NTOSH$ are all defined in terms of the other variables so that the deflation procedures do not alter any of the identities of the model. The basic commercial policy variables are deflated by a purchasing-power-parity index which is the ratio of the Korean wholesale price index to the wholesale price index of major trading partners.

Tables 8–10A through 8–10G give the actual values of the raw data used and Tables 8–11A through 8–11D give the values of the derived endogenous and exogenous variables.

TABLE 8-10A
Raw Data in Billions of Constant 1965 Won

Year	RY	RYNA	RI	RIA	RNFI	RGRC	RIVG
1953	421.93	218.60	35.28	4.04	9.42	—	36.13
1954	447.36	228.30	41.66	3.45	7.56	—	3.53
1955	474.54	250.50	48.98	4.53	7.75	162.87	0.95
1956	480.47	268.20	52.77	5.07	7.38	161.04	−11.32
1957	522.73	292.20	61.31	6.48	7.59	156.64	16.90
1958	551.69	305.40	57.79	5.35	7.59	180.61	9.45
1959	575.84	332.20	59.29	5.99	7.75	186.66	−3.73
1960	589.07	345.10	61.71	6.97	7.38	176.40	2.04
1961	613.61	345.10	65.26	8.35	5.79	192.47	6.81
1962	634.97	382.60	84.05	6.72	6.48	194.39	−15.25
1963	693.03	422.50	105.95	10.28	6.79	186.53	22.93
1964	750.31	436.00	93.33	10.66	6.53	218.38	20.85
1965	805.85	494.20	117.64	13.67	7.65	229.01	−0.15
1966	913.82	567.90	190.63	23.16	13.08	235.12	8.40
1967	995.16	668.30	232.09	19.24	21.53	238.91	−12.40
1968	1127.32	796.50	325.63	23.82	22.24	239.97	−12.47
1969	1306.19	935.80	407.76	24.26	23.04	246.20	30.08
1970	1422.33	1055.00	416.76	25.06	10.17	253.51	14.34

Year	RILG	RMG	RXG	RMOS	RXOS	RT
1953	36.13	91.67	10.64	1.83	13.30	49.92
1954	39.66	64.57	6.82	2.12	9.50	34.92
1955	40.61	86.95	4.91	2.57	13.83	39.84
1956	29.29	100.88	6.98	3.69	10.19	74.63
1957	46.19	117.12	7.09	6.61	13.80	83.07
1958	55.64	99.87	5.65	7.25	18.87	75.50
1959	51.91	80.02	6.29	7.85	21.20	54.59
1960	53.95	90.40	9.69	10.24	21.39	61.31
1961	60.76	82.30	11.89	9.00	26.75	46.93
1962	45.51	112.90	15.45	7.43	27.87	63.74
1963	68.44	143.56	23.78	9.98	22.80	66.65
1964	89.29	104.83	32.51	9.93	23.49	50.96
1965	89.14	120.15	47.80	9.44	29.12	53.95
1966	97.54	192.87	69.09	13.54	51.59	58.29
1967	85.14	263.59	87.82	17.73	82.81	59.76
1968	72.67	374.93	133.66	35.56	99.97	63.01
1969	102.75	468.83	183.02	47.40	122.38	64.65
1970	117.09	513.69	252.93	64.85	117.72	45.23

TABLE 8–10B
Raw Data in Billions of Won at Current Prices

Year	CY	CYDP	CSH[a]	CSC[a]	CGS[a]
1953	48.18	44.14	3.44	2.24	1.11
1954	66.88	60.23	2.97	3.31	0.35
1955	116.06	106.33	3.87	5.00	1.32
1956	152.44	140.25	−3.08	6.57	8.50
1957	197.78	179.63	9.55	8.85	8.18
1958	207.19	183.78	7.85	10.20	7.65
1959	221.00	190.85	3.11	12.35	7.18
1960	246.69	212.69	−2.65	13.11	11.91
1961	296.82	260.16	2.51	17.25	14.10
1962	348.58	295.71	−10.48	25.25	21.62
1963	487.96	421.98	6.15	35.60	24.57
1964	696.79	617.14	11.06	46.44	34.75
1965	805.85	696.87	2.30	62.66	49.74
1966	1032.04	886.32	42.05	76.66	62.19
1967	1242.35	1043.24	11.73	97.59	88.25
1968	1575.65	1286.04	15.26	121.93	133.97
1969	2047.11	1701.32	114.41	149.44	159.51
1970	2545.92	2081.66	84.19	182.85	206.43

Year	CSTD[b]	CDTR	CITR	CGT
1953	—	0.99	1.70	0.41
1954	—	1.27	3.29	0.50
1955	—	1.90	5.22	0.50
1956	—	2.32	6.74	0.61
1957	—	4.37	10.42	1.93
1958	—	4.89	12.64	3.08
1959	—	6.02	16.19	2.17
1960	1.92	6.46	18.73	1.51
1961	2.18	8.44	19.98	0.64
1962	2.58	9.09	28.65	3.23
1963	3.62	12.18	30.94	0.0
1964	3.14	16.63	33.92	−1.89
1965	5.06	22.14	47.13	0.35
1966	14.16	38.03	72.31	5.27
1967	22.71	53.46	98.66	3.69
1968	28.36	81.00	147.71	23.22
1969	33.11	115.01	196.90	31.75
1970	45.58	145.01	250.37	7.84

a. Includes current account transfers from abroad.

b. Before 1960, savings were estimated as a residual. Since then separate estimation of savings has resulted in a statistical discrepancy between savings and gross domestic capital formation.

TABLE 8–10C

Raw Data in Millions of Dollars, Dollar Prices

Year	DMGS	DMG	DCKL	DCKS	DMA	DXG
1953	—	345.40	—	—	—	40.10
1954	—	243.30	—	—	—	25.70
1955	337.30	327.60	0.0	−0.90	15.30	18.50
1956	394.00	380.10	0.0	−3.20	−18.70	26.30
1957	466.20	441.30	0.0	−2.90	4.10	26.70
1958	403.60	376.30	0.0	7.00	−45.30	21.30
1959	331.10	301.50	0.80	−0.60	−15.10	23.70
1960	379.20	340.60	2.60	0.60	−14.50	36.50
1961	344.00	310.10	0.20	−2.00	−30.30	44.80
1962	453.40	425.40	2.80	−6.70	56.50	58.20
1963	578.50	540.90	42.60	18.40	55.80	89.60
1964	432.40	395.00	10.30	−3.30	2.70	122.50
1965	488.30	452.70	19.10	−2.50	−16.20	180.10
1966	777.70	726.70	177.20	6.40	−119.20	260.30
1967	1060.00	971.90	233.40	45.20	−118.20	345.40
1968	1546.60	1412.60	383.10	13.20	−3.00	503.60
1969	1945.00	1766.40	372.10	56.50	−95.00	689.60
1970	2149.60	1940.00	292.10	122.40	29.20	922.80

Year	DMGR	DMC	DMK	DMI	DXGM
1953	—	—	—	—	0.90
1954	—	—	—	—	1.20
1955	6.36	25.42	57.02	189.81	1.40
1956	31.19	32.54	42.81	238.16	1.50
1957	84.33	40.98	41.94	235.57	3.10
1958	51.05	30.56	36.25	234.21	2.40
1959	17.53	16.08	41.81	209.75	3.00
1960	20.56	17.00	40.07	217.15	5.50
1961	30.21	15.65	42.39	195.80	8.50
1962	33.55	20.10	68.56	291.56	10.60
1963	107.23	24.14	113.17	314.54	39.60
1964	60.78	13.27	69.17	259.87	58.50
1965	54.44	16.28	73.23	319.66	107.00
1966	61.30	25.17	168.35	461.60	153.80
1967	76.57	40.48	305.27	573.79	215.40
1968	129.35	93.93	517.58	721.57	338.40
1969	250.33	129.84	571.64	870.90	481.60
1970	244.78	140.55	572.46	1025.44	651.50

TABLE 8–10D
Exchange Rate and Export Premia, Won per Dollar

Year	OR	RXS
1953	6.50	0.0
1954	18.00	8.50
1955	30.00	48.10
1956	50.00	52.90
1957	50.00	58.90
1958	50.00	64.00
1959	50.00	84.70
1960	62.50	83.90
1961	127.50	14.60
1962	130.00	0.0
1963	130.00	39.80
1964	214.30	39.70
1965	265.40	0.0
1966	271.30	0.0
1967	270.70	0.0
1968	276.60	0.0
1969	288.20	0.0
1970	310.70	0.0

TABLE 8–10E
Tariffs, Tariff Equivalents, and Export Subsidies in Billions of Won at Current Prices

Year	TM	PX	SX	SXTAXD	SXTAXI
1953	0.30	0.0	0.0	0.0	0.0
1954	0.84	0.22	0.0	0.0	0.0
1955	1.15	0.89	0.0	0.0	0.0
1956	1.50	1.39	0.0	0.0	0.0
1957	2.38	1.57	0.0	0.0	0.0
1958	4.39	1.36	0.02	0.0	0.0
1959	8.29	2.01	0.03	0.0	0.0
1960	10.20	3.06	0.04	0.0	0.0
1961	5.56	0.65	0.35	0.0	0.0
1962	6.93	0.0	1.18	0.31	0.26
1963	6.71	3.57	1.70	0.53	0.57
1964	8.51	4.86	3.26	0.99	1.20
1965	12.85	0.0	6.86	2.84	2.69
1966	18.00	0.0	12.93	5.02	5.33
1967	25.41	0.0	20.88	7.72	8.22
1968	37.88	0.0	37.78	11.13	19.26
1969	44.72	0.0	49.45	17.21	22.55
1970	50.92	0.0	76.48	26.50	34.70

TABLE 8–10F
Price Indexes

Year	WPI	WPIG	WPIOG	WPITP
1953	—	—	—	93.10
1954	—	—	—	94.70
1955	27.80	25.70	28.10	92.40
1956	36.60	41.10	34.30	96.70
1957	42.50	47.20	40.10	100.40
1958	39.90	38.70	39.60	97.20
1959	40.80	33.90	42.60	97.70
1960	45.20	40.60	46.10	97.90
1961	51.20	50.30	51.40	98.30
1962	56.00	53.30	56.50	97.60
1963	67.50	84.50	64.20	98.30
1964	90.90	106.70	87.80	98.50
1965	100.00	100.00	100.00	100.00
1966	108.80	105.00	109.40	102.80
1967	115.80	117.00	115.70	104.00
1968	125.20	130.00	124.50	105.60
1969	133.70	152.70	130.80	108.80
1970	145.90	168.60	142.50	112.80

TABLE 8–10G
Other Data

Year	PR	PU	NRD	NRF	NLR
1953	—	—	0.0480	0.0369	0.1830
1954	—	—	0.0900	0.0361	0.1830
1955	13.33	8.09	0.1200	0.0370	0.1830
1956	13.45	8.85	0.1200	0.0420	0.1830
1957	13.59	9.36	0.1200	0.0462	0.1830
1958	13.75	9.86	0.1200	0.0434	0.1830
1959	14.13	10.17	0.1120	0.0500	0.1750
1960	14.56	10.43	0.1000	0.0516	0.1750
1961	14.51	11.19	0.1210	0.0497	0.1750
1962	15.10	11.34	0.1500	0.0500	0.1640
1963	15.27	11.92	0.1500	0.0501	0.1570
1964	15.55	12.41	0.1500	0.0499	0.1590
1965	15.81	12.94	0.1790	0.0506	0.1850
1966	15.78	13.59	0.2640	0.0600	0.2600
1967	16.08	13.99	0.2640	0.0599	0.2600
1968	15.91	14.84	0.2610	0.0668	0.2580
1969	15.59	15.82	0.2390	0.0821	0.2400
1970	15.35	15.96	0.2280	0.0848	0.2400

TABLE 8–11A
Endogenous Variables

Year	YNA	Y	DTR	INT	SG	GC
1953	218.60	421.93	8.67	12.26	9.72	—
1954	228.30	447.36	8.50	16.39	2.34	—
1955	250.50	474.54	7.77	16.64	5.40	162.87
1956	268.20	480.47	7.31	16.52	26.79	161.04
1957	292.20	522.73	11.55	21.25	21.62	156.64
1958	305.40	551.69	13.02	21.97	20.37	180.61
1959	332.20	575.84	15.69	20.58	18.71	186.66
1960	345.10	589.07	15.43	20.37	28.44	176.40
1961	345.10	613.61	17.45	29.81	29.15	192.47
1962	382.60	634.97	16.56	39.56	39.38	194.39
1963	422.50	693.03	17.30	34.41	34.90	186.53
1964	436.00	750.31	17.91	27.36	37.42	218.38
1965	494.20	805.85	22.14	34.28	49.74	229.01
1966	567.90	913.82	33.67	48.09	55.07	235.12
1967	668.30	995.16	42.82	58.68	70.69	238.91
1968	796.50	1127.32	57.95	78.58	95.85	239.97
1969	935.80	1306.19	73.38	97.10	101.78	246.20
1970	1055.00	1422.33	81.01	111.43	115.33	253.51

Year	IVG	MG	ILG	SC	YDP	SH
1953	36.13	—	36.13	19.62	386.55	−6.00
1954	3.53	—	39.66	22.14	402.88	16.34
1955	0.95	1.69	40.61	20.44	434.76	14.87
1956	−11.32	8.28	29.29	20.71	442.05	1.61
1957	16.90	22.38	46.19	23.39	474.76	8.34
1958	9.45	13.55	55.64	27.16	489.36	11.45
1959	−3.73	4.65	51.91	32.18	497.28	11.83
1960	2.04	5.46	53.95	31.31	507.88	−3.78
1961	6.81	8.02	60.76	35.66	537.82	2.89
1962	−15.25	8.90	45.51	46.00	538.66	0.86
1963	22.93	28.46	68.44	50.56	599.32	−9.05
1964	20.85	16.13	89.29	50.01	664.54	−5.56
1965	−0.15	14.45	89.14	62.66	696.87	7.51
1966	8.40	16.27	97.54	67.88	784.79	41.37
1967	−12.40	20.77	85.14	78.17	835.67	39.99
1968	−12.47	34.33	72.67	87.24	920.11	43.68
1969	30.08	66.44	102.75	95.35	1085.55	64.05
1970	14.34	64.81	117.09	102.15	1162.96	58.16

TABLE 8–11A (concluded)

Year	INA	I	CK	DC	MC	MK
1953	31.24	35.28	—	421.81	—	—
1954	38.21	41.66	—	445.49	—	—
1955	44.45	48.98	0.0	480.47	6.75	15.13
1956	47.70	52.77	0.0	524.69	8.64	11.36
1957	54.83	61.31	0.0	543.14	10.88	11.13
1958	52.44	57.79	0.0	566.35	8.11	9.62
1959	53.30	59.29	0.21	579.19	4.27	11.10
1960	54.74	61.71	0.69	599.76	4.51	10.64
1961	56.91	65.26	0.05	591.83	4.15	11.25
1962	77.33	84.05	0.74	634.20	5.33	18.20
1963	95.67	105.95	11.31	667.14	6.41	30.04
1964	82.67	93.33	2.73	705.08	3.52	18.36
1965	103.97	117.64	5.07	747.69	4.32	19.44
1966	167.47	190.63	47.03	812.47	6.68	44.68
1967	212.85	232.09	61.94	900.00	10.98	82.79
1968	301.81	325.63	101.68	998.27	24.93	137.38
1969	383.50	407.76	98.76	1102.62	34.46	151.72
1970	391.70	416.76	78.62	1187.75	37.22	151.58

Year	XGM	X	MI	M	SK	IV
1953	0.24	10.64	—	91.67	—	—
1954	0.32	6.82	—	64.57	—	—
1955	0.37	4.91	50.38	86.95	3.82	22.67
1956	0.40	6.98	63.21	100.88	−5.81	9.11
1957	0.82	7.09	62.52	117.12	0.32	11.81
1958	0.64	5.65	62.16	99.87	−10.17	8.29
1959	0.80	6.29	55.67	80.02	−4.17	9.22
1960	1.46	9.69	57.63	90.40	−3.69	2.50
1961	2.26	11.89	51.96	82.30	−8.57	8.16
1962	2.81	15.45	77.38	112.90	13.22	15.46
1963	10.51	23.78	83.48	143.56	19.69	10.76
1964	15.53	32.51	68.97	104.83	−0.16	−3.66
1965	28.40	47.80	84.84	120.15	−4.96	0.99
1966	40.82	69.09	122.51	192.87	−29.94	1.13
1967	54.77	87.82	155.62	263.59	−19.37	7.69
1968	89.81	133.66	191.52	374.93	2.71	14.99
1969	127.82	183.02	231.15	468.83	−10.22	−0.40
1970	178.57	252.93	271.52	513.69	40.80	21.54

TABLE 8–11B
Basic Commercial Policy Variables

Year	ORD	XPX	SOX	TAM
1953	—	—	—	—
1954	—	—	—	—
1955	99.71	159.87	0.0	11.67
1956	132.10	139.77	0.0	10.43
1957	118.12	139.14	0.0	12.74
1958	121.80	155.91	2.29	28.42
1959	119.73	202.82	3.03	65.84
1960	135.37	181.72	2.37	64.86
1961	244.79	28.03	15.00	34.42
1962	226.57	0.0	35.34	28.39
1963	189.32	57.96	27.63	18.07
1964	232.22	43.02	28.84	23.35
1965	265.40	0.0	38.09	28.39
1966	256.34	0.0	46.93	23.40
1967	243.12	0.0	54.29	23.48
1968	233.30	0.0	63.28	22.62
1969	234.53	0.0	58.35	20.60
1970	240.21	0.0	64.08	20.29

TABLE 8–11C
Derived Commercial Policy Variables

Year	XPM	SUBM	SUBX	SXDT	TAR	MARDEV
1953	—	—	—	0.0	2.63	—
1954	—	—	—	0.0	5.62	—
1955	9.03	20.70	159.87	0.0	4.70	—
1956	9.67	20.10	139.77	0.0	4.73	—
1957	8.42	21.16	139.14	0.0	6.29	—
1958	8.83	37.25	158.20	0.0	11.69	—
1959	15.94	81.79	205.85	0.0	21.60	0.106
1960	19.47	84.34	184.10	0.0	24.36	0.165
1961	4.05	38.47	43.03	0.0	11.49	0.200
1962	0.0	28.39	35.34	0.56	12.62	0.076
1963	9.60	27.67	85.59	0.75	9.53	0.006
1964	13.34	36.69	71.86	1.07	9.16	0.004
1965	0.0	28.39	38.09	2.84	12.85	0.060
1966	0.0	23.40	46.93	4.45	15.94	0.088
1967	0.0	23.48	54.29	6.19	20.35	−0.002
1968	0.0	22.62	63.28	7.96	27.10	−0.035
1969	0.0	20.60	58.35	10.98	28.53	−0.024
1970	0.0	20.29	64.08	14.80	28.45	0.001

TABLE 8–11D
Other Exogenous Variables

Year	YA	G	IA	PK	NFI	MST
1953	203.40	13.84	4.04	—	9.42	−61.39
1954	219.10	28.16	3.45	—	7.56	−42.30
1955	224.10	23.71	4.53	27.12	7.75	−51.10
1956	212.20	1.77	5.07	18.58	7.38	−81.13
1957	230.60	17.47	6.48	19.45	7.59	−90.26
1958	246.30	26.31	5.35	17.27	7.59	−87.12
1959	243.70	39.16	5.99	9.74	7.75	−67.94
1960	244.00	31.71	6.97	11.25	7.38	−72.46
1961	268.50	29.60	8.35	14.25	5.79	−64.68
1962	252.40	29.36	6.72	−0.69	6.48	−84.18
1963	270.60	26.35	10.28	9.31	6.79	−79.47
1964	314.30	17.01	10.66	5.23	6.53	−64.52
1965	311.60	19.53	13.67	−1.39	7.65	−73.63
1966	345.90	42.63	23.16	10.35	13.08	−96.34
1967	326.90	51.16	19.24	8.36	21.53	−124.84
1968	330.80	67.78	23.82	9.46	22.24	−127.42
1969	370.40	97.24	24.26	57.64	23.04	−139.63
1970	367.40	105.56	25.06	43.24	10.17	−98.10

Year	RPG	POP	GP	RD	LR	RF
1953	—	—	—	0.0480	0.1830	0.0369
1954	—	—	—	0.0900	0.1830	0.0361
1955	0.91	21.42	162.13	0.1200	0.1830	0.0370
1956	1.20	22.30	141.44	0.1200	0.1830	0.0420
1957	1.18	22.95	151.16	0.1200	0.1830	0.0462
1958	0.98	23.61	176.51	0.1200	0.1830	0.0434
1959	0.80	24.30	178.28	0.1120	0.1750	0.0500
1960	0.88	24.99	172.98	0.1000	0.1750	0.0516
1961	0.98	25.70	191.26	0.1210	0.1750	0.0497
1962	0.94	26.44	170.24	0.1500	0.1640	0.0500
1963	1.32	27.19	181.00	0.1500	0.1570	0.0501
1964	1.22	27.96	223.10	0.1500	0.1590	0.0499
1965	1.00	28.75	214.41	0.1790	0.1850	0.0506
1966	0.96	29.37	227.25	0.2640	0.2600	0.0600
1967	1.01	30.07	205.74	0.2640	0.2600	0.0599
1968	1.04	30.75	193.17	0.2610	0.2580	0.0668
1969	1.17	31.41	209.84	0.2390	0.2400	0.0821
1970	1.18	31.31	203.04	0.2280	0.2400	0.0848

(continued)

TABLE 8–11D (concluded)

Year	RINF	MNC	NTOSH	XGP	RT
1953	—	—	−7.79	10.40	49.92
1954	0.309	—	−8.16	6.50	34.92
1955	0.636	13.00	−9.77	4.54	39.84
1956	0.297	9.40	−10.84	6.58	74.63
1957	0.193	10.21	−14.51	6.27	83.07
1958	−0.007	6.43	−11.50	5.01	75.50
1959	0.022	4.33	−11.49	5.49	54.59
1960	0.091	12.16	−10.27	8.23	61.31
1961	0.155	6.91	−18.63	9.63	46.93
1962	0.135	3.09	−18.43	12.64	63.74
1963	0.283	−4.83	−18.09	13.27	66.65
1964	0.319	−2.15	−18.67	16.98	50.96
1965	0.077	−2.90	−22.95	19.40	53.95
1966	0.129	2.73	−36.55	28.27	58.29
1967	0.105	−6.57	−40.53	33.05	59.76
1968	0.120	−13.23	−43.66	43.85	63.01
1969	0.121	−14.95	−73.73	55.20	64.65
1970	0.142	−11.45	−63.67	74.36	45.23

NOTES

1. The implicit production function which we use is
$$YNA_t = f(INA_{t-1}, INA_{t-2}, \ldots, INA_{t-T})$$
where INA_t is the investment in nonagricultural sectors in period t. We also assume that depreciation takes place at a rate γ with respect to earlier years investment and that investment enters the function f in a logarithmic form, i.e.,
$$YNA_t = \alpha + \beta [\log_e(INA_{t-1}) + \gamma \log_e(INA_{t-2}) + \ldots + \gamma^{T-1} \log_e(INA_{t-T})]$$
Defined recursively, this becomes (approximately for very large T)
$$YNA_t = (\alpha - \gamma \alpha) + \gamma YNA_{t-1} + \beta \log_e(INA_{t-1})$$
The estimate of the coefficient γ is the estimated depreciation rate.

2. The test for an increasing incremental capital-output ratio was suggested by Albert Fishlow.

3. The sample period was extended to 1971, since preliminary data for 1971 were available for YNA.

4. This is the incremental capital-output ratio on a net basis, i.e., allowing for estimated depreciation.

5. ρ is the coefficient of autocorrelation as estimated in the terminal iteration of the Cochrane-Orcutt technique.

6. These elasticities are estimated from the regression equations by multiplying the coefficient of Y by the ratio of the means of DTR and Y or INT and YNA as the case may be.

7. The current rate of inflation and the rate of inflation lagged once were sufficient

to explain expected rates of inflation. The rate of inflation lagged more than once had little explanatory power.

8. Several readers of the draft manuscript commented that they did not understand how corporate savings could be affected positively by the interest rate. It is sometimes argued, for example, that marginal efficiency of investment is the relevant variable because corporations save only to invest in productive capacity. This is a common fallacy and represents a failure to understand the concept of reservation demand. Self-financed investment by a tightly controlled corporation, typical in Korea, represents a decision not to distribute profits for the purpose of increased consumption and a decision not to seek outside financing, but rather to retain profits for financing investment. As for the substitution effect, a higher interest rate makes self-financing more attractive than outside financing for both working and fixed capital and saving a better choice than consumption. Of course the income effect works in the opposite direction so that the coefficient of the interest rate has no a priori sign and must be determined empirically.

9. For example, the Medium Industry Bank and the Korea Development Bank.

10. Loan rates of commercial banks were more than 24 percent over the latter 1960s which corresponds to a real interest rate of more than 10 percent.

11. These elasticities were determined with respect to percentage changes in the total effective exchange rate, i.e., $ORD + SUBM$.

12. We made no attempt to specify the structure so that the system would be triangular. After the model was specified a priori we attempted to triangularize the matrix.

Chapter 9

Effects of the Exchange Rate Regime on Growth: A Simulation Approach

The econometric model estimated in the previous chapter establishes a framework within which we can appraise the influence of commercial policy on the growth and structure of the South Korean economy. In chapters 6 and 7 we have already attempted to assess the effect of commercial policy on the efficient allocation of investment. It is difficult, however, to use the analysis of efficiency to determine the total effect on growth. Most studies of the static efficiency loss that results from tariffs and quantitative restrictions indicate that the loss is at most only a very small fraction of current output. Far more important may be the consequences of commercial policy for savings and investment relationships, export and import patterns, availability of foreign exchange, and government budgets. The strength of these relationships may have such bearing on the growth process that the growth effects very much outweigh the static efficiency effects.

COMMERCIAL POLICY VARIABLES

The basic commercial policy variables to be considered are: (1) the official exchange rate; (2) the export premium per dollar of exports which arises from a multiple exchange rate system that favors export earnings; (3) other subsidies and subsidy equivalents per dollar of exports; (4) tariffs and foreign exchange taxes per dollar of imports. All basic commercial policy variables are computed on a purchasing-power-parity basis.

The basic commercial policy variables are combined to form a number

164

of derived commercial policy variables. The effective exchange rate on imports is a combination of the official exchange rate, tariffs and foreign exchange taxes per dollar of imports, and total export premia per dollar of imports. That is, the cost of imports is raised above the official rate not only because of tariffs and foreign exchange taxes but also because some imports are financed by purchases of export dollars under the multiple exchange rate system. The effective exchange rate on exports is a combination of the official exchange rate, the export dollar premium, and the total of other subsidies per dollar of export. The overall effective exchange rate is defined as the weighted average effective exchange rate on exports and imports (where the weights are exports and imports). Finally, the rate of devaluation is defined as the percentage increase in the overall effective exchange rate averaged over the current year and the two previous years.

INTERACTIONS BETWEEN BASIC COMMERCIAL POLICY VARIABLES AND THE BEHAVIOR OF ECONOMIC AGGREGATES

A major effect of the commercial policy variables is the influence of the effective exchange rate for exports on export performance and of the effective exchange rate for imports on import demand. The export performance, of course, affects the availability of foreign exchange required to finance purchases of imported capital goods for investment and imported raw materials and intermediate goods for current production. The demand for imports affects the amount of foreign exchange required to finance a given level of production or investment.

The rate at which devaluation of the overall effective exchange rate takes place affects the real private cost of servicing foreign loans. The more rapid the rate of devaluation, the greater the local cost of financing foreign loans and the lower the demand for foreign commercial capital imports. A drop in the level of foreign capital imports reduces the availability of foreign exchange to finance imports for current production as well as for investment *and* reduces total savings and investment because of the reduction in foreign savings.

The *way* in which various effective exchange rates are maintained also affects macroeconomic relationships. To the extent that exports are encouraged by tax subsidies, either direct or indirect, the government budget is affected. An increase in export subsidies of this sort, at given levels of government expenditure, reduces government savings and hence total investment. Encouragement of exports by a multiple exchange rate system, however, does not have the same adverse effect on government revenues.

Similarly, tariffs and foreign exchange taxes affect government revenues.

If the aggregate elasticity of demand for imports is less than unity, an increase in the average tariff rate increases government revenues and savings at a given level of government expenditures. Purchases of export certificates which carry import entitlement, while they add to the local currency cost of imports beyond the official exchange rate, do not yield government revenue in the same way as tariffs.

The *net* effect of all these relationships and interactions is difficult to determine a priori. The interactions are too complex. For example, an increase in import tariffs reduces the demand for imports and hence conserves foreign exchange but may reduce government revenues if the aggregate elasticity of import demand is greater than unity.[1] The conservation of foreign exchange makes more rapid growth possible when the supply of foreign exchange is limited, but a reduction in government revenues, if it curtails government savings and investment, hinders growth. Similarly, an increase in the rate of devaluation boosts export earnings while reducing import demand and thus fosters more rapid growth when foreign exchange is scarce. But by also reducing the inflow of foreign commercial capital a higher rate of devaluation tends to retard growth. The net effect of various policies depends on a complex set of interrelations among the parameters of the aggregate behavioral functions. In this chapter, we shall perform some experiments on a simulation model using different policy strategies to attempt to determine the efficacy of various exchange rate policies in promoting growth. Our results will be analyzed to determine the important parameters and relationships.

THE SIMULATION MODEL

The basis of the simulation model is the econometric model estimated in the previous chapter. In more general form the model may be written as follows.

$$B \cdot \psi_t + \Gamma_1 \phi_{1t} + \Gamma_2 \phi_{2t} + \Gamma_3 \phi_{3t} + \Delta \psi_{t-\tau} + e_t = 0 \qquad (9\text{-}1)$$

where ψ_t is a vector of endogenous variables, ϕ_{1t} is a vector of basic commercial policy variables, ϕ_{2t} is a vector of derived commercial policy variables, ϕ_{3t} is a vector of all other exogenous variables in the model, $\psi_{t-\tau}$ is a vector of predetermined endogenous variables and e_t is a vector of error terms. B, Γ_1, Γ_2, Γ_3, and Δ are matrixes of parameters of the model and are estimated in the previous chapter. The variables in the system and the structure of the matrixes are given in tables 8–1 through 8–5.

In addition to the basic econometric model set forth in (9–1), the simulation model includes a number of equations that give the derived commercial policy variables as functions of the basic commercial policy variables and a number of inequality constraints which the system must satisfy. The first derived commercial policy variable, export premia per dollar of *imports,* is export premia per dollar of *exports* multiplied by total exports and divided by total imports.

$$\phi_{2,1,t} = XPM_t = (XPX_t \cdot X_t) / M_t \qquad (9-2)$$

Total tariffs and tariff equivalents per dollar of imports, i.e., the difference between the official exchange rate and the effective rate on imports, is the second derived commercial policy variable and is the sum of tariffs and foreign exchange taxes per dollar of imports and export premia per dollar of imports.

$$\phi_{2,2,t} = SUBM_t = TAM_t + XPM_t \qquad (9-3)$$

Similarly, total subsidies and subsidy equivalents per dollar of exports is the sum of export subsidies on exports and export premia per dollar of exports.

$$\phi_{2,3,t} = SUBX_t = SOX_t + XPX_t \qquad (9-4)$$

Subsidies on exports in the form of internal tax relief is expressed as a fraction of total export subsidies times a factor required to express these total subsidies in 1965 prices.[2]

$$\phi_{2,4,t} = SXDT_t = \alpha_1 SOX_t \cdot X_t \cdot \alpha_{2t} \qquad (9-5)$$

Total tariffs and foreign exchange taxes are equal to the effective tariff rate (i.e., total tariffs and foreign exchange taxes per dollar of imports) times total imports multiplied by the factor α_{2t} required to express these revenues in terms of 1965 prices.

$$\phi_{2,5,t} = TAR_t = TAM_t \cdot M_t \cdot \alpha_{2t} \qquad (9-6)$$

The rate of devaluation is the percentage rate at which the overall effective exchange rate devalues. The overall effective exchange rate is a weighted average of the effective exchange rate on imports and exports. The effective exchange rates on exports and imports are

$$RX_t = ORD_t + SUBX_t \qquad (9-7)$$

and

$$RM_t = ORD_t + SUBM_t \qquad (9-8)$$

respectively. The overall or average effective exchange rate is

$$R_t = (RX_t \cdot X_t + RM_t \cdot M_t) / (X_t + M_t) \qquad (9-9)$$

The rate of devaluation, then, is

$$RDEV_t = (R_t - R_{t-1}) / R_{t-1} \qquad (9-10)$$

The moving average rate of devaluation is the last derived commercial policy variable:

$$\phi_{2,6,t} = MARDEV_t = (RDEV_t + RDEV_{t-1} + RDEV_{t-2})/3 \quad (9\text{--}11)$$

The model is also subject to a number of inequality constraints. The first set of them refers to the level of foreign exchange reserves at the end of year t denoted by $LFXR$. The level of foreign exchange reserves is determined recursively from period to period.

$$LFXR_{t+1} = LFXR_t + \Delta LFXR_t \quad (9\text{--}12)$$

where the change in reserves in year t is denoted by $\Delta LFXR_t$.[3] The level of foreign exchange reserves must be greater than some minimum fraction of imports and less than some maximum fraction of total imports.

$$LFXR_{t+1} \geqq \alpha_3 M_t \quad (9\text{--}13)$$

$$LFXR_{t+1} \leqq \alpha_4 M_t \quad (9\text{--}14)$$

The purpose of these constraints is to require reserves which are "adequate" but not "excessive" where the policy parameters α_3 and α_4 define adequacy and excessiveness in terms of a fraction of imports.

Similarly, inventory levels are constrained to be greater than a minimum fraction of total income and less than some maximum fraction of total income.

$$LIV_{t+1} \geqq \alpha_5 Y_t \quad (9\text{--}15)$$

$$LIV_{t+1} \leqq \alpha_6 Y_t \quad (9\text{--}16)$$

where the level of inventories at end of year t is determined recursively as follows:

$$LIV_{t+1} = LIV_t + IV_t \quad (9\text{--}17)$$

where IV_t is the level of investment in inventories in year t (excluding grain inventories). Unless inventory levels are restricted to be greater than some fraction of total income, investment will not be constrained by availability of savings, i.e., investment could be financed by unlimited drawing down of inventories. The upper limit on inventories is to ensure that production is limited by total effective demand.

METHOD OF SIMULATION

The simulations of the model expressed in equations (9–1) through (9–17) were performed over the period 1960 to 1970 with several variations of the values of the basic commercial policy variables. These are:

$\phi_{1,1,t} = ORD_t$, official exchange rate on a purchasing-power-parity basis;

$\phi_{1,2,t} = XPX_t$, export premia per dollar of exports;

$\phi_{1,3,t} = SOX_t$, subsidies per dollar of exports;

$\phi_{1,4,t} = TAM_t$, tariffs and foreign exchange taxes per dollar of imports.

The parameters α_1, α_3, α_4, α_5, and α_6 are also basic policy parameters. These were set at values we regarded as reasonable, given past experience. The proportion of export subsidies in the form of internal tax relief (α_1) was, in fact, set equal to its historical value for each year from 1960 to 1970. In the final simulations values of α_3 through α_6 were set as follows:

$\alpha_3 = 0.17$, lower limit on foreign exchange as a proportion of imports;

$\alpha_4 = 0.35$, upper limit on foreign exchange as a proportion of imports;

$\alpha_5 = 0.05$, lower limit on inventories (excluding grains) as a proportion of output;

$\alpha_6 = 0.14$, upper limit on inventories (excluding grains) as a proportion of output.

Historically, over the period 1960 to 1970, foreign exchange reserves ranged from 17 to 67 percent of total imports while inventories ranged from 10 to 14 percent of total GNP. If the historical upper limit on foreign exchange reserves is maintained in the simulations, considerable reserves are accumulated for some of the simulation runs. To translate excess reserves into extra growth, an upper limit of 35 percent, or four months' imports, is postulated as reasonable. Similarly we use a lower limit of 5 percent on inventories as a percent of output to allow a tighter regime that facilitates faster depletion of inventories to finance investment.

In addition to the variations in these values and parameters, we use two policy adjustment variables, EC_t and IG_t. EC_t is an excess capacity variable that comes into play whenever foreign exchange reserves or inventories are inadequate. We assume that the government will attempt to adjust to a balance of payments crisis (inadequate reserves) or an inflationary gap (pressure on inventories indicating that desired investment exceeds savings) by pursuing deflationary monetary and fiscal policies that generate excess capacity in the economy. IG_t is a variable denoting a change in total investment induced by government policies, including inflationary or deflationary monetary policy and direct government investment. We assume that in addition to excess capacity, the government is able to reduce investment when a balance of payments problem arises or an inflationary gap emerges. Conversely, when reserves are excessive or inventories large, the government tries to increase total investment.

The model is nonlinear because of the relationships (9–2), (9–6), (9–9), and (9–10). Rather than use a general nonlinear solution technique such as Gauss-Seidel, a special solution technique was devised for this particular model which takes advantage of the rather simple nature of the nonlinearities. The nonlinear solution technique is described in the appendix to this chapter.

At each period of time in the simulations, the constraints (9–13) through (9–16) are checked. If foreign exchange reserves are less than the required minimum level relative to imports or inventories are below the minimum level relative to income—constraints (9–13) and (9–15) violated—the excess capacity variable EC_t is increased and the level of investment is reduced by lowering IG_t.[4] If there are excess reserves or excess inventories—constraints (9–14) and (9–16) violated—investment is increased by increasing IG_t. These policy adjustments are continued in an iterative fashion until the constraints violated are satisfied. Initially the policy values EC_t and IG_t are set equal to zero in each period; so if none of the constraints are violated there is no excess capacity and no government-induced changes in investment.

SIMULATION EXPERIMENTS

Using the model described above, two sets of simulation experiments were performed to determine the behavior of the macroeconomic aggregates over the period 1960 to 1970. The first set of experiments involved variations in the "pure" effective exchange rate, a completely unified exchange rate with no subsidies on exports and no tariffs or tariff equivalents on imports. With a "pure" effective exchange rate, there are no distortions of international prices and the exchange rate regime is completely liberal. These experiments are designed first of all to determine how much can be gained by complete liberalization and secondly to estimate various "equilibrium" exchange rates.

The second set of experiments involved variations, positive and negative, in the basic commercial policy variables in comparison with their historical values. The official exchange rate (ORD) was varied between 80 and 120 percent of its historical value. The exchange rate premium per dollar of export (XPX) was varied between 0 and 200 percent of its historical value to determine the effect of the multiple exchange rate system. Subsidies per dollar of exports (SOX) were varied between 0 and more than 500 percent of their historical value, and tariffs and foreign exchange tax per dollar of imports (TAM) were varied between 0 and more than 300 percent of their historical value.

In all of the experiments, we assume some "optimal" solution in the sense that there exists some combination of basic commercial policy variables that maximizes a "well-behaved" utility function defined with respect to the endogenous macro-variables. We did not, however, attempt to define such a utility function and use optimization techniques to determine the maximum value of the utility function. Rather, we looked at two separate "performance indicators" for each simulation run: (1) the discounted value of total GNP from 1960 to 1970, and (2) the discounted value of consumption. Neither is really an appropriate measure of utility. The discounted value of consumption may be high because savings and investment are low in the last few years so that future growth beyond 1970 is sacrificed for consumption from 1960 to 1970. The discounted value of GNP may be high because consumption is low so that future growth beyond 1970 is bought at the price of low consumption from 1960 to 1970. One growth path, however, may dominate another in the sense that both consumption and total income are higher. This is, in fact, the situation most frequently encountered in our simulation runs so that there is no practical conflict between maximization of income or consumption.

The use of optimization techniques presents problems beyond the appropriate definition of a utility function. The model is complex and nonlinear, involving 40 equations and inequalities in each time period. Thus there are more than 400 constraints from 1960 to 1970 and they would impose formidable computational difficulties on a nonlinear optimization model. Simulation enables us to determine "near optimal" solutions. Furthermore, we are able to examine the time path of the macro-aggregates for selected sets of policy choices which would not be possible if we used an optimization model.

EQUILIBRIUM EXCHANGE RATES

The first set of experiments were intended to determine the exchange rate that would result in a growth path which, if subsidies, taxes, and tariffs on foreign trade were eliminated, would be similar to the path the economy actually followed from 1960 to 1970. Variations above and below this "equilibrium" rate were also made to determine the behavior of the discounted value of output and consumption during the same period.

The first step was to set the official exchange rate so that the purchasing-power-parity effective exchange rate (without tariffs and subsidies) was equal to the historical purchasing-power-parity effective rate (including taxes, tariffs, and subsidies). This experiment yielded a growth performance somewhat inferior in GNP, but superior in consumption (Figure 9–1). The reason for the poorer growth in GNP is that government revenues from tariffs and foreign exchange taxes are reduced and government savings decline. The economy runs into inflationary pressures, especially in 1968 and 1969. Investment tends to exceed available savings, both domestic and foreign. Reduction of inventories violates the inventory (i.e., savings-investment) constraint in the model.

FIGURE 9–1

**Income and Consumption over Time: Pure Effective Exchange Rate Equal
to Historical Exchange Rate Including Taxes and Subsidies**

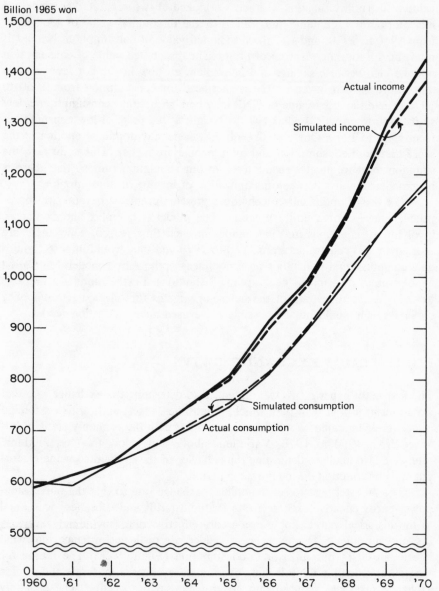

Deflationary fiscal and monetary policies reduce investment and generate excess capacity, thus slowing the economy's growth. Consumption, by contrast, rises because reduced government revenues lead to increased disposable income.

The next step was to vary the "pure" effective exchange rate above and below the actual historical value of the effective exchange rate. The results in terms of the total discounted values of GNP and consumption are shown in Figure 9–2. If the "pure" rate is reduced to 99.5 percent of the historical effective rate, the results are slightly better, both for output and consumption, but the results are not significantly different. If the "pure" rate is reduced much below 99.5 percent, the results are worse, both for output and consumption.

FIGURE 9–2

Behavior of Discounted Values of Income and Consumption
with Variations in the Pure Effective Exchange Rate

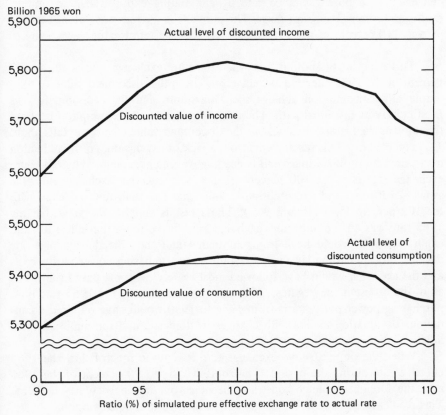

For example, if the pure effective exchange rate is reduced to only 90 percent of the historical values, the total discounted value of income drops by more than 4 percent and of consumption by about 2 percent. This poorer performance is caused by a foreign exchange constraint encountered in the middle of the decade. Investment must be reduced and excess capacity appears. Similarly, if the pure effective exchange rate is raised above 99.5 percent of the historical levels, consumption and income growth are constrained by a lack of savings. Savings are insufficient because of the decline in foreign savings $(M-X)$ brought about by the tendency of imports to contract more than exports when the pure effective exchange rate is reduced.

Conventional economic wisdom asserts that the 1965 exchange rate was an equilibrium rate and that if its purchasing-power-parity value had been maintained, it would have been unnecessary to increase export subsidies to maintain balance of payments equilibrium. This hypothesis was tested in the following way: The 1965 effective purchasing-power-parity exchange rate was converted to a pure exchange rate by eliminating export subsidies, import tariffs, and foreign exchange taxes. The pure exchange rate was varied between 90 and 110 percent of the 1965 effective exchange rate for the years 1964 to 1970.

This experiment showed that when the pure exchange rate is set at 102 percent of the 1965 effective exchange rate, both the discounted value of total output and consumption achieve their maximum and the economy follows most closely its historical path. The discounted value of consumption is about the same as the historical value, but the discounted value of income falls about 1.2 percent short. This result stems from a lack of savings due to the reduction in government tariff revenues and hence in government savings. When the pure exchange rate is set at 100 percent of the 1965 effective exchange rate, the growth of income and consumption is somewhat less than that achieved with the 102 percent level (Figure 9–3). These results support the view that the 1965 rate was an "equilibrium" exchange rate in the sense that all tariffs and export subsidies could have been eliminated and the official exchange rate devalued to approximately the 1965 rate on a purchasing-power-parity basis and the economy would have followed most closely the same path in terms of all of the economic aggregates. Of course, maintenance of the 1965 rate on a purchasing-power-parity basis from 1964 to 1970 would have required a continuous devaluation in line with changes in domestic and international price inflation, that is, a gliding peg exchange rate.

When the pure effective exchange rate is reduced much below the 1965 effective rate during the period 1964 to 1970, say to 90 percent of the 1965 rate, the foreign exchange constraint becomes binding, particularly in 1965. This results in considerably less growth in income and consumption.

The behavior of the discounted values of income and consumption is

FIGURE 9–3

**Behavior of Discounted Values of Income and Consumption with Pure Effective
Exchange Rate Valued Relative to 1965 Effective Exchange Rate**

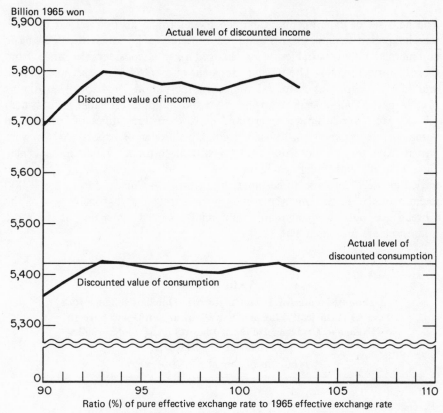

erratic when the pure effective exchange rate is set between 93 and 102 percent of the effective rate. Local maxima for both income and consumption
occur at 93, 97, and 102 percent. At 93 percent, there are some excess foreign exchange reserves in 1967. This helps growth. At 97 percent, excess
foreign exchange reserves accumulate in 1966 and 1967. Policy variables then
come into play, stimulating investment and increasing output. The result is
more rapid growth in those years, but it leads to an inflationary gap and a
savings-investment constraint in 1968 and 1969. At 102 percent, excess foreign exchange reserves appear even earlier, in 1964, but the savings-investment
constraint takes effect earlier and more persistently from 1966 through 1970.
The erratic behavior, then, is caused by the interaction of the savings-investment and foreign exchange constraints.

MANIPULATION OF COMMERCIAL POLICY VARIABLES

The next set of experiments attempted to determine an optimal set of commercial policy variables. This required simulations in which the four basic commercial policy variables were changed over a considerable range from their historical values. The official exchange rate (ORD) was set at 80, 100, and 120 percent of its historical values for the period 1964 to 1970. Export premia per dollar of export arising from the multiple exchange rate system (XPX) were varied between zero and more than three times their historical values in successive steps. Other subsidies per dollar of export (SOX) were varied from zero to more than five times their historical values in sequence. Finally, tariffs and foreign exchange taxes per dollar of imports (TAM) were varied between zero and three times their historical values.[5] More than 1,000 experiments were run and the results demonstrate the responsiveness of the Korean economy to changes in commercial policy. Only a few of the more interesting are presented here.[6]

TABLE 9–1

Discounted Value of Total Output with Official Exchange Rate at Its Historical Value and Variations in Tariffs and Foreign Exchange Taxes per Dollar of Import (TAM) and Subsidies per Dollar of Export (SOX)

(billions of won at 1965 prices)

SOX as a Percent of Historical Value	TAM as a Percent of Historical Value				
	80	120	160	200	240
0	5,830	5,891	5,920	5,985	nf
40	5,852	5,886	5,928	5,999	nf
80	5,850	5,882	5,938	6,015	nf
120	5,840	5,887	5,952	6,026[a]	nf
160	5,839	5,897	5,953	6,013	nf
200	5,838	5,880	5,928	5,988	nf
240	5,820	5,853	5,894	5,937	nf
280	5,795	5,813	5,869	5,868	nf
320	5,752	5,776	5,807	5,820	nf

NOTE: nf—not feasible.

a. Maximum value of discounted value of output from 1960 to 1970.

First, we discuss variations in export subsidies per dollar of exports (*SOX*) and tariffs and foreign exchange taxes per dollar of imports (*TAM*), holding the official exchange rate constant at its historical values. Table 9–1 gives the figures for the discounted value of output over the period 1960 to 1970 and Table 9–2 gives the discounted value of consumption over the same period for this set of experiments. The figures marked *a* in these tables give the maximum values of discounted output and consumption. The optimal value of discounted output exceeds the historical level, 5,860, by 4 percent; the optimal value of discounted consumption exceeds the historical level, 5,421, by about 1 percent. The underscored numbers in tables 9–1 and 9–2 represent combinations of values for *TAM* and *SOX* which result in *both* greater consumption *and* greater output over the period 1960 to 1970 than the historical values. Both the maximum value of output and the maximum value of consumption lie within the region for which both output and consumption exceed historical values. Thus one could maximize the discounted value of output without lowering the discounted value of consumption below its historical value. Alternatively, one could maximize the discounted value of consumption without lowering the discounted value of output below its historical value.

TABLE 9–2

Discounted Value of Consumption with Official Exchange Rate at Its Historical Value and Variations in TAM and SOX

(billions of won at 1965 prices)

SOX as a Percent of Historical Value	TAM as a Percent of Historical Value				
	80	120	160	200	240
0	5,396	5,407	5,398	5,408	nf
40	5,416	5,411	5,411	5,424	nf
80	5,423	5,417	5,424	5,442	nf
120	5,425	5,428	5,441	5,458	nf
160	5,433	5,443	5,452	5,462a	nf
200	5,442	5,443	5,447	5,458	nf
240	5,440	5,437	5,438	5,439	nf
280	5,435	5,423	5,433	5,410	nf
320	5,418	5,410	5,407	5,393	nf

NOTE: nf—not feasible.
a. Maximum value of discounted value of consumption from 1960 to 1970.

The maximum discounted values of output and consumption occur at very nearly the same combinations of the values of SOX and TAM (with the official exchange rate held at its historical value). The level of tariffs and foreign exchange taxes per dollar of imports (TAM) is double the historical level and the level of export subsidies is somewhat greater than the historical level (+20 percent in the case of maximum output and +60 percent in the case of maximum consumption). The increased value of TAM results in increased government revenues. Since the level of government expenditures is assumed to be exogenous, the effect is to increase government savings. The increase in the value of SOX tends to reduce government revenues, but since export subsidies are increased by a smaller percentage than tariffs, since exports are less than total imports, and since only part of export subsidies have a direct budgetary impact, the net effect is a substantial increase in government savings which increases total investment and accelerates growth. The increase in SOX and TAM both generates extra foreign exchange accumulation through increased exports and reduces imports. The accumulation of foreign exchange also makes possible increased investment and growth. The time path of output and consumption is shown in Figure 9–4 for the case in which the discounted value of output is maximized. By 1970, the simulated value of output exceeds the historical value by 95 billion won (constant prices) or almost 7 percent. Furthermore, historical values of output and consumption in the simulation are almost equaled or exceeded every year from 1960 to 1970. Thus the increase in SOX and TAM results in a dynamically more efficient growth path.

The doubling of TAM does not involve very high tariffs and foreign exchange taxes. In 1970, for example, tariffs (there were virtually no foreign exchange taxes) were only about 7 percent of imports so that doubling it would imply a tariff rate of about 14 percent. If tariffs and foreign exchange taxes are raised much above this level, however, the simulation run becomes unfeasible because some of the smaller import items turn negative. This result is inevitable whenever import demand functions are specified to be linear. Even if the specification were more realistic, the imposition of higher tariffs would probably lead to diminished growth by making the demand for imports very elastic. As tariffs are raised, import demand eventually decreases by a larger percentage; government tariff revenues drop; government savings are smaller; and investment and growth decline.

If export subsidies are raised by more than 20 percent above historical levels, growth in output also declines. This occurs because of the reduction in government revenue and savings which in turn decreases investment. In the simulation run with export subsidies higher than 120 percent of historical values and tariffs double historical values, the savings-investment constraint is violated in 1966 and 1967. Investment has to be curtailed because savings

FIGURE 9–4

Time Paths of Consumption and Output with SOX Equal to 120 Percent of Historical Values and TAM Equal to 200 Percent of Historical Values

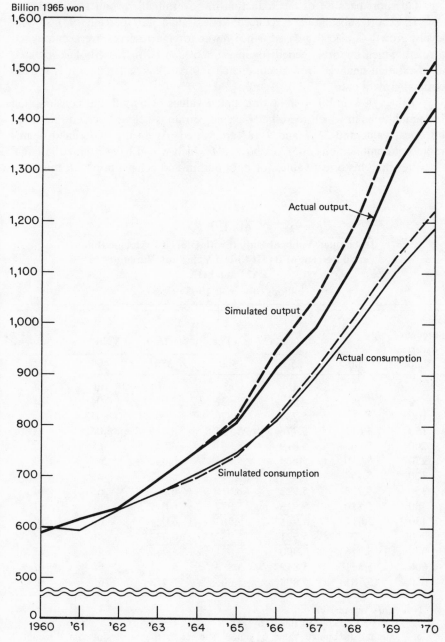

Billion 1965 won

are deficient, and in consequence growth is correspondingly diminished. Savings fall short because of the reduction in government revenues and savings.

If export subsidies are reduced to less than 120 percent of historical levels, growth is also decreased, since fewer foreign reserves are accumulated through which imports needed for investment can be increased. The increase in investment financed from accumulated reserves is smaller than it is for the optimal growth path.

Tables 9–3 and 9–4 show discounted values of output and consumption for simulations in which the official exchange rate is held 20 percent below its historical value and *SOX* and *TAM* are varied. Again the underlined figures represent combinations of *SOX* and *TAM* which would have resulted in equal or better than historical values for both output and consumption. In this case,

TABLE 9–3

**Discounted Value of Output with Official Exchange Rate
at 80 Percent of Its Historical Value and Variations in
TAM and SOX**

(billions of won at 1965 prices)

SOX as a Percent of Historical Value	*TAM* as a Percent of Historical Value					
	200	250	300	350	400	450
0	nf	nf	nf	nf	nf	nf
50	nf	nf	5,832	5,964	6,046	nf
100	nf	5,731	5,879	6,003	6,055	nf
150	5,612	5,776	5,911	6,029	6,065[a]	nf
200	5,663	5,819	5,951	6,041	nf	nf
250	5,710	5,863	5,985	6,042	nf	nf
300	5,754	5,901	6,018	6,019	nf	nf
350	5,796	5,922	6,010	6,007	nf	nf
400	5,810	5,943	5,977	6,019	nf	nf
450	5,812	5,961	5,963	6,034[b]	nf	nf
500	5,827	5,921	5,962	6,032	nf	nf
550	5,846	5,900	5,931	5,985	nf	nf
600	5,831	5,849	5,883	5,931	nf	nf
650	5,781	5,808	5,806	5,918	nf	nf

NOTE: nf—not feasible.
a. Maximum discounted value of output.
b. Maximum discounted value of output subject to the constraint that discounted value of consumption exceeds historical value.

TABLE 9–4

Discounted Value of Consumption with Official Exchange Rate at 80 Percent of Its Historical Value and Variations in TAM and SOX

(billions of won at 1965 prices)

SOX as a Percent of Historical Value	TAM as a Percent of Historical Value					
	200	250	300	350	400	450
0	nf	nf	nf	nf	nf	nf
50	nf	nf	5,274	5,312	5,319	nf
100	nf	5,253	5,306	5,340	5,332	nf
150	5,217	5,286	5,331	5,362	5,346	nf
200	5,255	5,319	5,363	5,378	nf	nf
250	5,293	5,355	5,393	5,390	nf	nf
300	5,330	5,388	5,423	5,389	nf	nf
350	5,366	5,412	5,431	5,397	nf	nf
400	5,387	5,438	5,426	5,417	nf	nf
450	5,403	5,464[a]	5,433	5,430	nf	nf
500	5,427	5,455	5,447	5,456	nf	nf
550	5,455	5,458	5,447	5,447	nf	nf
600	5,462	5,443	5,436	5,435	nf	nf
650	5,446	5,436	5,408	5,388	nf	nf

NOTE: nf—not feasible.
a. Maximum discounted value of consumption.

the maximum discounted value of output and the maximum discounted value of consumption require widely divergent policies. Output is maximized whenever export subsidies are increased 50 percent and tariffs 300 percent above their historical values. The discounted value of consumption, however, is far smaller than its historical value. The discounted value of consumption is maximized whenever export subsidies are raised 350 percent and import duties 150 percent above historical values. The former case emphasizes tariffs; the latter case emphasizes export subsidies. In both cases, additional growth results from accumulations of foreign exchange reserves which allow increased investment. Increased export subsidies, however, lead to relatively more consumption because the reduction of direct tax revenues as a means of subsidy results in an increase of disposable income.

Since the two objectives of output maximization and consumption maximization are divergent, one might determine the maximum discounted value of output subject to the constraint that the discounted value of consumption be at least as great as its historical value. This point is reached whenever tariffs are 250 percent and export subsidies 350 percent above historical values. Perhaps an even better solution is achieved by increasing export subsidies 400 percent above historical values while holding tariffs at 250 percent. A large jump in consumption follows but only a small loss in output. The values of output and consumption are roughly similar to those in the prior case in which the official exchange rate is equal to its historical value. The difference is that when the official exchange rate falls below its historical value, tariffs and subsidies have to be raised to very high levels to increase the availability of foreign exchange. The high tariffs generate the revenue required to offset the loss in revenue caused by export subsidies.

TABLE 9–5

**Discounted Values of Output and Consumption with Official
Exchange Rate at 120 Percent of Its Historical Value
and Variations in TAM and SOX**

(billions of won at 1965 prices)

SOX as a Percent of Historical Value	Output				
	TAM as a Percent of Historical Value				
	0	10	20	30	40
0	5,717	5,713	5,738	5,745[a]	nf
10	5,690	5,717	5,726	5,740	nf
20	5,697	5,707	5,713	5,729	nf
30	5,684	5,693	5,714	5,712	nf
40	5,671	5,694	5,702	5,688	nf

SOX as a Percent of Historical Value	Consumption				
	TAM as a Percent of Historical Value				
	0	10	20	30	40
0	5,373	5,366	5,376[a]	5,376[a]	nf
10	5,358	5,370	5,370	5,374	nf
20	5,365	5,366	5,365	5,370	nf
30	5,358	5,359	5,367	5,361	nf
40	5,352	5,362	5,361	5,348	nf

NOTE: nf—not feasible.
a. Maximum values.

Table 9–5 gives the discounted values of consumption and output when the official exchange rate is set 20 percent greater than its historical value. In this case the maximum values of output and consumption occur with the same values of SOX and TAM. Furthermore, the maximum values are below historical values and far below the maximum values achievable when the official exchange rate is set equal to or 20 percent below historical values (see tables 9–1 through 9–4). In the experiments in which the level of the official exchange rate is kept high, foreign exchange is no problem. Growth is inhibited by a lack of savings. The maximum for both output and consumption is reached when export subsidies are set at zero and tariffs at only 30 percent of historical values. If export subsidies are raised or if tariffs are reduced, government revenue and savings decline and further exacerbate the savings-investment constraint. When tariffs are raised, some minor imports become negative. Yet even if nonlinear import demand functions were specified, an increase in tariffs would probably lead to an elastic demand and less revenue which would also aggravate the savings-investment constraint. We conclude, then, that if the official exchange rate values had been greater, growth in output and consumption would have been smaller.

CONCLUSIONS

The experiments performed on the simulation model suggest that commercial policy has been an important factor in South Korea's growth. They indicate, however, that in promoting exports through subsidies and low tariffs, the government has sacrificed revenues with the result that growth·has been less than optimal. This conclusion assumes that if government revenues had been increased, they would have been set aside, as savings, for investment. The South Korean government deserves credit for keeping the growth of current expenditures low and for channeling some funds into productive investments. But the question remains whether they could have achieved a greater success had the revenues at their disposal been larger.

The experiments also support the view that the 1965 exchange rate was an equilibrium rate in the sense that all subsidies and tariffs could have been eliminated and the same historical growth still achieved. This definition of equilibrium exchange rate differs somewhat from the usual one, the rate that would equilibrate demand and supply of foreign exchange. This more traditional definition, however, is not very useful. Since monetary and fiscal policies help determine the demand for and supply of foreign exchange, there may be one or more equilibrium exchange rates for each possible set of government policies. It is more interesting to consider the optimal combination of policies —exchange rate, fiscal, and monetary. Our experiments show that the optimal "pure" exchange rate is slightly higher than the actual (about 102 percent of the historical) and is combined with more expansionary monetary and fiscal policies. If subsidies and taxes on exports and imports are combined with exchange rate policy, the optimal exchange rate is about equal to the historical rate. The optimal rate should be combined, however, with higher import duties (or fewer exemptions) and roughly similar export subsidies.

APPENDIX: SOLUTION OF THE NONLINEAR SIMULATION MODEL

The simulation model given by equations (9–1) through (9–17) is nonlinear because of equations (9–2), (9–6), (9–9), and (9–10). The way in which the nonlinear solution is obtained involves first the solution for YNA_t. See equation (8–2).

$$YNA_t = -281.8254 + 0.9413 YNA_{t-1} + 80.0668 \log_e (INA_{t-1})$$

$$+ \hat{e}_{1,t} - EC_t \qquad (9\text{–}18)$$

All the variables on the right hand side are predetermined; $\hat{e}_{1,t}$ is the estimated residual from the regression equation (8–2) and EC_t^* is excess capacity, a policy adjustment variable. The value of the derived commercial policy variable $SUBX_t$ can be determined from (9–4), since it is the sum of two basic commercial policy variables SOX_t and XPX_t. Then exports of manufactured goods can be determined from

$$XGM_t = -241.4847 + 0.3323 YNA_t + 0.2629 ORD_t \qquad (9\text{–}19)$$

$$+ 0.1471 SUBX_t + \hat{e}_{19,t}$$

where ORD_t is also a basic commercial policy variable and $\hat{e}_{19,t}$ is the estimated residual from regression equation (8–27). Equation (8–29) may be used next to determine the value of total exports X_t as the sum of XGM_t and primary product exports XGP_t, which is exogenous to the model. Equation (9–2) may be used then to obtain a first estimate of XPM_t as follows:

$$XPM_t = (XPX_t \cdot X_t)/M_t^o \qquad (9\text{–}20)$$

where M_t^o is the actual historical value of imports in year t. This enables us to obtain initial first estimates of all the remaining derived commercial policy variables $\phi_{2,t}^o$ from equations (9–3) through (9–11).

After initial estimates of the derived commercial policy variables have been determined, initial estimates of the endogenous variables of the linear econometric model (9–1) may be obtained recursively by inverting the B matrix.

$$\psi_t = -B^{-1}\Gamma_1\phi_{1t} - B^{-1}\Gamma_2\phi_{2t}{}^0 - B^{-1}\Gamma_3\phi_{3t} \qquad (9\text{-}21)$$

$$-B^{-1}\Delta\psi_{t-\tau} - B^{-1}\hat{e}_t$$

where $\hat{e}_t$ are the estimated residuals from the regression equations used to estimate the linear system. Note that although the exogenous variables, ϕ_{1t}, $\phi_{2t}{}^0$, and ϕ_{3t} and the predetermined variables $\psi_{t-\tau}$ will change from simulation to simulation, we continue to use the estimated error terms $\hat{e}_t$ derived from the regressions on the original data. The justification for this is the assumption that the error terms are assumed to be uncorrelated with the exogenous variables, and we would like to determine the path of the economy under different assumptions concerning the values of the commercial policy variables.

The solution of (9–21) results in a new estimate of total imports:

$$M_t{}^1 = MC_t{}^0 + MK_t{}^0 + MI_t{}^0 + MG_t{}^0 + MNC_t \qquad (9\text{-}22)$$

which may differ from the original estimate $M_t{}^0$. If this new estimate is substituted in (9–20) for the original estimate $M_t{}^0$ and the remaining derived commercial policy variables are determined from equations (9–3) through (9–11), we obtain a second estimate of the derived commercial policy variables $\phi_{2,t}{}^1$. Similarly, a second estimate of the endogenous variables ψ_t is determined by solving (9–21) recursively with $\phi_{2,t}{}^1$ substituted for $\phi_{2,t}{}^0$. This process is repeated as often as is necessary until the successive estimated values of total imports differ by an arbitrarily small amount.

NOTES

1. We must also assume that the supply of imported goods is infinitely elastic.
2. In terms of the original data,
$$\alpha_{2t} = RY_t \cdot WPI_t / (OR_{1965} \cdot WPITP_t \cdot CY_t)$$
3. In terms of our original data, the change in reserves is
$$\Delta LFXR_t = -SK_t + DCKS_t \cdot (RMG_t + RMOS_t) / DMGS_t$$
See tables 8–8 and 8–9 for definitions of the variables.
4. Income and investment are reduced by 1:3.
5. It should be kept in mind that export subsidies and tariffs were a relatively small percent of the effective exchange rate (e.g., 13 percent and 9 percent, respectively, in 1965); so that a doubling or tripling is equivalent to a much smaller change in the effective exchange rate.
6. Export premia were very small during the period covered by the simulations. Variations in XPX, export premia per dollar of exports, did not make much of a difference to our experiments, so none of those results are reported here.

Chapter 10

The Foreign Exchange Regime and Resource Allocation

Any foreign exchange regime can have a substantial effect on the allocation of resources.[1] Protective tariffs encourage the movement of resources into import substitution industries rather than into export industries or into strictly domestic production. The exchange rate also influences the allocation of resources. When overvalued, it discourages investment both in export and in import-substituting industries and makes investment in domestic enterprise (i.e., nontradables) more attractive. In time, however, an overvalued currency leads to balance of payments pressure, which in turn prompts restrictions on imports. Controls on the use of foreign exchange, quantitative controls on imports and multiple exchange rates are some of the techniques available to government and all of them have substantial effects on investment incentives and the allocation of resources.

It is difficult to determine whether the changes in the structure of prices and incentives caused by the foreign exchange regime lead to more or less efficiency in resource allocation. Much of the literature on trade and development presumes that any substantial deviation of the exchange rate from a unified equilibrium rate, large deviations in effective tariffs, and all import controls cause resources to be allocated inefficiently. According to this view, world prices of tradable commodities reflect the true opportunity costs of producing them. Thus tariffs, controls, and multiple exchange rates, which distort world market prices, lead to inefficiencies.

There are many reasons to question this view. The protection of infant industry, the need to raise revenues from tariffs, and the ability to achieve social and political goals through manipulation of the price mechanism argue

186

in favor of some divergence between world market and domestic prices. World market prices, however, provide a standard by which the effects of the foreign exchange regime on resource allocation can be appraised. Large divergences from world market prices suggest the possibility, when other justifications are lacking, that allocation of resources is inefficient.

STANDARD MEASUREMENT TECHNIQUES

A simple measure of the divergence between world market and domestic prices is the legal tariff. If foreign supply is perfectly elastic, and if imports are free from quantitative controls, and if domestic demand for a protected commodity is great enough to sustain imports despite the extra cost, then the legal tariff is both equal to and the cause of the divergence between world market and domestic prices. In Korea, however, the legal tariff is seldom a good measure of this discrepancy. First, quite a number of commodities are exempt from duties, particularly intermediates imported for use in the production of exports. Many capital goods are exempted from legal tariffs as well. Second, a number of tariffs are virtually prohibitive, so that many commodities are not imported. Domestic production is sufficient to satisfy local demand at or below the world market price plus tariff. In these two cases, the legal tariff overstates the actual degree of protection. Third, many imports are subject to controls. The domestic price of such commodities can be higher than the world market price plus tariff if the demand at that price exceeds the amount of imports the quota allows.

For our study of protection in Korea it was thus necessary to compare world market and domestic prices directly. The divergence between the two can be expressed as a percentage of the world price:

$$t_n = \frac{pd - pw}{pw} \qquad (10\text{--}1)$$

where pd is the domestic price of a commodity and pw is the world market price.[2] We call t_n the rate of nominal protection or nominal tariff rate to distinguish it from the legal tariff rate.[3]

Neither legal nor nominal tariff rates provide clear indications of how tariffs or quantitative restrictions divert resources. A much better measure is the rate of effective protection, because it takes into account the intermediates required for production along with primary factors. Effective rates of protection measure protection in relation to the returns to primary factors engaged in separate processing activities. When intermediate inputs are traded, protective measures influence resource allocation according to their effect on factor returns in various processing activities. For example, if the value added in automobile assembly is only 10 percent of the total value of the car, and if imported automobile parts are free of duties and QRs, while the tariff on the final product is 100 percent, then the effective incentive to assemble automobiles is exceedingly high. For the effective rate of protection would be not 100 percent but $100/(.10)$ or 1000 percent.

The general formula for the effective rate of protection, t_{ej}, for activity j is: [4]

$$t_{ej} = \frac{p_{dj} - \Sigma_i a_{ij} p_{di}}{p_{wj} - \Sigma_i a_{ij} p_{wi}} - 1,   \tag{10-2}$$

or

$$t_{ej} = \frac{p_{wj}(1 + t_{nj}) - \Sigma_i a_{ij} p_{wi}(1 + t_{ni})}{p_{wj} - \Sigma_i a_{ij} p_{wi}} - 1   \tag{10-3}$$

$$= \frac{t_{nj} p_{wj} - \Sigma_i a_{ij} t_{ni} \, p_{wi}}{p_{wj} - \Sigma_i a_{ij} p_{wi}}$$

where p_{dj} is domestic price of commodity j, p_{wj} is its world market price, a_{ij} is the input-output coefficient giving the input of commodity i per unit of output of commodity j, and t_{ni} is the nominal protection rate for commodity i. The effective rate of protection is the percentage difference between domestic value added—the numerator of the first term on the right-hand side of (10-2) —and value added in world market prices—the denominator of the first term on the right-hand side of (10-2). Equation (10-3) shows that the effective rate of protection may also be expressed in terms of rates of nominal protection on commodity j and the rates of protection on all the inputs into commodity j. For example, if the rate of nominal protection on all inputs is zero (i.e., $t_{ni} = 0$ for all i), then the effective rate of protection is merely the tariff rate divided by value added at world market prices. The higher the rate of protection on inputs i relative to the rate of protection on output j, the lower the rate of effective protection.

This formula assumes that all intermediate inputs are tradable, so that protection affects only factor rewards in the specific processing activity. When the existence of nontradable intermediate inputs is admitted, it becomes somewhat unclear whether protection affects only the factor rewards in the primary processing activity or those in the domestic industries producing nontradables as well. Two conventions have grown up to compute effective protection where there are nontradable inputs. Under the Balassa convention, protected value added includes only that in the specific processing activity (see Balassa and Associates [1971]). Corden (1971) proposed an alternative formulation that takes into account the indirectly generated value added in those domestic industries which supply nontradable commodities. His argument is that protection affects the factor rewards in the domestic nontradable sectors as well. Thus one should measure the effective incentive to domestic resources in both the final processing stage and in those industries which supply nontradable inputs. The Corden measure of effective protection is the percentage deviation between the value in domestic prices and that in world market prices of the value added generated directly in the production of commodity j and indirectly in the production of nontradable inputs into commodity j. One must invert that part of the input-output matrix referring to nontradable goods to perform the Corden calculation.[5]

The interpretation of effective incentives as we have measured them is not straightforward, for it is not clear whether a high incentive rate is indicative of a high level of incentives (i.e., high excess profits) for factors to move into a particular activity, or a high degree of inefficiency (i.e., wasteful use of all resources used) in the production of a commodity, or a combination of both. High tariffs and other forms of protection may encourage some small efficient producers to expand beyond an efficient scale. Excess profits of the marginal producers may be eliminated, but inframarginal producers may be reaping profits in the form of producers' surplus. If domestic demand is limited, however, the excess profits may remain for all producers. On the other hand, the protected industries may be high-cost industries at all levels of output so that no excess profits are made by any producers. Similarly, low or negative effective incentive rates may indicate factor rewards below their opportunity costs or a high degree of efficiency. "High" and "low" in this context are to be understood in relative terms rather than as absolute magnitudes.

Furthermore, effective protection rates may not even indicate the direction in which resources will tend to flow in response to incentives. If this is generally true, the interpretation of effective protection becomes even more difficult.[6]

EXTENSIONS AND VARIATIONS USED IN MEASURING PROTECTION

An important refinement made here is the notion of effective subsidy in contrast to effective protection. Subsidies in the form of income tax exemptions, accelerated depreciation, and special low interest rates to finance specific activities are not included in the usual measures of effective protection, even though such subsidies may provide particular sectors with substantial incentives. Therefore, we have calculated rates of effective subsidy as well as rates of effective protection. Subsidies affecting direct tax and interest liabilities do not change value-added at world market prices; they do, however, affect the composition of value-added and profits after taxes. These subsidies are incorporated into a measure of effective subsidy in the following way:

The total direct tax liabilities of all firms were reapportioned to each sector on the basis of its share in the total tax base; i.e., we assumed that each firm would have paid the average tax rate on its net income under a neutral tax policy. The difference between the reapportioned tax liability and a sector's actual tax liability is the estimated tax subsidy. The subsidy could, therefore, be negative as well as positive, depending upon whether the sector actually paid a higher or lower tax rate than the average; the algebraic sum of all estimated tax subsidies is zero.

Interest subsidies were determined in analogous fashion. To compute the interest that would be paid under a neutral credit policy, we assumed that all sectors paid the same average interest rate on outstanding loans, that rate being determined as the ratio of total interest payments by all sectors to total loans outstanding. The interest subsidy to a sector is thus the difference between total interest payments at the average interest rate and the actual interest payments of a sector. The algebraic sum of all interest subsidies is zero.

Total direct tax and interest subsidies were added to value added in domestic prices.[7] This adjusted value added is divided by value added at world market prices, and the ratio (minus one) is the effective subsidy rate. Since the sum of all subsidies is zero, the weighted average of all effective subsidy rates is equal to the weighted average of all effective protection rates, where the weights are world market price value added.

Another important extension in this study is to calculate two separate rates of protection or subsidy, one applying to domestic sales, the other to export sales. Prices to the producer of both outputs and inputs are quite different for production for export. Specifically, exports particularly benefited from the following types of preferential treatment in addition to direct tax and interest subsidies:

(1) export production was completely exempt from indirect taxes on both inputs and output;

(2) imports of both intermediate and capital goods for export production were tariff exempt;

(3) exports received an additional subsidy for inputs in the form of a wastage allowance;[8]

(4) a number of export sectors paid subsidized rates for railroad transport and electricity.

All of these factors changed the prices paid for inputs used to produce exports and were taken into account in calculating the effective incentive rates for exports. In addition, exports were frequently priced below the domestic market price. One reason for this difference might be that exported commodities were of lower quality than those consumed domestically. But a more likely explanation is that monopolies or cartels among producers, sustained by import quotas and tariffs, enforced discriminatory pricing. Finally, most tax and interest subsidies apply to production for export but not to production for domestic sale. All of the export incentives described in chapters 3·and 6 that were in effect in 1968 were incorporated in our estimates, except for import prepayment deposits and the implicit export-import link subsidy. Both of these measures were quantitatively unimportant in 1968. We should also note that special incentives to emergent import-substituting activities were taken into account as well.

In total, a number of distinct measures of effective protection and subsidy rates were calculated for Korea for 1968. Effective protection and subsidy rates were calculated by both the Balassa (see Balassa and Associates [1971]) and Corden methods. In both cases, depreciation is deducted from value added. Estimates of effective incentives were obtained separately for export and domestic sales.

THE DATA BASE

Our estimates are based on 1968 domestic and world-market prices, 1968 trade and output flows, and input-output coefficients from a 1966 input-output table. A synthetic input-output table for 1968 derived from the 1966 table is available. However, we believe that the double-deflation and trend extrapolation method used to estimate the 1968 coefficients yields unreliable estimates. We prefer to use the 1966 coefficients in the belief that they are better estimates of the 1968 coefficients than those of the extrapolated 1968 table.

The 1966 table contains 299 producing sectors. The table was aggregated to 160 sectors, of which 150 are tradable-goods-producing sectors. Effective rates of protection and subsidy were calculated for these 150 sectors separately.

The 150 tradable goods sectors were further aggregated in two different ways: (1) by eleven industrial groups, and (2) by four trade categories, namely export industries, import-competing industries, industries that export and are also import-competing, and industries that are neither export oriented nor import-competing (the latter industries called non-import-competing industries). Details of these industrial classifications appear in Table 6–6 and the accompanying text.

Data on world market prices and domestic prices were obtained by means of a survey.[9] A list of commodity groups for which price comparisons were to be made was prepared from the Bank of Korea's 1966 input-output data tabulated at the level of 2,000 commodity groups (comparable input-output information for 1968 was not available). Of the 2,000 groups, price observations were obtained for selected commodities in 365 of them, which in total accounted for 70.8 percent of aggregate commodity domestic sales and 78.2 percent of commodity exports in 1966. The principal criterion for selecting a commodity group for inclusion in the survey was that it had a relatively large share in sectoral output. Priority was further given to non-import-competing commodity groups, to products subject to quantitative restrictions, and to export commodities.

The major sources of domestic price information were individual producers, producers' associations such as the Korea Chamber of Commerce, and various government agencies including the Ministry of Finance, the Economic Planning Board, the Bank of Korea, and the Korea Development Bank. Export and import prices for those commodities actually exported or imported were obtained from domestic records of the transactions. Export prices were not estimated for other commodities. For commodities not actually imported in 1968, import prices were estimated from Korea's export price (if relevant) or, in a majority of the cases, from wholesale prices (exclusive of indirect taxes) in Japan and, less frequently, in the United States. A single price comparison was obtained for a majority of the commodity groups; however, in a number of cases, comparative price information for several commodities within a commodity group was collected.

All world market prices are stated c.i.f., this being the appropriate basis for determining protection of sales on the domestic market. Domestic prices are ex-factory f.o.b. net of indirect taxes.

Other data required to compute effective rates of protection and subsidy included rebates on overhead charges (electricity and rail transport), indirect tax rates and exemptions, legal tariff rates and exemptions on imported inputs, wastage allowance rates, direct tax credits and reductions, and interest rates actually paid. These data were collected from published sources where possible and through the cooperation of various Korean government agencies. Tariff rates include those intended to soak up excess profits on imports subject to quantitative restrictions. Estimates of wastage allowance subsidies, which could not be obtained directly from government, were pieced together from other sources.

NOMINAL RATES OF PROTECTION AND QUANTITATIVE RESTRICTIONS

The 1968 price data gathered from the survey for the most part followed the pattern expected. In some cases the price data on domestic and foreign sales exhibited peculiar characteristics. Differences in quality between domestic and foreign products explained some of these peculiarities, and errors that usually accompany this kind of price data may have accounted for others. In cases where domestic and foreign price comparisons indicated that these factors seemed to be involved, adjustments were made in the data where appropriate. The information used to make the adjustments included (1) the relationship between the price difference as shown by the survey and the legal and actual tariff rates; (2) the relative importance of exports and imports within the commodity group; (3) the type of import control imposed on the commodity.

Domestic prices of imported products generally exceeded world prices. Where they did not, the lower domestic price usually reflected poorer quality. There were some exceptions, however. Negative nominal protection for all petroleum products, the most notable example, is explained by government controls. All crude petroleum is imported and refined domestically in a regulated industry. Local petroleum prices provide substantial subsidies to domestic consumers.

As mentioned above, among goods for which both export and import prices were available, export prices tended to be lower than import prices. This can be explained by quality differences or market imperfections.

Goods primarily for export exhibited three different patterns. First, the export price of primary products tended to be higher than the domestic price. Because this is not possible in perfectly competitive markets, except where government controls on exports appear to cause differential pricing, we assumed that in most cases the difference stemmed from the inferior quality or packaging of the domestic product. Ginseng (a medicinal root) and dried seaweed, however, are special cases, because exports of both are controlled by the government. The only commodity for which we could find evidence of an export tax was ginseng, where the nominal rate of protection on both domestic and export sales was negative. A government monopoly buys up the entire ginseng crop at harvest and sells it at home and abroad for a much higher price than what it pays the farmer. The export price of dried seaweed is higher because almost all of it goes to Japan; the price is negotiated by the Korean and Japanese governments. In contrast to its involvement in the ginseng trade, the government acts only as a sales agent in the export of seaweed.

In the second pattern exhibited by export commodities, export prices tended to be the same as domestic prices. Exports conforming to this pattern included both primary and manufactured products.

The third pattern, which mostly applied to manufactured products, showed the domestic price substantially higher than the export price. This might be explained in a number of ways. Many of these commodities, particularly textiles, earn large tariff duty remissions and tax breaks for export sales. But when they are sold locally, they are subject to these duties and taxes. Consequently, export and domestic prices are bound to differ. In some cases, however, pricing may have been noncompetitive and discriminatory. Negotiations between the government and exporters' associations set export quotas firm by firm and the size of export subsidies. By acting through manufacturers' associations in the domestic market, the exporters may have been able to form a cartel for the restriction of sales.

Nominal protection estimates gauge the relative importance of quantitative restrictions in 1968. Since nominal protection seldom exceeded the legal tariff, it is tempting to conclude that QRs added little to the protection provided by the tariff structure. However, to make this conclusion valid, it is necessary to separate the regular tariff from the special tariff which in many instances was used to mop up the scarcity premiums resulting from the QRs. Recall that the legal tariff rate was composed of two elements: the regular rate which was legislated and the special rate which was administered.

Special tariffs were imposed on 123 commodity groups (out of a total of 365) within the sample; these accounted for 13.7 percent of total domestic sales within the sample.

The weighted-average special tariff on the 116 manufacturers subject to it was 9.8 percent compared with a legal tariff rate of 83.9 percent.[10] Thus the special tariff played a relatively modest role in the protection system, at least for manufactures.

Among primary products, the weighted-average special tariff rate on the seven commodities subject to it was 207.1 percent. This result, however, was dominated by red pepper for which the special tariff was 217 percent. Without red pepper the weighted average of the special tariff for primary products was 80.2 percent compared with a legal tariff rate of 81.1 percent. Thus QRs had more effect on primary products than on manufactures.

Final judgment on the importance of QRs rests on a comparison of nominal protection with the *regular* tariff rate (i.e., excluding the special tariffs). The following estimates are weighted averages over all commodities for which nominal protection exceeded the *regular* tariff rate:

Trade Category	Number of Commodity Groups	Nominal Protection Rate	Regular Tariff Rate
X	5	64.9%	56.5%
NIC	46	66.2	26.9
IC	22	41.5	18.0
XIC	4	98.6	38.7
All	77	62.6	26.6

Except for the commodity groups in the export category, QRs did afford some commodities significant additional protection. The major groups so protected include barley and wheat, red pepper, chickens, worsted yarn, steel sheet and wire rod, wire and cable, cotton shirting, several chemical products including synthetic staple fiber, and several metal products including tools. These 77 commodity groups, however, accounted for only 11.4 percent of total domestic sales within the sample, so that in total effect, QRs were relatively unimportant, even though they were imposed on competitive imports in the markets for commodities representing 75.6 percent of all domestic sales in the sample. (That figure, however, represents a biased estimate of the imposition of QRs relative to total domestic sales, for a commodity group's inclusion in our sample was based, in part, on the imposition of QRs.)

AVERAGE PROTECTION

The average levels of incentives for agriculture, mining, and manufacturing are summarized in tables 10-1 and 10-2. The averages of legal and nominal protection are weighted by domestic sales volumes in world market prices, while those for effective protection and subsidy are weighted by value-added in world market prices. The results are striking in a number of ways.[11]

First, nominal rates of protection are well below legal tariff rates, which indicates considerable tariff redundancy. Tariffs are particularly redundant in manufacturing, where the average legal rate of protection was 58.8 percent and the average nominal rate was 10.7 percent (Table 10-1), compared with agriculture and mining where the spread is much narrower. Tariff redundancy

TABLE 10-1

Average Incentive Rates by Major Industry Grouping, 1968

(percent)

	Agriculture	Mining	Total Primary	Manufac- turing	Total
Average legal protection	36.0	9.6	34.1	58.8	49.4
Average nominal protection	16.6	6.9	15.9	10.7	12.6
Average effective protection					
Balassa	18.1	2.9	17.1	−0.9	9.9
Corden	17.5	2.5	16.4	−0.7	8.4
Average effective subsidy					
Balassa	22.1	4.7	20.9	−6.5	10.0
Corden	21.3	4.1	20.1	−4.7	8.5

SOURCE: All tables in Chapter 10 are drawn from Annex tables 2.A through 2.C, Westphal and Kim (1974).

TABLE 10–2

Average Incentive Rates in Manfacturing by Trade Category, 1968

(percent)

	Export Industries	Import- Competing Industries	Non-Import- Competing Industries	Export & Import- Competing Industries	Total
Average legal protection	53.7	55.4	64.1	46.3	58.8
Average nominal protection	5.2	31.6	5.0	23.1	10.7
Average effective protection					
Balassa	−10.7	91.7	−16.1	45.2	−0.9
Corden	−8.1	50.2	−12.4	28.7	−0.7
Average effective subsidy					
Balassa	−13.4	90.7	−23.7	37.9	−6.5
Corden	−10.2	49.6	−18.2	24.1	−4.7

NOTE: Trade categories are defined in Chapter 6.

within manufacturing was greatest in the export industries and the non-import-competing industries (Table 10–2). In the export and non-import-competing industries, the nominal tariff was only about one-tenth of the legal tariff; while in the import-competing sectors, the implicit tariff was more than 50 percent of the legal tariff. Given that quantitative restrictions played a relatively minor role, tariff redundancy was natural in industries where there were few imports.[12] The overall level of tariff redundancy in Korea is thus very high for three reasons: many tariffs, though relatively low in absolute magnitude, are prohibitive; exemptions and reductions of tariff levies are common; and because much of Korean industry is export oriented, even though protected by tariffs on the domestic market.

Second, agriculture is much more highly protected than mining or manufacturing. Average nominal protection is 16.6 percent for agriculture, 10.7 percent for manufacturing, and only 6.9 percent for mining. The difference in effective protection between major industries is even larger. By the Balassa measure, for example, the average rate of effective protection for agriculture is 18.1 percent, only 2.9 percent for mining, and a negative 0.9 percent for manufacturing. More protection for agriculture than for manufacturing is very unusual in other countries.

Third, the average level of protection and subsidy is quite low in Korea compared with other countries, because the exchange rate in 1968 was not greatly overvalued. The level of protection for manufacturing is especially low, a negative 6.5 percent according to the Balassa measure of effective subsidy. The average level of effective protection for all sectors is only about 10 percent.

The low level of protection for manufacturing is partly influenced by the inclusion of processed food and beverages and tobacco in the manufacturing sector (the line dividing processed food, in particular, from primary production is quite arbitrary, for much of the food processing is done in the primary sector). If these are excluded, the level of incentives to manufacturing increases. The average effective subsidy rate is no longer negative, but slightly positive (less than 1 percent). It nonetheless remains well below the average for the primary, processed food, and beverage and tobacco sectors taken together.

INCENTIVES TO DOMESTIC AND EXPORT SALES

Differential rates of effective protection for and subsidy to domestic sales compared with export sales are summarized in tables 10–3 and 10–4. Table 10–3 shows that in every industrial sector, except intermediate products I and transport equipment, effective *protection* for export sales is negative. The large positive effective protection for intermediate products I is due almost entirely to plywood, which receives substantial protection through the wastage allowance on imported roundwood. Wood is extremely scarce in Korea and imports are controlled. Plywood manufacturers are given generous wastage allowances for export production so that they have substantial excess wood which they can sell domestically or process into goods for domestic sale.

Table 10–4 also indicates a pattern of low and negative effective protection for exports. The rate of protection for the export sales of export industries (X) is slightly positive, while for all other industries it is negative. This difference, however, is again due to plywood. Exclude plywood and the average level of protection becomes negative.

The basic reason for the near zero or negative rates of protection for export sales is that exporters purchase tradable intermediate inputs at world market prices, just as they sell their products at world market prices. Imported inputs are automatically purchased at world market prices, since for exporters they are duty free. Inputs purchased domestically are not more expensive than comparable imports, otherwise they would have been imported. Thus exporters operate, so far as commodities are concerned, at world market prices. For nontradable, domestically produced inputs, however, *nominal*

TABLE 10–3

Effective Protection for and Subsidy to Export and Domestic Sales by Industry Group, 19
(percent)

Industry[a]	Balassa Measure			Corden Measure		
	Export	Domestic	Average	Export	Domestic	Ave
Effective Protection						
Agriculture, forestry, and fishing	−16.1	18.5	18.1	−15.3	17.9	1
Processed food	−2.7	−18.2	−17.0	−2.2	−14.2	−1
Beverages and tobacco	−1.9	−19.3	−18.6	−1.7	−15.5	−1
Mining and energy	−1.0	4.0	2.9	−0.9	3.5	
Construction materials	−5.2	−11.5	−11.3	−3.9	−8.8	−
Intermediate products I	31.0	−25.5	−19.5	18.6	−18.8	−1
Intermediate products II	−0.2	26.1	24.2	−0.2	17.4	1
Nondurable consumer goods	−1.9	−10.5	−8.5	−1.4	−8.0	−
Consumer durables	−4.7	64.4	51.0	−3.0	39.8	3
Machinery	−12.7	44.2	42.9	−4.6	29.5	2
Transport equipment	53.1	163.5	163.9	−13.1	83.2	8
Effective Subsidy						
Agriculture, forestry, and fishing	−9.9	22.5	22.1	−9.4	21.7	2
Processed food	2.3	−25.2	−23.0	1.8	−19.6	−1
Beverages and tobacco	14.5	−25.8	−24.2	12.6	−20.8	−1
Mining and energy	3.0	5.1	4.7	2.7	4.5	
Construction materials	5.9	−16.9	−15.9	4.4	−12.9	−1
Intermediate products I	43.4	−29.7	−21.9	26.0	−21.9	−1
Intermediate products II	17.5	19.6	19.5	11.6	13.1	1
Nondurable consumer goods	5.4	−20.6	−14.7	4.1	−15.7	−1
Consumer durables	2.4	38.2	31.3	1.5	23.6	1
Machinery	5.2	31.5	30.9	1.9	21.0	2
Transport equipment	−22.8	158.7	159.1	−5.6	80.8	8

a. Industrial groups are defined in Chapter 6.

protection is positive. This makes the *effective* protection for the *output* for export of some industries slightly negative.[13] For other industries, effective protection is slightly positive because wastage allowance subsidies and utility rebates outweigh nominal protection for nontradable inputs. Most wastage allowance subsidies, about one-half of the total, go to plywood manufacture.

TABLE 10–4

Effective Protection for and Subsidy to Export and Domestic Sales in Manufacturing by Trade Category, 1968

(percent)

Trade Category[a]	Balassa Measure			Corden Measure		
	Export	Domestic	Average	Export	Domestic	Average
Effective Protection						
Export industries (X)	4.6	−18.0	−10.7	3.4	−14.0	−8.1
Import-competing industries (IC)	−8.6	93.1	91.7	−3.9	51.1	50.2
Non-import-competing industries (NIC)	−0.8	−16.4	−16.1	−0.7	−12.6	−12.4
Export and import competing industries (XIC)	−2.1	72.8	45.2	−1.4	46.1	28.7
All manufacturing industries	3.1	−1.4	−0.9	2.2	−1.1	−0.7
Effective Subsidy						
Export industries (X)	13.5	−26.2	−13.4	9.8	−20.4	−10.2
Import-competing industries (IC)	35.3	91.4	90.7	15.8	50.2	49.6
Non-import-competing industries (NIC)	6.1	−24.3	−23.7	5.0	−18.7	−18.2
Export and import-competing industries (XIC)	8.7	55.0	37.9	5.6	34.8	24.1
All manufacturing industries	12.4	−8.9	−6.5	8.9	−6.5	−4.7

a. Trade categories are defined in Chapter 6.

Thus except for plywood and some minor exports, effective protection for export sales tends to be close to zero or negative.

In striking contrast, effective subsidy to exports is positive among all industries except agriculture and transport equipment (see Table 10–3). When industries are grouped by trade category (see Table 10–4), the rates of subsidy for their export sales are positive in all categories. This clearly demonstrates the overwhelming importance of tax and credit preferences for exports in the total system of export incentives.[14] Just as tax and interest preferences raised effective incentives to export sales, they lowered them to domestic sales except in agriculture where virtually no direct taxes were levied. Tax rates were also below average in mining and energy. The average level of effective subsidy to all manufactured export sales is 12.4 percent, and to domestic sales, −8.9 percent. A bias in favor of export sales is rarely encountered in the incentive systems of developing countries, and this makes the Korean case all the more unusual. This bias is even greater than the 12.4 percent subsidy to exports, since the effective incentives to domestic sales were negative.

The rank correlation coefficient between *effective protection* and *effective subsidies* (Balassa measure) on sales to the export market is only .15, which is barely significant at the .05 level. Thus the major explicit incentives to export activity not only came from credit and direct tax preferences, but these policies also had a powerful influence on the inter-industrial structure of export incentives. The rank correlation between these measures on sales to the domestic market, however, is .95. The major incentive policy addressed to production for the domestic market was the structure of nominal protection rates, and therefore estimates of effective protection are reasonably good predictors of the net effect of all policy instruments operating within the protected domestic market. There is virtually no correlation between effective subsidies to export sales and to domestic sales; there is thus no stable overall relationship between the incentives offered a sector for its domestic sales and those for its exports.[15]

In the industrial sectors classified as export and import-competing (XIC), and in the import-competing sector (IC), the incentive was much higher to domestic sales than to exports, while in the export (X) and non-import-competing (NIC) sectors the reverse was true. The explanation for this marked difference appears to be the way in which newer export commodities are often promoted through linking highly profitable domestic sales to satisfactory export performance by individual producers. High levels of protection for the domestic market should thus be interpreted as an incentive to export various goods, for example certain kinds of textile products, fertilizers, and electrical products. Most of these products appear in the former two classifications.

Relative incentives are somewhat different in the primary product industries, where incentives are lower for export sales in general than for domestic sales. The average effective subsidy rate for exports of primary products was −2.7 percent and for domestic sales it was 21.6 percent. The bias against exports is particularly marked in agriculture. However, the effective subsidy rate for exports in nearly all the export mining sectors was positive and for domestic sales it was negative.

VARIABILITY IN RATES OF PROTECTION

Table 10–5 displays frequency distributions for various measures of incentives at the 150-sector level. The degree of dispersion increases as the measure of protection includes more of the incentive policies. That is, legal tariff rates have the least dispersion, nominal protection rates have more, effective protection rates even more, and effective subsidies the most dispersion.

Rates of effective protection are subject to some extreme values, ranging from −18404.7 percent to +1929.1 percent.[16] The extremes occur in those sectors that have a near zero value-added in world market prices. Errors of measurement and aggregation can easily lead to extreme values when value added is near zero. To remove the effects of the extreme values, all sectors having a protection or subsidy rate greater than 500 percent on either the Balassa or Corden measure were eliminated from the sample and a coefficient of variation (unweighted) was calculated for the reduced sample. The coefficient of variation for the Balassa effective protection rate dropped from 36.7 to 3.2, but the relative ranking of the various measures of variability remained the same except that between the Corden and Balassa measures of protection. Over the entire set of sectors, the Corden rates vary less than the Balassa rates, largely because the Corden measure defines value added in world market prices more inclusively. As a result, there is less tendency toward extreme values, since value added in world prices is greater in absolute value. The variability in export protection was much less than for domestic protection or subsidy. For the reduced sample, export variability was still less but not significantly so.

Effective protection and subsidy rates are more variable than legal and nominal protection rates because the value-added denominator of the former is substantially smaller than the value-of-output denominator of the latter and not because of an escalation of nominal rates at higher processing stages. Average nominal protection for inputs is larger than nominal protection for output in most industrial groups. The only one of the eleven groups in which there was any marked escalation of protection was transport equipment. At the 150-sector level, there were numerous instances of both positive and reverse escalation of nominal protection, though reverse escalation predominated.[17]

Table 10–6 lists the 20 (of the 150) sectors that had the highest rates of effective protection for domestic sales. For the most part, these high rates of protection arose because of low value-added at world market prices, i.e., high nominal protection of the output and low nominal protection of the inputs. In some cases, the high rates of protection can be traced to a single commodity group within the sector and do not characterize the sector as a whole. For example, the high rate for vegetables reflects a high rate of protection for just one vegetable, red peppers, but this vegetable nevertheless accounts for a large portion of the average Korean food budget.

Most of the highly protected sectors are import-competing or both export and import-competing industries. In nine cases, value added in exports at the prices received and paid by the producer (i.e., domestic prices) is negative

TABLE 10–5

Frequency Distributions of Incentives Measures in 150-Sector Sample

Value in Percent: Greater Than or Equal to	Less Than	Legal Tariff	Nominal Protection	Effective Protection Balassa Export	Effective Protection Balassa Domestic	Effective Protection Balassa Average[a]	Effective Protection Corden Average[a]	Effective Subsidy Balassa Export	Effective Subsidy Balassa Domestic	Effective Subsidy Balassa Average[a]	Effective Subsidy Corden Average[a]
−∞	−100			1	6	6	1	2	7	6	1
1000	∞				3	3	2		3	3	2
500	1000				5	4	1	1	4	5	5
200	500	1			5	5	3	2	6	5	5
150	200				3	4	4		4	4	4
100	150	12	2		8	8	8	1	6	5	9
90	100	9	2		2		2	6	1	2	1
80	90	10	1		1	2	4	1	3	1	2
70	80	10	3	1	1	1	2	1	3	4	1
60	70	9	1		4	5	5	2	3	3	3
50	60	12	8		4	3	2	1	1	1	4
40	50	16	8		2	2		2	4	5	4
30	40	13	7	1	4	4	5	2	2	2	2
20	30	21	19	2	6	4	7	12	5	5	7
10	20	6	25	2	11	13	14	16	10	11	14
1	10	18	31	16	13	15	19	41	16	17	20
−1	1	13	39	17	1	2	3	13	1	3	3

−10 −1			87	21	23	29	26	9	13	21
−20 −10		1	13	20	19	24	13	21	20	23
−30 −20		1	2	14	15	6	4	16	16	15
−40 −30		1	2	5	4	5	1	11	11	4
−50 −40		1	4	6	5	2	2	6	4	2
−60 −50				3	1			3	1	1
−70 −60			1	1	2	2		3	2	2
−80 −70							1	1	1	
−90 −80										
−100 −90		1	1	1				1		
Over entire sample										
Simple average	49.2	18.1	−3.5	−66.1	−31.1	23.7	10.5	−115.4	−29.6	21.8
Coefficient of variation[b]	.8	1.4	5.2	23.2	36.7	13.3	9.1	13.9	37.5	13.4
Over reduced sample[c]										
Simple average	48.0	13.1	−3.5	20.8	20.2	10.3	11.4	14.1	15.9	7.7
Coefficient of variation[b]	.8	1.4	3.2	3.3	3.2	3.7	3.5	4.7	4.0	5.1

a. These columns refer to weighted average effective incentives where weights are value added at world prices in domestic sales and export sales.

b. Coefficient of variation, standard deviation divided by the mean.

c. Excludes those sixteen sectors for which one or more measures of effective incentives exceeds 500 percent or for which value added in world market prices is negative.

TABLE 10-6

Sectors Having High Effective Protection for Domestic Sales, 1968
(percent)

Sector	Negative Value Added	Effective Subsidy Rate	Effective Protection Rate	World Price Value-Added Coefficient	Nominal[a] Input Protection	Nominal Protection on Output
Vegetables		150.4	139.7	.59	19.6	91.0
Raw salt		113.9	133.1	.59	28.8	90.3
Worsted and woolen yarns	b	333.8	383.2	.08	31.0	60.4
Cotton fabrics		176.2	169.5	.11	11.1	27.9
Silk fabrics		233.8	260.6	.19	17.5	64.3
Synthetic dyes	c	141.4	136.7	.20	32.1	53.3
Paint and printing ink		145.9	144.8	.27	39.3	67.8
Steel sheet and bars	c	131.9	138.7	.12	13.0	28.6
Steel pipes	d	−3186.6	−3417.7	−.02	34.6	110.6
Galvanized and plated steel	c	160.7	127.0	.15	27.8	42.6
Insulated wire and cable	e	1463.1	1654.8	.03	29.8	76.3

Measuring instruments		114.9	120.6	.37	26.7	61.1
Photographic materials	f	1228.9	1274.6	.06	22.8	100.4
Household electronic equipment	f	68.5	114.0	.38	46.0	72.1
Electric appliances		449.0	558.9	.15	35.8	113.5
Watches and clocks		152.0	160.2	.29	36.1	71.7
Machinery components		114.6	127.2	.33	30.2	62.0
Transformers	f	195.8	225.2	.26	38.3	87.6
Railroad equipment	f	204.8	202.4	.09	39.7	55.1
Motor vehicles	f	241.8	247.7	.23	44.0	90.0

NOTE: All protection and subsidy rates pertain to sales on the domestic market and are based on the Corden convention.

a. Nominal input protection $= \dfrac{\Sigma_i t_{ni} a_{ij}}{\Sigma_{ij} a_{ij}}$ in the notation used in equations (10–2) and (10–3).

b. Value added negative for exports at world market prices, Balassa measure only.

c. Value added negative for exports at both world market and domestic prices, Balassa measure only.

d. Value added negative for all sales in world market prices and export sales in domestic prices, both Balassa and Corden measures.

e. Value added negative for all sales in world market prices with Balassa measure, for export sales only with Corden measure, and export sales in domestic prices.

f. Value added negative for all sales in world market prices and export sales in domestic prices, Balassa measure only.

205

under the Balassa convention. The implication in these cases, to which we return below, is that exports are sold at a loss. In five cases, total value added is negative in world market prices. We doubt the inference that production in these sectors was absolutely inefficient. Rather, in these sectors world-price value added is very small and slight errors of measurement or aggregation can result in a negative magnitude. Nominal protection rates were estimated from a sample of commodities that was too small to cover the whole range produced in any one of the 150 sectors. Input-output coefficients are aggregates for the whole sector and do not necessarily apply to the specific commodities whose prices were measured.

Exports may in fact be sold at a loss by private producers if export of a particular commodity raises profits on domestic sales, or if, in the more extreme case, exporting makes it possible to gain access to the profitable domestic market. For example, credit availability, import licenses for inputs, and favorable tax treatment were dependent, through government policies, on export performance. In such cases, the true subsidy to exports includes at least a part of the profits realized on the domestic market, for these profits could not be fully realized under the Korean system except by exporting. We have not tried to incorporate this phenomenon in our measure of effective incentives to export sales, though it does show up in the average incentives to the sector's total sales. Of the nine commodities with negative value added for exports in domestic prices, all were well protected in the domestic market. All except photographic materials were import-competing products with exports less than 4.0 percent of output. Photographic materials exports were 20.6 percent of output, but were also import competing.

EFFECTIVE INCENTIVES AND RESOURCE ALLOCATION

If high levels of effective incentives reflect high profit rates, then investment should flow toward those sectors with high effective incentives. This would show up either in rapid import substitution or rapid growth of exports for goods with high levels of effective incentives. On the other hand, if there is no correlation between effective incentives and growth of the ratio of imports to total supply or exports to total production, then effective incentives are more likely to reflect relative inefficiency. Table 10–7 lists rank correlation coefficients between various measures of effective incentives and resource allocation.

Neither the share of exports in total output nor growth contributions of exports are significantly related to effective *protection*. However, export trade shares and growth contributions are significantly and positively related to effective rates of *subsidy*. This result is striking, for it demonstrates the importance of tax and credit preferences among the various export subsidies, and

TABLE 10–7

**Rank Correlation Coefficients between Effective
Incentives and Resource Allocation**

	Share of Exports in Output 1968	Growth Contribution of Exports 1960–68
Exports		
Effective protection to exports		
Balassa	−.16	−.15
Corden	−.13	−.06
Effective subsidy to exports		
Balassa	.29	.26
Corden	.28	.32

	Share of Imports in Total Supply 1968	Growth Contribution of Import Substitution[a] 1960–68
Imports		
Effective protection to domestic sales		
Balassa	.32	−.14
Corden	.32	−.15
Effective subsidy to domestic sales		
Balassa	.40	−.14
Corden	.39	−.15

NOTE: The correlations were obtained at the 117-sector level where time series data on resource allocation are available. Correlation coefficients of greater than .16, .20, and .27 (in absolute value) are significant at the .10, .05, and .01 levels under a two-tailed test.

a. These are the contributions of import substitution to total growth of the sector. See Chapter 6 for an explanation.

suggests that export incentives had a positive influence on the expansion of exports.

Imports prompt the opposite conclusion. Since the correlation between the share of imports in total supply and effective incentives is significant and positive, it suggests that import substitution had progressed the *least* in those sectors where the level of effective incentives to domestic sales was high. The correlations between effective incentives to domestic sales and growth contributions are not significant, though they are negative, which is what we would expect if import substitution had progressed the least in sectors where incentives were large. Thus, effective subsidies to domestic sales seem to indicate relative inefficiencies while effective subsidies to exports seem to indicate profit incentives.

Tables 10–8 and 10–9 present data at the 117-sector level for the major exporting and import-substituting sectors. The exporting sectors within manufacturing are those that contributed more than 1 percent to the growth of manufactured exports between 1960 and 1968. The exporting sectors within the primary group are those that contributed the most to the growth of primary exports. Import-substituting sectors have been identified only within manufacturing and are those that contributed more than 1 percent of the total import substitution contribution to manufacturing ouput growth. Because of rising import shares in other sectors, the import-substituting sectors accounted for well over three times the total import substitution that took place within manufacturing. Some sectors are classified as both major export and major import-substituting, and they are designated in the tables.

The pattern discerned in the correlation analysis does not hold uniformly for the major export and import-substituting sectors; nonetheless some regularity is discernible. Most of the exporting sectors received positive effective subsidies to exports; several received subsidies that were higher than average. The effective subsidy to exports exceeded the subsidy to domestic sales in 13 of the 19 manufacturing sectors (compare the export subsidy rate with the average in Table 10–8). In the other 6 sectors, however, subsidies were biased in favor of domestic sales. Given that exports were sometimes subsidized by linking sales and various preferences in the profitable domestic market to export performance, the export effective subsidy rate in these cases probably seriously understates the incentives to export activity.

Our analysis does not prove that resource allocation was affected by policy or that it was relatively efficient; it merely demonstrates that the available information is reasonably consistent with these contentions. Incentives policies are only one of many forces that determine changes in economic structure. It is therefore somewhat surprising to find any correlation at all in the hypothesized direction. However, we cannot reject the counter-hypotheses that these correlations merely reflect errors of measurement or are meaningless because our data do not really measure what needs to be measured.

FACTOR INTENSITY OF TRADE

It is difficult to assemble evidence about the efficiency of Korea's rapid growth that is conclusive. The preceding analysis demonstrates that the level and dispersion of incentives was relatively modest, but it does not prove that resource allocation was efficient. Here we investigate the question of efficiency by using an additional partial measure: the relative factor intensity of Korea's exports and imports. Apart from considerations of natural resource and labor skill endowments, Korea's comparative advantage, at least within manufacturing, should lie in exporting products that are labor intensive and in importing goods that are capital intensive.

Our analysis of the factor intensity of Korea's trade follows the pioneering work of Leontief (1954). Using labor and capital input coefficients at the 117-sector level for 1968, we have calculated the direct as well as the total factor input requirements associated with Korea's exports and imports.[18] Total labor and capital requirements include both direct and indirect labor and capital requirements by sector per unit of production, export, or import. The indirect factor requirements are determined by inverting the input-output table for 1966 at the 117-sector level.

Imports can be treated in two different ways. First, all imports can be classified by one of the 117 sectors and capital and labor requirements calculated as if the imports were produced using the Korean sectoral coefficients. Second, clearly noncompeting imports, i.e., imports not produced in Korea, can be excluded and remaining imports classified by sector.[19] The results reported here include noncompeting imports, except for a few primary products not found in Korea, in the bundle of imports that is considered to be replaced. This procedure facilitates comparisons over time, since the imports considered to be noncompetitive in the compilation of the tables changed from year to year.

In the calculation of the total factor input coefficients, the matrix of intermediate input coefficients includes the requirements for those inputs that were actually imported. Certainly it does not make sense to calculate the factor requirements to replace some imports without also assuming that intermediate imports would also be replaced.[20] If total factor input coefficients for imports and exports are to be consistent, the same input-output matrix must be used in both cases. This does mean, however, that calculation of the total factor input coefficients relating to exports assumes that *all* intermediate input requirements would be produced domestically. Given that some imports of intermediate inputs were related to export production, our calculations overstate the "actual" total factor employments associated with export activity.[21]

For those years for which detailed input-output statistics are available, Table 10–10 exhibits the average direct and total capital and labor ratios for exports and imports of primary and manufactured products separately as well as for total imports and exports (including services and social overhead). For purposes of comparison, the comparable input coefficients for domestic production are also shown.

TABLE 10-8
Effective Incentives to Major Export Sectors, 1968
(percent)

Sector	Share in Total		Share of Exports in Output		Export Growth Contribution[a]	Effective Subsidy Rate[b]	
	Export Growth 1960–68	Output Growth 1960–68	1960	1968		Export	Average
Primary sectors—Total	2.7	26.4	3.7	2.5	1.2	-2.7	20.9
of which:							
Metallic ores	1.7	.3	67.4	70.5	78.0	2.8	-.1
Nonmetallic minerals	1.0	.9	23.8	15.9	13.6	2.8	-4.2
Industrial crops	1.0	1.7	4.8	6.1	6.8	-39.3	3.5
Fishing	.9	2.7	11.0	6.3	3.7	11.9	1.8
Total for sectors listed	4.6	5.6					
Manufacturing sectors—Total	97.3	73.6	2.6	11.4	15.1	12.4	-6.5
of which:							
Silk yarn	4.4	.6	48.4	83.7	90.1	-5.2	-7.4
Knit products	13.0	1.9	.0	57.8	78.7	3.1	9.8
Misc. metal products	1.4	.2	.8	25.7	74.3	8.4	-1.8

Other fabrics	5.1	.8	.0	36.2	72.8	20.0	1.1
Other manufactured products[c]	8.9	1.5	13.0	59.0	69.0	3.8	21.8
Lumber and plywood[c]	19.3	3.8	.7	42.6	57.6	94.7	-6.6
Processed seafoods	5.1	1.4	17.4	33.6	42.0	-.7	-57.2
Worsted and woolen fabrics	1.1	.3	.2	10.6	39.7	-9.0	-2.3
Apparel and accessories[c]	11.3	3.3	1.1	29.7	39.4	7.9	-24.7
Electronics	3.4	1.0	3.9	37.5	37.6	.3	62.8
Rubber products	3.7	1.2	5.5	22.5	34.0	.6	-44.6
Misc. textile products[c]	2.0	.7	8.5	24.8	32.0	1.8	24.8
Rope and fishing nets[c]	1.3	.5	6.6	22.7	25.9	21.1	-11.8
Slaughtering, meat and dairy products	2.1	1.1	.5	10.0	22.2	28.2	-8.3
Cotton fabrics	2.1	1.1	9.2	15.7	21.7	350.4	298.4
Electric equipment[c]	1.2	.7	6.4	19.9	20.8	22.9	155.5
Cement[c]	1.4	1.7	1.2	8.2	9.2	7.1	-13.4
Processed tobacco[c]	2.3	4.5	.1	4.5	5.9	18.5	-38.8
Petroleum products[c]	1.9	6.1	.0	3.7	3.7	2.1	-69.8
Total for sectors listed	91.0	32.4					

a. Sectors appear in order of the contribution of exports to their growth; see Chapter 6 for an explanation.
b. According to the Balassa convention.
c. Both a major export and a major import-substituting sector because of aggregation.

211

TABLE 10-9

Effective Incentives to Major Import-Substituting Sectors, 1968

Sector	Share of Sector in: Import Substitution in Manufacturing[a] 1960–68	Growth of Manufactured Output 1960–68	Share of Imports in Total Supply 1960	Share of Imports in Total Supply 1968	Import Substitution Contribution[a]	Effective Subsidy Rate[b] Domestic	Effective Subsidy Rate[b] Average
Manufacturing sectors	100.0	100.0	22.4	25.3	3.2	-8.9	-6.5
Fertilizers	58.3	2.4	96.5	41.7	76.3	46.5	47.0
Petroleum products	133.1	8.2	100.0	6.0	51.5	-73.1	-69.8
Sewing machines	3.2	.3	59.4	31.7	41.0	4.9	4.2
Misc. electrical equipment	8.1	.7	58.0	7.2	34.9	-822.6	-802.9
Hemp and flax yarns	1.3	.1	47.5	.6	32.9	181.0	179.1
Electrical products	5.2	.5	64.9	13.4	31.6	82.6	78.4
Drugs	18.5	2.0	36.9	14.3	28.8	-36.4	-36.3
Steel ingots	11.0	1.3	28.8	7.4	26.5	-29.1	-29.1
Paper and paperboard	9.7	1.2	34.5	9.1	25.0	4.2	4.2
Basic inorganic chemicals	3.1	.5	51.3	42.1	21.8	32.8	32.3
Cosmetics and toothpaste	2.8	.4	60.0	1.8	21.8	3.0	3.0

Cast and forged steel	4.2	.6	26.0	4.0	20.5	−17.3	−17.2
Other manufactured products[c]	12.4	2.0	78.3	21.4	19.7	47.4	21.8
Refined sugar	7.4	1.4	38.6	19.9	17.0	−50.6	−49.3
Electrical equipment[c]	4.3	.9	82.5	61.4	15.7	160.8	155.5
Cement[c]	8.6	2.3	9.8	3.8	11.6	−15.1	−13.4
Grain milling	8.6	2.5	5.9	6.0	11.2	−13.3	−13.3
Steel sheet and bars	6.8	2.1	48.3	48.7	10.3	1451.6	1592.8
Rope and fishing nets[c]	2.2	.7	12.7	6.4	9.3	−20.2	−11.8
Glass products	1.6	.7	29.0	10.9	6.6	−16.4	−15.9
Misc. textile products[c]	2.0	1.0	11.7	2.9	6.4	31.7	24.8
Apparel and accessories[c]	8.3	4.5	9.0	1.2	5.9	−37.5	−24.7
Other paper products	2.1	1.2	14.3	5.5	5.6	−10.7	−10.4
Other clay and stone products	1.2	.7	11.7	3.2	5.5	−21.8	−21.2
Processed tobacco[c]	5.7	6.1	7.3	.1	3.0	−42.4	−38.8
Coal products	1.3	1.9	1.3	.0	2.2	45.4	45.4
Lumber and plywood[c]	1.7	5.2	2.6	.4	1.0	−46.6	−6.6
Total	332.7	51.4					

a. Sectors appear in order of the contribution of import substitution to their growth; see Chapter 6 for an explanation.
b. According to the Balassa convention.
c. Both a major export and a major import-substituting sector because of aggregation.

TABLE 10–10

Factor Intensity of Trade

	Labor (thousand man-years per billion won of output measured in 1965 constant domestic prices)		Capital[a] (ratio of capital to output)		Labor-Capital Ratios (thousand man-years per billion won of capital in world prices)			
	1960	1968	1960	1968	1960	1963	1966	1968
Direct factor requirements								
Primary products								
Domestic output	10.86	10.74	.65	.63	16.60	17.20	17.08	17.16
Exports	7.54	6.27	.92	1.10	8.19	6.89	6.15	5.69
Imports	11.06	11.28	.67	.73	16.58	15.91	16.13	15.48
Manufactured products								
Domestic output	1.63	1.53	.55	.58	2.97	2.89	2.67	2.64
Exports	1.87	1.89	.69	.53	2.72	3.02	3.24	3.55
Imports	1.29	1.54	.62	.66	2.09	1.93	1.98	2.33
Total factor requirements								
Primary products								
Exports	9.84	8.29	1.49	1.73	6.55	5.75	5.13	4.81
Imports	12.99	13.06	1.08	1.16	11.99	11.50	11.90	11.30
Manufactured products								
Exports	7.89	7.91	2.11	1.83	3.74	3.71	4.09	4.29
Imports	5.06	5.56	1.84	2.03	2.77	2.40	2.40	2.74

a. Capital includes inventories and is measured in world prices; output is measured in constant 1965 domestic prices.

In every observation year, manufactured exports had higher direct and total labor-capital ratios than did manufactured imports. On the other hand, primary exports were more capital intensive than primary imports. A large share of Korea's primary exports are capital-intensive minerals, whereas minerals are only a small share of primary imports. Primary imports include a large share of labor-intensive agricultural products.

Even though there was a steady fall in the direct labor intensity of manufacturing production, the composition of Korea's manufactured exports shifted from 1960 to 1968 so as to increase the direct labor-capital ratio in manufactured exports by approximately 30 percent. Korea's manufactured exports were less labor intensive than average manufacturing in 1960, but far more labor intensive by 1968. The direct labor intensity of manufactured imports was less than that of manufacturing production throughout the period. The total labor-capital ratio for Korea's manufactured imports declined slightly between 1960 and 1968. Thus, at the same time that Korea's manufactured exports were becoming more labor intensive, her manufactured imports were tending to become a bit more capital intensive. The result was that in 1960, the total labor-capital ratio in manufactured exports was 35 percent higher than that in manufactured imports; by 1968, the ratio was more than 56 percent higher.

The total labor intensity of exports was greater than the direct labor intensity. That is, intermediate products produced for export industries have been even more labor intensive than the direct production of the exports themselves.

VALUATION OF OUTPUT AND GROWTH RATES AT WORLD MARKET AND DOMESTIC PRICES

In order to use the input-output tables of 1955, 1960, 1963, 1966, and 1968 for calculating contributions to growth, they were deflated to both constant 1965 domestic market prices and world market prices. At constant world prices, the compound annual growth rates between 1955 and 1968 for primary, manufactured, and total commodity output were 5.5, 14.0, and 9.8 percent. These growth rates are almost identical with those obtained when constant domestic prices are used as aggregation weights. This result is noteworthy: similar comparisons in other countries have shown that the growth rate in constant domestic prices often exceeds the rate of growth in constant world market prices.[22] Growth rates are usually much higher when constant domestic prices are used because it is usually the highly protected sectors, i.e., those with high domestic prices relative to world market prices, that are the fastest growing. In Korea, rates of protection were not very high and the relatively more protected sectors did not grow very much more rapidly than the less protected. That growth rates are nearly identical and very high, whether measured in domestic or international prices, suggests that Korea's growth has been relatively efficient if world market prices are taken to reflect true opportunity costs and domestic prices represent real marginal utilities.[23]

Our figures also show one other respect in which the Korean economy stands out: revaluation in world prices generally raises the contribution of the primary sectors to total growth because these sectors are usually less protected than manufacturing. In Korea, however, primary activity has received more protection than manufacturing (both nominal and effective), so that revaluation increases (if only slightly) the relative contribution of manufacturing. The contribution of the primary sectors to the growth of total commodity output between 1955 and 1960 was 26.3 percent in constant domestic prices and 25.0 percent in constant world prices.

CONCLUSIONS

Effective protection or subsidy rates may indicate either excess profits or gross inefficiency. If rates are low, however, they leave little room for much of either. The low average incentive rates and the relatively small dispersion in South Korea are presumptive evidence that Korean development has been efficient.

This hypothesis is buttressed by other data. Domestic prices and international prices differ so little that the growth rate of the economy remains very high when measured by constant world prices instead of by domestic prices. Thus Korea's growth cannot be regarded as spurious in the sense that growth was dominated by the inefficient production of overpriced goods.

The emphasis in South Korea has been on the expansion of labor-intensive manufactured exports. Of course, if all considerations of natural resource bias, labor skills, infant industries, and risk and uncertainty are taken into account, it may have been more advantageous for South Korea to take a much different path. Nevertheless, the presumption is strong that a poor country like South Korea has a comparative advantage in labor-intensive expansion. Thus all the evidence taken together suggests that South Korea has followed the path of efficiency.

NOTES

1. This chapter summarizes a more extensive report on our investigations published in Westphal and Kim (1974). That report discusses both methodology and results in far greater detail.

2. The world market price is expressed in terms of domestic currency at the prevailing exchange rate. Note that this formula implies that nominal protection is equivalent, from a resource allocation point of view, to an actual tariff rate, were it to be imposed at the same level. As Bhagwati (1965) has shown, this is not always true where markets are imperfect. In fact, when domestic production or quotas are monopolized, the nominal rate tends to be greater than the equivalent tariff. Thus our nominal protection rates may be overestimates of the protective effects of QRs in an equivalent tariff sense. See also Shibata (1968) and Bhagwati (1968).

3. As used here, legal and nominal tariffs correspond to the explicit and implicit tariffs defined in Appendix A.

4. This formula assumes all intermediate inputs are tradables.

5. Ray (1973) analyzes three different ways of measuring protection: (1) the Corden method, (2) what Ray calls the Balassa method but is actually a method used only in earlier writings of Balassa (e.g., see Balassa 1965), and (3) what Ray calls the Scott measure but is actually the measure used in more recent writings by Balassa. See Balassa and Associates (1971). Ray shows that the Scott (i.e., late Balassa) method has limited significance for resource allocation and that the Corden measure has even somewhat more significance. In this study we use these two methods only.

An alernative to both the Balassa and Corden measures of effective protection is a measure called the domestic resource cost (DRC) of foreign exchange, which is either earned through exports or saved through domestic production. This measure, developed independently by Bruno (1972) and Krueger (1972) attempts to calculate the real domestic resource cost of value added domestically for any particular product. It requires the calculation of shadow prices of domestic inputs, an exercise which we have not attempted here.

6. See Bhagwati and Srinivasan (1973), Bruno (1973), and Ramaswami and Srinivasan (1970).

7. The adjusted value added so measured is an estimate of what value added in the sector would have been if there were no tax and credit preferences and net factor returns were unaltered from their actual value under the incentives policies.

8. For a definition of the wastage allowance, see Chapter 4.

9. The survey was jointly financed by USAID, Korea Mission, and the Economic Planning Board, Republic of Korea, to whom we are grateful. Westphal and Kim (1974), Annex Table 1, presents the full results of the price comparison survey after necessary adjustments by the authors.

10. Figures were averaged by using domestic sales flows in world market prices as weights.

11. For comparisons with other countries, see Balassa and Associates (1971).

12. Theoretically one would expect tariff redundancy only in products for which there were no imports at all. Empirically, however, "products" are aggregations of several product lines and prices and tariffs are averages of the aggregates.

13. Positive nominal protection on nontradables is due to protection on inputs to their production and to indirect taxes levied on their sale, even to exporters.

14. Total export subsidies in 1968 amounted to 8.4 percent of the total value of commodity exports. This figure excludes tariff and indirect tax exemptions, as these are not subsidies in relation to prices at world market values. Direct tax subsidies were 1.1 percent of total commodity exports while interest subsidies were 4.5 percent.

15. These statements hold equally whether one uses the Balassa or Corden measures of effective incentives. The rank correlations between Balassa and Corden estimates in every particular case are very high, always well above .95.

16. Negative rates of effective protection and subsidy less than −100.0 in algebraic

value occur where value added in world market prices is negative, i.e., where the world value of inputs exceeds that of the output. They thus indicate absolute inefficiency, assuming there are no errors of measurement. See Guisinger (1969).

17. Legal tariff rates, in fact, exhibit a pattern of positive escalation; that is, tariffs rise with the stage of processing. Nominal protection rates, which are the relevant measures, do not exhibit positive escalation except in some cases.

18. For estimates of the sectoral labor coefficients, we have relied upon the labor input coefficient estimates provided along with the Bank of Korea's 1966 input-output table (Bank of Korea, *Economic Statistics Yearbook, 1969,* p. 383, Labor Coefficients Based on Workers). These data are given at the 43-sector level only; we have assumed that the same labor input coefficient pertains to all of the sectors at the 117 level that comprise a single sector at the 43-sector level. For estimates of the capital-output ratios we have relied upon Kee Chun Han's (1968) exhaustive retabulation of the 1968 National Wealth Survey. By virtue of the estimation method, the capital-output ratios for the manufacturing sectors give marginal rather than average input coefficients. Nonetheless, for estimates of average capital-output ratios in 1968, they are considered superior to the average ratios obtained from the National Wealth Survey. We experimented with several other sets of capital-output ratio estimates; the basic conclusions are not sensitive to the set of estimates employed. Constant 1965 price input-output data on production, exports, and imports were used to calculate factor input requirements. The factor input coefficients were deflated to obtain the proper input coefficients per billion won of output in 1965 prices. The 1966 117-sector input-output matrix, deflated to 1965 prices, was used to obtain total factor input requirements. We have omitted real estate and ownership of dwellings, iron scrap, and other scrap from the calculation of input requirements.

19. Details on these and related methodological issues and computational results are available from the authors.

20. Estimates of input-output coefficients for noncompetitively imported intermediate inputs are not directly available from the original input-output tables. We applied a simple method of proportional estimation by row and column sums to estimate these coefficients.

21. Calculations of the factor intensity of exports based on the input-output table for domestically produced inputs are given in Hong (1973). His results concerning the relative factor intensities of exports and imports are consistent with ours.

22. See Little, Scitovsky, and Scott (1970), pp. 70–76 and Balassa and Associates (1971), pp. 32–34. These authors examine GDP growth rates rather than total commodity output growth rates and use effective protection measures for a single year to deflate value added to constant world market prices rather than nominal protection measures for a single year to deflate output; otherwise the calculations are quite similar.

23. See Bhagwati and Hansen (1973) for a discussion of the implications of measuring growth rates at domestic or international prices.

Chapter 11

An Overview

In the preceding chapters we have examined the history and the complex details of foreign exchange and trade policy and have discussed quantitative measures of the effects of these policies on efficiency and growth. In this chapter we evaluate the influence of South Korea's economic growth on employment and income distribution. We also assess the main factors at work in the rapid growth of the South Korean economy since the early 1960s, particularly the role of foreign exchange and trade policy, by drawing as much as possible on our previous analysis. Then after summarizing the lessons of the two liberalization episodes, we shall caution against hasty generalizations from the South Korean experience.

EFFECTS OF GROWTH ON EMPLOYMENT

The rapid growth of the Korean economy was documented in Chapter 2. Before discussing the causes of this performance, however, it is appropriate to analyze its effects on employment and income distribution.

In fact, the rapid growth of the 1960s was accompanied by a steady decline in the rate of unemployment, particularly in the nonfarm sector (Table 11–1). In addition, the nonfarm proportion of the population was steadily rising, exceeding 50 percent by 1970. At the same time, farm population declined not only relatively but also absolutely from a peak of 16.1 million in 1967 to a low of 14.4 million in 1970.

Unemployment declined because job opportunities in the nonagricultural

219

TABLE 11–1

Farm and Nonfarm Population and Unemployment, 1957 to 1972

	Farm Population (millions)	Nonfarm Population (millions)	Nonfarm Population as Percent of Total Population	Unemployment Rate (percent)	Nonfarm Household Unemployment Rate (percent)
1957	13.6	9.4	40.8	5.9	na
1958	13.8	9.9	41.8	6.2	na
1959	14.1	10.2	41.8	5.8	na
1960	14.6	10.5	42.0	7.5	na
1961	14.5	11.4	43.9	7.9	na
1962	15.1	11.5	43.3	8.3	na
1963	15.3	12.0	44.1	8.2	16.4
1964	15.6	12.4	44.5	7.7	14.4
1965	15.8	12.8	44.8	7.4	13.5
1966	15.8	13.5	46.0	7.1	12.8
1967	16.1	13.8	46.1	6.2	11.1
1968	15.9	14.5	47.8	5.1	8.9
1969	15.6	15.4	49.7	4.8	7.8
1970	14.4	17.1	54.3	4.5	7.4
1971	14.7	17.4	54.2	4.5	7.4
1972	14.7	18.0	55.1	4.5	7.5

NOTE: na—not available. Since the coverage and method of labor force survey changed in 1963, the labor force statistics available for the period prior to 1963 were not consistent with those for the later period. All data other than total population given in this table for 1960–62 were therefore estimated by linking the old survey data with the new data (two different survey results were available for 1963).

SOURCE: Bank of Korea, *Economic Statistics Yearbook, 1973*, p. 6; Economic Planning Board, *Major Economic Indicators*, July 1973, p. 96; Economic Planning Board, *Korea Statistical Yearbook*, various issues prior to 1964.

sectors rapidly increased. Table 11–2 shows that the rate of growth of population dropped steadily throughout the 1960s. From a high of 3.2 percent per annum in 1961, it declined to 1.8 percent by 1970. The growth of the total labor force, however, showed a fairly high rate of increase from 1960 to 1972, although there were ups and downs reflecting moderate changes in participation rates. The farm labor force has declined since 1965, decreasing at a rate of 2.1 percent in 1971.

Job opportunities expanded rapidly, particularly in the manufacturing sector, the leading sector of the economy (Table 11–3). At the same time, growth in manufacturing stimulated rapid increases in output and employment in other nonagricultural sectors.

TABLE 11-2

Population and Labor Force Growth, 1960 to 1972

	Total Population (millions)	Growth Rate of Total Population (percent)	Population 14 Years and Older (millions)	Growth Rate of Population 14 Years and Older (percent)	Total Labor Force (millions)	Growth Rate of Total Labor Force (percent)	Farm Labor Force (millions)	Growth Rate of Farm Labor Force (percent)	Non-farm Labor Force (millions)	Growth Rate of Nonfarm Labor Force (percent)
1960	24.70	—	14.16	—	7.74	—	4.93	—	2.82	—
1961	25.50	3.2	14.50	2.4	7.94	2.6	4.85	-1.6	3.11	10.3
1962	26.23	2.9	14.85	2.4	8.15	2.7	5.06	4.4	3.10	-0.3
1963	26.99	2.9	15.09	1.6	8.34	2.3	5.09	0.6	3.25	5.0
1964	27.68	2.6	15.50	2.7	8.45	1.3	5.17	1.6	3.28	0.9
1965	28.33	2.4	15.94	2.8	8.86	4.9	5.23	1.2	3.63	10.7
1966	28.96	2.2	16.37	2.7	9.07	2.4	5.28	0.1	3.79	4.4
1967	29.54	2.0	16.76	2.4	9.30	2.5	5.20	-1.5	4.10	8.2
1968	30.17	2.1	17.17	2.5	9.65	3.8	5.26	1.2	4.39	7.1
1969	30.74	1.9	17.64	2.7	9.88	2.4	5.26	0.0	4.63	5.5
1970	31.30	1.8	18.25	3.5	10.20	3.2	5.20	-1.1	5.00	8.0
1971	31.85	1.8	18.98	4.0	10.54	3.3	5.09	-2.1	5.45	9.0
1972	32.42	1.8	19.72	3.9	11.06	4.9	5.41	6.3	5.65	3.7

SOURCE: Economic Planning Board, *Annual Report on the Economically Active Population, 1972*; *Major Economic Indicators*, July 1973, p. 96; and *Korea Statistical Yearbook*, various issues.

TABLE 11–3

Employment, Earnings, and Output in Nonagricultural Sectors, 1957 to 1972

	Monthly Earnings of Production Workers in Manufacturing (won)	Seoul Consumer Price Index (1970 =100)	Price Deflated Earnings (1970 prices)	Rate of Growth of Price Deflated Earnings (percent)	Employ.[a] ment in Manufacturing (thousands of persons)	Rate of[a] Growth of Employment in Manufacturing (percent)	Value Added in Manufacturing (billions of won constant 1970 prices)	Growth of Value Added in Manufacturing	Non-[a] agricultural Employment	Rate of[a] Growth of Nonagricultural Employment	Nonagricultural Value Added (billions of won constant 1970 prices)	Rate of Growth of Nonagricultural Value Added (percent)
1957	2,030	26.1	7,778	—	409	—	94.65	—	2,086	—	564.29	—
1958	2,170	25.3	8,577	10.3	413	0.9	103.25	9.1	1,946	-6.7	589.03	4.4
1959	2,350	26.4	8,902	3.8	456	10.5	112.78	9.2	1,938	-0.4	635.80	7.9
1960	2,330	28.6	8,147	8.5	438	-4.0	122.00	8.2	2,149	10.9	663.15	4.3
1961	2,610	30.9	8,447	3.7	446	1.8	125.79	3.1	2,547	18.5	662.28	-0.1
1962	2,780	32.9	8,450	0	511	14.5	142.34	13.2	2,580	1.3	728.81	10.1
1963	3,180	39.7	8,010	-5.2	610	19.3	166.96	17.3	2,825	9.5	796.26	9.3
1964	3,880	51.4	7,549	-5.8	637	4.4	177.86	6.5	2,974	5.3	827.40	3.9
1965	4,600	58.4	7,877	4.3	772	21.2	213.35	20.0	3,396	14.2	927.05	12.0
1966	5,420	65.4	8,287	5.2	833	7.9	249.87	17.1	3,547	4.5	1,051.27	13.4
1967	6,640	72.5	9,159	10.5	1,021	22.6	306.77	22.8	3,906	10.1	1,218.23	15.9
1968	8,400	80.6	10,422	13.8	1,170	14.6	389.67	27.0	4,354	11.5	1,437.04	18.0
1969	11,270	88.7	12,706	21.9	1,232	5.3	473.03	21.4	4,589	5.4	1,669.01	16.1
1970	14,561	100.0	14,561	14.6	1,284	4.2	560.01	18.4	4,829	5.2	1,864.67	11.7
1971	17,349	112.3	15,449	6.1	1,336	4.1	659.21	17.7	5,190	7.5	2,078.36	11.5
1972	20,104	125.6	16,006	3.6	1,445	8.2	762.79	15.7	5,213	0.4	2,262.70	8.9

SOURCE: Bank of Korea, *Economic Statistics Yearbook*, various issues; Economic Planning Board, *Korea Statistical Yearbook*, various issues.

a. Since the coverage and method of labor force survey changed in 1963, the labor force statistics available for the period prior to 1963 were not consistent with those for the later period. All data other than total population given in this table for 1960–62 were therefore estimated by linking the old survey data with the new data (two different survey results were available for 1963).

Growth in employment opportunities in manufacturing was rapid mainly because of large increases in investment and output which created a demand for workers. The growth in output was achieved through labor-intensive methods. In many other countries rapid growth in manufacturing output is accompanied by a rapid increase in labor productivity because of a trend toward more capital-intensive methods. In Korea, by contrast, manufacturing employment grew very rapidly between 1957 and 1967, at 9.6 percent per annum, while labor productivity lagged behind at an annual rate of increase of about 2.6 percent. From 1967 to 1972, however, productivity increased much more, at an average of 11.9 percent per annum. These changes were a function of variations in the growth in real wages. In 1959, real monthly earnings of manufacturing workers reached a peak of 8,902 won in terms of 1970 prices (Table 11–3). By 1964 real monthly earnings had declined to 7,549 won but they began to rise again in 1965. After surpassing the 1959 level in 1967, they registered spectacular growth until 1970. This increase continued, though at a somewhat slower rate, until 1972. By 1971, the 1964 level of earnings had doubled. The rapid growth in real wages since 1967 was the result of increasing tightness in the labor market and shortages of skilled labor. In contrast to the earlier period 1957 to 1967, it was correlated with much more rapid increases in labor productivity and slower growth in employment. Between 1967 and 1972, the growth rate of employment dropped to 7.2 percent a year.

Even though manufacturing employment grew less rapidly after 1967, the rate of growth from 1957 to 1972 averaged 8.8 percent per annum. Meanwhile, total nonagricultural employment increased by 6.3 percent per annum. One reason for this good performance was the government's willingness to allow wage rates to be set by competitive forces. Labor was not thoroughly unionized nor did the government press for minimum wages. Nonagricultural wages more accurately reflected the opportunity cost of labor in the traditional agricultural sector than they do in the typical less developed country where government policies combined with union pressures keep wages in the modern sector artificially high. Furthermore, by permitting the South Korean price structure to remain largely consistent with world prices, the government provided incentives to concentrate production in labor-intensive exports and home goods and to import capital-intensive goods rather than to substitute for imports. Labor absorption was rapid, at least until the very late 1960s when labor shortages began to appear and wages started to rise very rapidly.

GROWTH AND INCOME DISTRIBUTION

Though it is difficult to determine the effect of South Korea's rapid growth on income distribution, bits and pieces of evidence suggest that the distribution has been quite even. In fact surveys reveal that among Korean households expenditure on consumption tends to be more nearly equal than it is elsewhere in the world and that from 1964 to 1970 this distribution seemed to improve.[1]

Farm incomes are a notable case in point, thanks to a land reform that was begun under the U.S. military occupation and completed by the Korean government in 1949. The net result seems to be a remarkably even division of land and income. Nor is there much disparity between farm and nonfarm income as the following table shows:[2]

	Average Monthly Wage for Farm Workers (won)	Average Monthly Wage for Manufacturing Production Workers (won)
1961	1,978	2,610
1964	3,657	3,880
1968	7,383	8,400
1971	13,432	17,349

Though manufacturing wages have generally been higher than farm wages, the cost of living is probably lower in the country where farm workers often till their own vegetable gardens. Of course most farm work is seasonal, but even so Korea appears to be free of the large differences between rural and urban income typical of other less developed countries.

This impression is reinforced by data on average farm household income.[3] Farm income and manufacturing wages can be compared as follows:[4]

	Average Total Farm Household Income (won)	Farm Household Income per Worker (won)	Annual Manufacturing Wage Income (won)
1964	125,692	56,618	46,560
1968	178,959	87,297	100,800
1971	356,382	179,990	208,128

Total farm income, including income in kind, far exceeds annual wage income of production workers in manufacturing, but farm income per worker was somewhat greater than nonfarm income per worker in 1964, a good agricultural year. In 1968 and 1971 farm income per worker was probably a bit less than the average manufacturing wage. Even if these calculations are only very rough, they lead to the same conclusion that rural-urban income disparities are small.

Wages in nonagricultural sectors have tended to follow manufacturing wages. Market forces set the rates and because there are no great imperfections in the market disparities between sectors do not arise. In Korea where vast pools of the unemployed and the underemployed are unknown, the working class, both urban and rural, which forms the great bulk of the population, lives on an income that is nearly uniform. If data on income distribution were available they would probably show that even the conspicuous wealth of a few entrepreneurs in Seoul is not enough to reverse the apparent pattern.

FACTORS PROMOTING RAPID GROWTH

The South Korean economy has not suffered from any constant deficiency in effective demand. Except for 1958–61 and 1964 when effective demand was restrained by either deflationary monetary and fiscal policy or by political turmoil, investment demand since the Korean War has tended to be excessive relative to the supply of savings, and inflation has been acute. The rate of return on investment has tended to be high as may be inferred from the large demand for loanable funds that persisted despite very high interest rates after 1965. Borrowing at these high rates increased continually throughout most of the period from 1963 to 1971 and finder's fees for loans were common. Although many bank loans were subsidized in one way or another and the average interest paid on them was probably only about two-thirds the official rate, marginal borrowers had to pay the high rates which indicates that the rate of return on marginal investments was at least as great. This inference is corroborated by direct measurements. For example, Gilbert Brown has estimated from national accounts data that the average rate of return on new investment was 20 to 30 percent. He also cites direct estimates based on data from eleven firms that in late 1965 the average rate of return was about 28 percent.[5]

The South Korean economy has exhibited the characteristics that theory would predict for an underdeveloped country where labor is abundant and capital scarce—a high rate of return on capital, vigorous investment demand, and meager investable resources. The main constraints on growth are savings and foreign exchange. The factors that foster rapid growth are those that sustain and complement heavy investment demand, those that increase the requisite supply of savings, those that earn the foreign exchange needed when the level of effective demand is high, and, finally, those that foster efficient resource allocation, evidenced by a very low incremental capital-output ratio. The combination of these four factors produces a result that tends to be self-sustaining;

for rapid growth stimulates demand in nearly all sectors of the economy. As investment proves ever more profitable, an accelerator effect comes into play. Growth generates still more growth and in the consequent enthusiasm, predictable setbacks turn out to be temporary as entrepreneurs become convinced that the resumption of growth is inevitable.

In addition to these factors, which in varying degrees influence the growth of most developing countries, there are some that are peculiar to Korea. Though they have not yet been analyzed in any detail, they ought to be mentioned for they contributed to a favorable environment for investors and helped sustain brisk investment demand. For example, the work force in Korea is highly educated by the standards of most less developed countries. In 1970 the adult literacy rate was 88 percent,[6] and the proportion of primary-school-age children attending primary school was 97 percent.[7] A highly educated work force, it might be argued, was more easily trained and was a factor in the high levels of efficiency and productivity achieved.

South Korea also has an abundant supply of entrepreneurial and managerial expertise. Although very few Koreans became managers under the Japanese colonial regime, it did not take them long to develop a managerial class after the liberation. A large proportion of them immigrated from North Korea, but many of the most successful entrepreneurs are of southern origin. No significant number of managers and entrepreneurs are foreign. Foreign direct investment has been exceedingly small, only about 7.4 percent of total foreign investments and loans between 1959 and 1971.[8]

Another advantage favoring Korea's economic development was the political stability that prevailed during the period of most rapid growth. Park Chung Hee has made economic development the symbol of his government's legitimacy.[9] His efforts have been aided by Korea's cultural homogeneity. Disputes over language and among ethnic groups have not been important in South Korean politics.

South Korean development has also benefited from the weakness of the labor movement which so far has produced few powerful, organized unions. In the Korean system of industrial organization, which in many ways is similar to the Japanese, employees tend to remain with one firm for life, loyal to their paternalistic employers. Because the labor force is docile and unaccustomed to collective bargaining, upward pressure on wages is negligible except when manpower is scarce. Stable real wage rates helped to keep profits high and to stimulate investment demand.

Finally, ties with Japan encouraged growth. Although their colonial regime was extremely unpopular, the Japanese did manage to build a strong industrial base in Korea before the war. Much of it was destroyed during the war, and the subsequent departure of Japanese managers was temporarily crippling. Nevertheless, the Japanese had shown that industrialization was possible in Korea and they had provided an example for the Koreans to imitate. Imitation seemed all the more sensible since the Japanese, who had an economy of their own to rebuild, appeared to know how the job should be done. Accordingly, the Koreans adopted the technology, the approach to labor relations, the expansionary psychology, and many of the government policies that had worked so well for the Japanese. As a result, the emphasis on export promotion, the system of trade and foreign exchange controls, and the close cooperation between the public and private sectors that are reputed to be characteristic of Japan alone are typical of South Korea as well.

Investment demand, however voracious, cannot by itself sustain economic development. It must be matched by a rate of savings that is high enough to finance the investments desired. Ample foreign exchange is also important, for shortages can restrict realized investment by curtailing the supply of imported raw materials and capital goods. And if inefficiencies in production go uncorrected, an economy can suffer from progressive debility. Having analyzed these issues in the preceding chapters, we shall now present our conclusions.

SUPPLY OF SAVINGS

The supply of savings, both domestic and foreign, was abundant during the 1960s but not large enough to satisfy total investment demand because of an inflationary gap that has persisted throughout most of the period since 1963.

Foreign Savings.

We noted in Chapter 7 that foreign savings have remained about 10 percent of GNP since 1960 (Table 7–4), while over the years their nature has changed. In the post-Korean War period, most foreign savings took the form of foreign aid grants from the United Nations and from U.S. bilateral assistance programs. In the early 1960s, foreign aid loans began to replace grants and then, from 1966 onwards, commercial loans from a variety of countries became the dominant source.

In Chapter 7, we estimated that foreign savings might have been responsible for about 4 percent of total growth, assuming the average capital-output ratio between 1960 and 1970 was about 2.5. That is, what appeared to be an annual growth rate of 10 percent might have been closer to 6 percent without the contribution of foreign savings. By the early 1970s, foreign savings had declined in importance for two reasons. Domestic savings were becoming more plentiful and because the capital-output ratio has tended to increase, growth per dollar of imported capital had apparently deteriorated.

Large importation of foreign capital led to heavy debt service by 1970. Since 1971 the burden has become less onerous.

Foreign commercial borrowing probably was excessive in the late 1960s. A divergence between social opportunity costs and the private costs of foreign capital made foreign borrowing more attractive than it should have been. The government originally encouraged all forms of foreign borrowing, but had to discourage short-term transactions after 1970 under an IMF standby agreement.

There is little evidence that reliance on foreign aid was inordinate. Because aid receipts were usually grants, especially in the early 1960s, they cost Korea little while yielding high rates of return. It is true that many of the grants may have discouraged domestic savings, but at the time, South Korea was desperately poor and needed the additional resources both for consumption and investment.

Domestic Private Savings.

Although foreign capital sparked the growth of the South Korean economy, domestic savings eventually sustained it. In 1960 domestic savings financed only about 20 percent of total gross investment. By 1972 this proportion had risen to about 75 percent (see Table 7–4).

Business savings (in constant 1970 prices) grew rather slowly after the Korean War, but since 1957, they increased quite rapidly, at an average rate of 11.8 percent per year between 1957 and 1972 (Table 11–4). As we showed in Chapter 8, business savings are moderately responsive to interest rates. The elasticity of business savings is 0.34 although the interest rate is still statistically a significant determinant of business savings (see equation (8–15) in Chapter 8). A more significant factor in business savings, however, is nonagricultural value added. As value added and profits increase, business savings tend to increase (there are no reliable profit data; nonagricultural value added might serve as a proxy). The elasticity of business savings with respect to nonagricultural value added was 0.67 between 1960 and 1970.

As Table 11–4 shows, household savings have been very erratic, being very sensitive to both the rate of inflation and the interest rate on time deposits (see equation (8–14) in Chapter 8). Household savings were substantial while prices were stable during the late 1950s and even greater in the latter '60s after the interest rate reform of September 1965 had raised the rates. During periods of low interest rates and high inflation, like the early 1960s, household savings were very low and at times quite negative.

At 1.82, household savings were much more elastic than business savings from 1955 to 1970 and they were also quite elastic with respect to the rate of inflation.

TABLE 11–4

Sources of Domestic Savings, 1953 to 1972

(billions of won, constant 1970 prices)

Year	Government Savings	Business Savings	Household Savings	Total
1953	19.47	39.30	−15.09	43.68
1954	4.67	44.13	36.93	85.73
1955	10.65	40.32	30.40	81.37
1956	52.47	40.56	8.77	101.80
1957	41.95	45.38	12.05	99.38
1958	39.43	52.58	22.42	114.43
1959	36.08	62.06	21.16	119.30
1960	54.63	59.91	0.55	115.09
1961	66.33	68.69	5.18	140.20
1962	67.03	88.29	0.59	155.91
1963	66.41	96.77	−17.50	145.68
1964	71.50	96.07	−18.02	149.55
1965	94.38	119.24	22.62	236.24
1966	103.48	128.57	80.65	312.70
1967	128.83	145.39	83.37	357.59
1968	174.90	161.81	86.24	422.95
1969	183.98	174.89	115.34	474.21
1970	206.43	182.85	92.67	481.95
1971	190.45	191.82	49.36	431.63
1972	132.69	241.24	99.73	473.66

NOTE: The estimates of savings include savings from transfers from abroad. Household savings include errors and omissions and exclude grain inventory changes.

SOURCE: Table 8–11A.

Government Savings.

Government savings and business savings have been about equally important in total savings since the Korean War (Table 11–4). Between 1953 and 1970, government savings grew quite rapidly, at an average annual rate of 15.7 percent. The growth was most substantial, however, after the 1964 tax reforms. From 1964 to 1970 government savings increased at a rate of 20.6 percent per annum.

Government savings multiplied both because of rapid growth in tax revenues and because of a slow rate of increase in current expenditures. Tax revenues rose sharply during the Korean War recovery, from about 5 percent of GNP in 1953 to more than 10 percent in 1959. By 1964, however, they had declined to 7.3 percent. After the 1964 tax reforms, revenues reached a peak of more than 16 percent of GNP in 1971 before declining slightly in 1972.[10] In addition, government monopolies contributed rapidly growing net surpluses which constituted almost 11 percent of central government revenues in 1972.[11]

Government current expenditures grew less rapidly than total government revenues from 1962 to 1970, when current expenditures declined from 78 percent of current revenues to about 62 percent. Between 1970 and 1972, current expenditures rose more rapidly than revenues. Much of the government nonrecurrent expenditures went to directly productive assets. Between 1963 and 1971, about 14 percent of total government loans and investments went into mining and manufacturing, 39 percent into electricity, transport, and communications, and 25 percent into agriculture, forestry, and fisheries.[12] The remainder was invested in housing, education, and other services. Some government savings were channeled to the private sector through government-financed loan funds of development banking institutions such as the Korean Development Bank and the Medium Industry Bank. In 1963, government funds accounted for more than one-half of all outstanding loans of the banking sector. After the interest rate reform of 1965, the commercial banks greatly expanded their loan portfolios, but even in 1970, government funds accounted for more than one-quarter of total outstanding loans by banking institutions.[13] In 1972, about one-sixth of total government savings was allocated to capital transfers of this type.[14]

SUPPLY OF FOREIGN EXCHANGE

One of the most striking features of the South Korean economy has been the rapid growth of foreign exchange earnings. Foreign exchange receipts on current account grew at an average annual rate of 26.2 percent between 1963 and 1972 (Table 11–5).

Invisible Earnings.

In the early 1960s, a high proportion of total foreign exchange receipts were invisibles and derived directly from the presence of a large contingent of UN (mostly U.S.) forces stationed in South Korea. Sales of local currency to UN forces, military procurement, and provision of electricity, transport, water, and other public utilities to UN installations accounted for almost one-half of,

TABLE 11-5

Foreign Exchange Receipts on Current Account, 1961 to 1972

(millions of dollars)

Year	Foreign Exchange Receipts[a]			Receipts from UN Forces and from U.S. Procurement			
	Total	Merchandise Exports	Other Current Receipts	Total	Won Sales	Procurement	Utilities
1961	166.2	42.6	123.6	79.7	35.7	38.4	5.6
1962	179.0	56.7	122.3	86.1	47.2	34.1	4.8
1963	177.2	85.2	91.8	58.3	30.5	22.1	5.7
1964	212.2	115.1	97.1	63.7	26.4	33.2	4.1
1965	298.0	172.2	125.8	74.0	34.1	35.7	4.2
1966	486.8	248.4	238.4	100.9	30.4	65.5	5.0
1967	695.4	320.2	375.2	147.1	35.3	106.7	5.1
1968	889.4	464.9	424.5	177.6	49.3	122.3	6.0
1969	1,102.0	604.9	497.1	207.0	43.1	155.7	8.2
1970	1,306.7	816.0	490.7	190.8	52.3	131.4	7.1
1971	1,523.4	1,036.8	486.6	173.5	61.3	106.0	6.2
1972	2,159.2	1,580.0	579.2	192.8	97.6	90.6	4.6

SOURCE: Bank of Korea, *Economic Statistics Yearbook, 1973,* p. 216; *1970,* p. 282; Economic Planning Board, *Korea Statistical Yearbook, 1972,* p. 406.

a. These figures understate total receipts because they only include transactions conducted through banking channels. For example, in 1971 export receipts totaled $1,132 million according to customs clearance.

and total invisibles about three-quarters of, all foreign exchange earnings in 1961. Receipts from UN forces and other invisibles were relatively stagnant between 1961 and 1965, however, so that by 1965 they accounted for about one-third of total earnings. The escalation of the U.S.' effort in Viet Nam after 1965 brought more troops to South Korea and an increase in military procurement, both for troops in South Korea and for those in Viet Nam. South Korean goods were exported to Viet Nam under military procurement contracts beginning in 1967 and a number of Korean construction firms became involved in military projects in South Viet Nam. Receipts from UN forces increased rapidly between 1965 and 1969, but other foreign exchange receipts grew even more quickly. After 1969, receipts from UN forces declined, and by 1971, only 36 percent of invisible earnings and 11 percent of total foreign exchange receipts could be attributed to U.S. military procurement and other earnings generated by the presence of UN forces in South Korea.

Exports.

The major reason for the very rapid growth in foreign exchange earnings was the growth of exports. As we indicated in Chapter 6 exports in the 1950s were negligible and followed an erratic pattern, ranging from a high of $40 million in 1953 to a low of $17 million in 1958 (Table 6–1). After 1958 exports began a pattern of uninterrupted growth, exceeding the 1953 level by 1961. From 1962 until 1973, the growth rate of exports averaged 44.8 percent per annum every year and reached a high of 98 percent in 1973. Exports increased from less than one-third of total current foreign exchange receipts, about one-eighth of the total value of imports in 1962, to three-quarters of all current foreign exchange receipts and almost 65 percent of the value of imports in 1972.

In Chapter 6, we noted that exports of South Korea are relatively import intensive so that the *net* foreign exchange earnings are substantially less than the gross earnings. Even if a correction is made for this fact, the ratio of exports to GNP and the rate of growth of exports are exceptionally high by international standards.

The reasons for the rapid growth of exports are somewhat elusive. Actually exports grew rapidly from a very low level in 1958. But prior to 1964, our econometric analysis in Chapter 6 indicated that neither exchange rates nor export subsidies could explain the growth of exports. In 1964, the exchange rate was unified and the sensitivity of exports to exchange rates and subsidies increased markedly. The estimated elasticity of exports with respect to the purchasing-power-parity official exchange rate was 6.16 and the estimated elasticity with respect to subsidies is 4.69. These very high elasticities, however, are suspect because of the limited time period and the few degrees of freedom. Nevertheless, recent experience confirms the impression that Korean exports are highly sensitive to the exchange rate (the latest year for which data were used in the econometric work reported in chapters 6 and 8 was 1970). The purchasing-power-parity exchange rate adjusted for realignments in Japanese and European currency revaluations against the dollar, increased about 10 percent in 1972 and another 10 percent in 1973 (Table 5–7). This was the result of a float of the won in the first half of 1972, the dollar devaluation in early 1972 and 1973, and the float of other currencies against the dollar. Exports increased 52 percent in 1972 and 98 percent in 1973.

The increased sensitivity of exports to exchange rates and subsidies may be due to the unification of exchange rates and the relative stability of the purchasing-power-parity effective exchange rate from 1964 to 1970. The elimination of multiple rates removes the uncertainties and administrative costs to the private entrepreneur in dealing with an unstable, multiple rate system.

The rapid growth of South Korea's exports cannot be explained simply in terms of those incentives subject to quantitative measurement. Other very important factors, perhaps even more important, are the government's attitudes and methods of operating. For example, government officials use moral and political suasion to urge private entrepreneurs to meet export targets. Firms who are successful in promoting exports receive favorable treatment by tax officials, an important incentive in a country where effective tax rates are set more by administrative procedures than by law. Entrepreneurs who are successful exporters are publicly acclaimed and feted by the President and other high officials.

With an atmosphere in which businessmen are certain that government will reward efforts to export, it is relatively easy to take the substantial risks of expanding production and capacity for export markets. A businessman cannot only expect tangible rewards for export performance, but knows that if he runs into financial difficulties, the government will provide some form of special treatment to help him out of his troubles.

Earnings on Capital Account.

The other major sources of foreign exchange were on capital account.

Official grant aid plus net capital inflows were many times greater than export earnings for some time after the Korean War. Capital imports reached $373 million or almost twenty times the level of exports in 1957 (Table 11–6). By 1964, export earnings exceeded capital account earnings for the first time since the Korean War. The growth of foreign borrowing in the latter 1960s, however, exceeded the growth of exports so that until 1969, capital imports exceeded export earnings. In 1970, restrictions on capital imports again reduced them below the level of exports. By 1972, exports were three times as large as capital imports.

DEMAND FOR FOREIGN EXCHANGE

Gold and foreign exchange holdings of South Korea have been relatively ample compared with total imports. In 1960 they were more than 50 percent of the total import bill. Despite the rapid growth of the economy from 1963 to 1972, end-of-the-year foreign exchange reserves were never less than one-quarter of the annual import bill and were as high as 37 percent of imports in 1964, the year of the exchange rate reforms (Table 11–6).

During the same period, substantial liberalization of the import regime took place. The average tariff level declined and quantitative restrictions were much less important than before 1963. The demand for imports was held in

TABLE 11-6

**Capital Account Transactions and Foreign Exchange Holdings,
1953 to 1972**

Year	Official Grant Aid ($ million)	Net Loan Capital Inflows[a] ($ million)	Net Capital Imports ($ million)	Ratio of Net Capital Imports to Merchandise Exports	Gold and Foreign Exchange Holdings[b] ($ million)	Percent of Imports
1953	193	112	305	7.62	109	—
1954	139	28	167	6.96	108	—
1955	240	−3	237	13.17	96	29
1956	298	14	312	12.48	99	26
1957	355	18	373	19.58	116	30
1958	319	−7	312	18.35	146	42
1959	229	−17	212	10.60	147	54
1960	256	−1	255	7.28	157	51
1961	207	19	226	5.51	207	73
1962	200	−16	184	3.35	169	43
1963	208	−104	204	2.34	131	26
1964	141	−26	115	.97	136	37
1965	135	9	134	.77	146	35
1966	122	218	340	1.36	245	36
1967	135	299	334	1.00	356	39
1968	121	422	543	1.10	391	30
1969	104	631	735	1.12	553	34
1970	85	582	667	.76	610	34
1971	64	662	726	.64	568	27
1972	51	530	581	.35	740	33

SOURCE: Bank of Korea, *Economic Statistics Yearbook, 1973,* pp. 222–223 and various issues prior to 1973.

a. Loan capital, both private and government, short term and long term, net of amortization payments.

b. Includes reserve position in IMF and special drawing rights.

check, mainly by exchange rate policy. The large devaluation of 1964 raised the effective exchange rate on imports from 207.39 won to the dollar on a purchasing-power-parity basis in 1963 to 283.79 won to the dollar in 1965 (Table 11–7). From 1965 to 1970, although the average effective rate declined, it remained higher than at any time during the earlier period 1955 to 1963—except for 1961 when there was a sharp devaluation.

Imports into South Korea are very sensitive to exchange rate changes.

TABLE 11–7

Effective Exchange Rate on Imports on Purchasing-Power-Parity Basis, and Growth of Imports, 1955 to 1970

Year	Official Exchange Rate[a] (won/dollar)	Tariffs and Tariff Equivalents[a] (won/dollar)	Purchasing-Power-Parity Effective Exchange Rate on Imports[a] (won/dollar)	Imports ($ million)	Growth Rate of Imports (percent)
1955	99.71	11.67	111.38	327	—
1956	132.10	10.43	142.53	380	16.2
1957	118.12	12.74	130.86	390	2.6
1958	121.80	28.42	150.22	344	−11.8
1959	119.73	65.84	185.57	273	−20.6
1960	135.37	64.86	200.23	305	11.7
1961	244.79	34.42	279.21	283	−7.2
1962	226.57	28.39	254.96	390	37.8
1963	189.32	18.07	207.39	497	27.4
1964	232.22	23.35	255.57	365	−26.6
1965	265.40	28.39	283.79	420	15.1
1966	256.34	23.40	279.74	680	61.9
1967	243.12	23.48	266.60	909	33.7
1968	233.30	22.62	255.92	1,322	45.4
1969	234.53	20.60	255.13	1,650	24.8
1970	240.21	20.29	260.50	1,804	9.3

SOURCE: Tables 8–10C and 8–11B.

a. The first three columns are won/dollar rates deflated by a purchasing-power-parity index, and represent averages over the year. The third column is the sum of the first two columns.

This is vividly illustrated by even a cursory look at the data in Table 11–7. In 1958 and 1959, imports dropped sharply, even though GNP grew at 5.5 and 4.4 percent in those years. In 1958, there was no devaluation of the official exchange rate, but a foreign exchange tax was instituted and a price stabilization program implemented, both of which raised the effective exchange rate on imports (on a purchasing-power-parity basis) about 15 percent. The imposition of the foreign exchange tax was equivalent to a devaluation for imports. Imports fell by 12 percent in 1958. Part of the reduction in imports was due to a fall in grain imports as domestic grain production increased sharply, but imports of consumer goods fell by 25 percent and imports of capital and intermediate goods were also reduced. In 1959, foreign exchange tax receipts quadrupled and the effective exchange rate was increased by another 23 percent. Imports fell by 21 percent. Although grain imports continued to fall, consumption goods imports fell by almost 50 percent and intermediate goods by almost 10 percent.[15]

In January and February of 1961 a large devaluation reduced the value of the won from 65 to 130 won to the dollar. Grain imports increased by 50 percent, but imports of consumer and intermediate goods imports were sharply reduced. The net result was a 7 percent decline in total imports even though GNP grew 4.2 percent.

In 1964, there was a very sharp reduction in imports of 27 percent. The official exchange rate was devalued almost 50 percent. The growth of GNP was 8.3 percent, but there were very substantial reductions in nearly all categories of imports, including a 50 percent decrease in consumer goods imports.

The evidence of the sensitivity of imports to exchange rates is corroborated by the regression analysis described in Chapter 8. The regressions which dealt with imports of consumption goods, capital goods, and intermediate goods, were stable regardless of the time period used. Linear regressions provided very good fits. The elasticities of imports with respect to the official exchange rate (*ORD*) and the level of tariffs and tariff equivalents on imports (*SUBM*) are shown in Table 11–8.

Consumption goods are by far the most elastic with respect to changes in exchange rates and tariffs. Imports of capital and intermediate goods are generally less than unit elastic with respect to the exchange rate, but imports of intermediate goods are fairly sensitive to changes in tariff rates. Since the supply of imports to Korea is probably close to infinitely elastic, it can be assumed that exchange rate changes have a powerful effect in reducing the dollar value of imports.

In the late 1960s, the demand for foreign exchange was augmented by the need to service foreign debt. Beginning in 1970 attempts were made to restrict the import of foreign capital. By 1971, debt service payments reached $326.6 million on debt of maturity greater than one year. But debt service payments were still only a small fraction of the total use of foreign exchange before 1971.

South Korea succeeded in restraining the demand for foreign exchange during the period of rapid growth from 1963 to 1972. A less developed economy, growing at more than 10 percent per annum, can be expected to run short of foreign exchange because of the rising demands for imports. Although imports rose rapidly through much of this period, import growth would have been much greater had it not been for frequent devaluations and maintenance of the purchasing-power-parity effective exchange rate for imports at a constant level. Furthermore, the stable exchange rate helped stimulate export receipts, which were used to finance an increasingly large share of the total import bill.

TABLE 11–8

Elasticity of Imports, Various Periods

Import Variable[a] (dependent variable)	Commercial Policy Variable[b] (explanatory variable)	Time Period			
		1955–59	1960–64	1965–70	1955–70
Imports of consumption goods (*MC*)	Effective exchange rate on imports (*ORD* & *SUBM*)	−2.09	−5.48	−1.43	−2.11
Imports of capital goods (*MK*)	Official exchange rate (*ORD*)	−0.86	−0.99	−0.21	−0.36
Imports of intermediate goods (*MI*)	Official exchange rate (*ORD*);	−0.57	−0.80	−0.33	−0.47
	Tariffs and tariff equivalents (*SUBM*)	−0.97	−1.36	−0.57	−0.79

NOTE: Elasticities based on regression equations (8–24), (8–25), and (8–26) in Chapter 8, and computed at the means of the variables.

a. In constant 1965 prices.

b. Purchasing-power-parity basis.

Although South Korean economic policies favored high effective exchange rates, especially for exports, these policies caused some loss in government revenues and savings. As our analysis in Chapter 9 indicated, less subsidization of exports and higher taxes on imports could have generated somewhat more growth. Nevertheless, the Korean performance was unusually good compared with the records of other less developed countries.

ECONOMIC EFFICIENCY

There is no conclusive way to determine whether the Korean economy has operated efficiently. Because the various empirical methods used in the literature all have their faults, caution is necessary in discussing measures of efficiency. It is clear, however, that in Korea inefficiency has not been sufficient to stifle very rapid growth over the decade beginning in 1963. Furthermore, most of the conventional measures analyzed in Chapter 10 suggest a low level of inefficiency.

Prior to the 1964 exchange rate unification and liberalizing reforms, the system of exchange rates and trade policy probably did foster inefficiency. Quantitative restrictions were very important and the exchange rates were various and widely divergent.

Since 1964, however, the government has followed different policies. Although liberalizing trends have waxed and waned, the fluctuations have been minor, never approaching the chaos of the late 1950s.

In Chapter 10, we analyzed the restrictiveness of the trade policy and exchange rate regime in 1968. We saw that in Korea the average level of nominal protection is low. For manufacturing, the level of nominal protection estimated from information on comparative international and domestic prices was about 10.7 percent in 1968 and is probably much lower today because average tariff levels have steadily declined. Quantitative restrictions are not an important cause of large differences between international and domestic prices. The 77 commodity groups receiving significant protection through quantitative restrictions in 1968 accounted for only 11 percent of total domestic sales.

Unlike many other countries, Korea does not maintain large differences in nominal protection between industry and agriculture. Average nominal protection was 16.6 percent for agriculture and 10.7 percent for manufacturing. General variability of protection among sectors is quite low. When the Korean economy is measured in constant international prices rather than constant domestic prices, the total and sectoral rates of growth do not differ significantly. Emphasis on export promotion has led to rapid growth in the most labor-intensive sectors.

The observations made in Chapter 10 suggest an efficient pattern of growth. Such inefficiencies that do arise stem from the protection of agriculture and import-competing manufactures. The effective subsidy in 1968 to agriculture was 21.3 percent (Corden definition) and to manufacturing −4.7 percent. Effective protection is also much higher for import-competing industries than for export industries and for domestic sales than for export sales in industries that sell in both export and domestic markets.

Policies that affect the incentive to import foreign capital can influence efficiency just as much as policies that affect exports and import substitutes. In Korea, the incentive to import short-term foreign capital during the 1960s was excessive. Domestic inflation, high real and nominal domestic interest rates, and a failure to devalue smoothly and adequately all contributed to an exaggerated demand for foreign loan capital.

Policies governing credit, interest rates, pricing, the subsidization and management of government enterprises, and taxation also bear on efficiency.[16]

Only partial allowance was made for these policies in our estimates of effective subsidy. It is clear, however, when they are taken into account, that both the total and the variability of effective subsidies increase.

ROLE OF THE LIBERALIZATION EPISODES

The major liberalization efforts in Korea took place in 1964 and 1965. Earlier attempts in 1961 and 1962 that had failed of full implementation prompted a return to the multiple exchange rate system in 1963.

There is no clear correlation between the liberalization of 1964–65 and the start of rapid growth. In fact, mining and manufacturing output, which had grown 14.1 percent in 1962 (constant 1970 prices), and 15.7 percent in 1963, registered a gain of only 6.9 percent in the first year of liberalization. Only a poor harvest made 1962 a bad year and only an excellent harvest made 1964 a good one (Table 2–4). The satisfactory performance of 1962 and 1963 was largely the result of expansionary fiscal policies whereas industrial performance suffered in 1964, despite liberalization, because fiscal and monetary stabilization were rigidly enforced.

Nor was the devaluation of 1964 associated with a sudden upsurge of exports. Having touched bottom in 1958, exports grew without interruption from 1959 on.

The main argument in defense of liberalization is that it laid the basis for a decade of sustained growth, whereas fiscal and monetary policies were responsible for brief deviations from a propensity for substantial real growth. It might also be argued that liberalization itself was less important as a direct influence on the economy than it was as the harbinger of 'a new approach to exchange rates and trade policy that favored rapid growth.

Since liberalization, the effective exchange rates on exports and imports have remained high (somewhat higher for exports than for imports—see Table 5–10) while foreign exchange has never become a severe constraint on growth. The devaluation of 1964 was followed by many others over the next eight or nine years, both floating devaluations and discontinuous changes in the value of the won. Exchange rates had great effect on export performance, particularly after the reforms of 1964, and as Chapter 6 demonstrates, the growth of exports has been the dominant factor in the growth of the economy as a whole. We conclude, therefore, that the unification of the exchange rates and the stability of the effective exchange rate were powerful stimuli to subsequent growth.

By contrast, the interest rate reform of September 1965 was probably of more intrinsic importance in its effect on the rate of growth. The interest rate reform greatly encouraged household savings which having been negative in

1964 became about one-quarter of total domestic savings in 1969. Business savings, which had been nearly stagnant from 1962 to 1964, more than doubled between 1964 and 1970. Even more important than this boost for savings was the effect of the interest rate reform on incentives to hold assets in different forms. Commercial bank time deposits became the more favored way to hold savings; the increase in commercial bank deposits far exceeded the increase in total savings.[17] Most loanable funds were controlled by the commercial banks. Though some of their lending was done at subsidized interest rates, thus encouraging inefficient use of resources, the commercial banks could lend in much greater volume than the unorganized money markets and operate with much lower overhead. The cost to large borrowers was also much lower if they borrowed from the commercial banks instead of from a myriad of small operators in the unorganized money market.

The reforms of August 1972 took a different tack. After 1965, no serious effort had been made to reduce the rate of inflation. Rather, high nominal interest rates and frequent devaluations were supposed to compensate for rapid inflation. With the reforms of 1972, low nominal interest rates, stability of the exchange rate, and less rapid price inflation were to be the basic elements of policy. According to McKinnon (1973), there are important flaws in this new policy. A major factor in increasing the money supply in Korea is the discount of export bills at very low rates of discount and low rates of interest on the bills themselves to exporters. The low rate of interest on the bills increases exporters' demand for this form of credit and the even lower discount rate encourages commercial banks to discount the bills at the Bank of Korea, thus increasing commercial bank reserves. In fact, in the first six months of 1973, the discount of export bills exceeded the increase in commercial bank reserves, the other sources of reserve creation having undergone a net decline. Because of the discount of export bills, which has become the main source of reserve creation, the Bank of Korea has lost effective control of the money supply. Under such conditions, it is unlikely that inflation can be held within reasonable bounds. Added to the inflationary difficulties is the rapid increase in prices of petroleum products and grains, both of which Korea imports in large amounts. The success of the new policies in the long run, however, will depend on finding ways to bring the money supply back under control.

CONCLUSIONS

The Korean experience over the decade since 1963, remarkable as it seems to have been, does not necessarily provide a model for other less developed countries. There have been a number of special factors operating which are not likely to be replicated in other countries. It was the confluence of those factors, no one of them separately, that led to successful growth. First, abundant foreign assistance, particularly during reconstruction after the Korean War, helped build the infrastructural base for subsequent growth, although the periods of high levels of foreign aid are not coterminous with the periods of most rapid growth. Only a few other countries, having special relationships with the United States because of U.S. foreign policy objectives, received as much per capita foreign aid.

Second, Korea was able to maintain high and growing levels of government savings. Rates of taxation and public enterprise profits rose sharply while the growth of current expenditures remained moderate. Probably such a performance is only possible in countries where political leaders are powerful and secure. In many less developed countries political power is fragmented, the political process is highly competitive, and ethnic and regional differences are acute. Policy-makers in such circumstances are unlikely to be able to control revenues and expenditures to the necessary degree. To maintain themselves in power, they must use government expenditures as a means of gaining the support of particular interest groups. Public enterprises are rarely profitable because staffing them becomes a form of dispensing political patronage and top management posts are filled according to political criteria. Costs are high and productivity low. Prices tend to be kept unrealistically low for fear of injuring powerful interest groups by allowing prices to rise. Higher rates of taxation yield returns only if they are accompanied by greater expenditures contrived for the benefit of particular interest groups.

Third, frequent devaluations, either of the discontinuous type or of the gliding peg variety, are seldom feasible where resistance is intense. Discontinuous devaluations typically raise prices sharply for many imported goods, particularly for nonluxuries which had not been subject to stringent import controls. Consumer groups and industrial end-users who would suffer in consequence may resist efforts to devalue. Even gliding devaluations, which raise prices of imported goods more gradually, are not always popular. When the Allende regime came to power in Chile, it abolished the gliding exchange rate and fixed the foreign-exchange value of the domestic currency, partly because the gliding peg was politically unpopular. Even Korea abandoned the gliding peg in 1972 because considerable resistance to devaluations had gathered among a wide variety of industrialists. Many Korean firms had accumulated large foreign debts and were financially precarious. Continuous devaluations increased the amount of their dollar-specified liabilities in terms of won. Other firms producing mainly for the domestic market saw the costs of imported inputs rising and joined the resistance. Exporters, always favored by subsidies of various sorts as well as by frequent devaluations, have not organized an effective counterforce, possibly because they feel they can always count on enough subsidization to make up for losses caused by a failure to devalue.

Fourth, government policies toward labor in Korea prevented real wages from rising except in response to labor shortages in the late 1960s. This affected growth in two ways. Profit rates and returns to capital were high, stimulating high levels of investment. Wage disparities did not arise among sectors; labor was efficiently allocated among sectors; and there were no large and growing pools of wasted labor in the form of unemployed workers. On the contrary, unemployment rates declined throughout much of the 1960s.

The lack of pressure from organized labor in South Korea is partly historical accident. During industrialization under the Japanese, labor organizations were suppressed and suppression has continued to the present day. In many other less developed countries, organized labor is powerful and political regimes are dependent on it for support. The demands of labor cannot be ignored in such circumstances and it would be foolish of the government to insist that wages be set by market forces.

Fifth, South Korea underwent a thoroughgoing land reform first under the U.S. military government and later under an indigenous Korean government. Japanese landowners were expropriated and the subsequent redistribution of land was evenhanded. This meant that no large numbers of landless laborers streamed into the cities in response to slight differences in urban and rural wage rates. No doubt workers migrated from country to city, but they did not overburden the system, since there were more jobs available in the cities than there were migrants to fill them, as the decline in urban unemployment rates reveals. The even distribution of land also meant that the organization of agricultural production could easily be made labor intensive. The result was an efficient use of resources where land and capital were scarce and labor superabundant.

A land reform like South Korea's is not easily duplicated in other countries. Large landholdings, which were in the hands of one group of foreigners, the Japanese, were expropriated initially by another group of foreigners, the Americans. But when an indigenous government attempts to expropriate land from major landholders who are politically powerful, the reforms are not likely to be so sweeping.

Sixth, Korean culture places a very high value on education. Since parents are willing to spend large amounts of their own funds for the education of their children, they support a vigorous system of high-quality private schools throughout the country. Thus, even though public expenditures on education in Korea are low by international standards, South Korea's literacy rate is one of the highest in the world. Korea also has a very high proportion of secondary school and university graduates. Because this large investment in human capital did not require a commensurate public expenditure, more public resources could be channeled instead into economic overheads and directly productive investments.

These special factors are lacking in many less developed countries and the combination of any number of them is rare indeed. Taiwan is the only less developed society where strong similarities to Korea are found.

These special factors, however, are not sufficient in themselves to explain the success of the South Korean economy. Economic policies made an important contribution: tax and government expenditure reforms, the interest rate reforms, the exchange rate reforms, and the general emphasis on export promotion and reliance on international prices were some of the most critical. There is some evidence that export promotion was a bit overdone—greater reliance on tariffs particularly as a source of revenue may have generated slightly more growth—but the bias toward exports was far preferable to a strong bias in favor of import substitution. The export bias allowed efficient industries to establish themselves without being limited in size by the domestic market. The export bias led to an increasingly open economy and generated a growing share of the foreign exchange that lessened the economy's dependence on foreign capital imports. The subsidization of exports led to some inefficient resource allocation but did not result in the same distortion of incentives which is often the result of import substitution. Quotas on imports or prohibitive tariffs can distort the structure of product prices much more than the instruments typically used to promote exports. Exports are subsidized by tax exemptions and rebates, subsidization of credit, and subsidization of inputs. The effect of these instruments on costs and prices is limited. For example, income tax exemptions can be applied only if a firm is profitable and only to the extent that profits are made. Subsidized electricity and transportation rates typically affect only a small proportion of costs. In theory a direct export subsidy could be made to have as large a distorting effect as any tariff or import quota. In fact, direct subsidies have rarely been used. There has always been a reluctance to use direct subsidies, partly because they must be appropriated as a specific government expenditure and the effect on the budget is obvious and direct. A tax exemption, however, does not appear directly in the budget either as an expenditure or as negative revenue. An import quota has no obvious impact on the government budget. An import tariff except when prohibitive makes a positive contribution to revenue.

Unfortunately, South Korea's economic gains have been accompanied by a great deal of political repression. Labor unions have been very much discouraged, and there exist many cases of employer abuse of unskilled workers, reminiscent of nineteenth century sweatshops in Western nations. The South Korean experience does illustrate, however, the effectiveness of price-oriented economic policies in initiating and sustaining rapid economic growth. The poor performance in the area of human rights and in the labor policy is tempered by a favorable performance in terms of income distribution and the existence of many benevolently paternalistic employers. The relevance of the

Korean experience to other less developed economies, however, is questionable at best because it was probably the combination of political, historical, and cultural circumstances found only in South Korea that made these policies succeed. In other circumstances they might not work.

NOTES

1. See Chenery, Duloy, and Jolly (1973), Chapter 2.

2. Economic Planning Board, *Major Economic Indicators, May 1972*, pp. 88–89. Farm wages are reported in terms of a daily wage rate. To get monthly earnings, the daily wage rate was multiplied by 23.

3. Bank of Korea, *Economic Statistics Yearbook*, various issues.

4. Average total farm household income is from Ministry of Agriculture and Forestry, *Report on the Results of Farm Economy Survey and Production Cost Survey of Agricultural Products (1972)*. Average total farm household income is divided by 2.22 workers per household in 1964, 2.05 workers per household in 1968, and 1.98 workers in 1971. These figures were estimated from the farm labor force estimates in Table 11–2 and the total number of farm households in Bank of Korea, *Economic Statistics Yearbook, 1973*, p. 104. Manufacturing wages are from p. 254 of the same publication.

5. Brown (1973), p. 205.

6. Literacy rate for population aged 13 and over from Economic Planning Board, "Briefing Materials to the President," June 11, 1973.

7. Ministry of Education, *Statistical Yearbook of Education, 1970*, pp. 138–139.

8. *Major Economic Indicators, 1961–1971*, Seoul, Economic Planning Board, May 1972, p. 81.

9. See Cole and Lyman (1971).

10. Bank of Korea, *Economic Statistics Yearbook, 1973*, pp. 258–259 and 288–289.

11. Bank of Korea, *Economic Statistics Yearbook, 1973*, pp. 290–291.

12. Economic Planning Board, *Major Economic Indicators, 1961–1971*, p .33.

13. Ibid., p. 35.

14. Bank of Korea, *Economic Statistics Yearbook, 1973*, pp. 288–289.

15. For data on grain imports and the breakdown of imports into consumption goods, capital goods, and intermediate goods, see Table 8–10C and definitions and sources in Table 8–8.

16. See Brown (1973) for an analysis of the efficiency aspects of a number of these policies.

17. Commercial bank deposits increased from 28 billion won in 1964 to 636 billion won in 1971; time and savings deposits increased from 9 to 467 billion won over the same period. See *Major Economic Indicators, 1961–1971*, p. 35.

Appendix A

Definition of Concepts and Delineation of Phases

DEFINITION OF CONCEPTS USED IN THE PROJECT

Exchange Rates.

1. *Nominal exchange rate:* The official parity for a transaction. For countries maintaining a single exchange rate registered with the International Monetary Fund, the nominal exchange rate is the registered rate.[1]

2. *Effective exchange rate (EER):* The number of units of local currency actually paid or received for a one-dollar international transaction. Surcharges, tariffs, the implicit interest foregone on guarantee deposits, and any other charges against purchases of goods and services abroad are included, as are rebates, the value of import replenishment rights, and other incentives to earn foreign exchange for sales of goods and services abroad.

3. *Price-level-deflated (PLD) nominal exchange rates:* The nominal exchange rate deflated in relation to some base period by the price level index of the country.

4. *Price-level-deflated EER (PLD-EER):* The EER deflated by the price level index of the country.

5. *Purchasing-power-parity adjusted exchange rates:* The relevant (nominal or effective) exchange rate multiplied by the ratio of the foreign price level to the domestic price level.[2]

Devaluation.

1. *Gross devaluation:* The change in the parity registered with the IMF (or, synonymously in most cases, de jure devaluation).

2. *Net devaluation:* The weighted average of changes in EERs by classes of transactions (or, synonymously in most cases, de facto devaluation).

3. *Real gross devaluation:* The gross devaluation adjusted for the increase in the domestic price level over the relevant period.

4. *Real net devaluation:* The net devaluation similarly adjusted.

Protection Concepts.

1. *Explicit tariff:* The amount of tariff charged against the import of a good as a percentage of the import price (in local currency at the nominal exchange rate) of the good.[3]

2. *Implicit tariff* (or, synonymously, tariff equivalent): The ratio of the domestic price (net of normal distribution costs) minus the c.i.f. import price to the c.i.f. import price in local currency.[4]

3. *Premium:* The windfall profit accruing to the recipient of an import license per dollar of imports. It is the difference between the domestic selling price (net of normal distribution costs) and the landed cost of the item (including tariffs and other charges). The premium is thus the difference between the implicit and the explicit tariff (including other charges) multiplied by the nominal exchange rate.[5]

4. *Nominal tariff:* The tariff—either explicit or implicit as specified—on a commodity.

5. *Effective tariff:* The explicit or implicit tariff on value added as distinct from the nominal tariff on a commodity. This concept is also expressed as the effective rate of protection (ERP) or as the effective protective rate (EPR).

6. *Domestic resources costs (DRC):* The value of domestic resources (evaluated at "shadow" or opportunity cost prices) employed in earning or saving a dollar of foreign exchange (in the value-added sense) when producing domestic goods.

DELINEATION OF PHASES USED IN TRACING THE EVOLUTION OF EXCHANGE CONTROL REGIMES

To achieve comparability of analysis among different countries, each author of a country study was asked to identify the chronological development of his country's payments regime through the following phases. There was no presumption that a country would necessarily pass through all the phases in chronological sequence.

Phase I: During this period, quantitative restrictions on international transactions are imposed and then intensified. They generally are initiated in response to an unsustainable payments deficit and then, for a period, are intensified. During the period when reliance upon quantitative restrictions as a means of controlling the balance of payments is increasing, the country is said to be in Phase I.

Phase II: During this phase, quantitative restrictions are still intense, but various price measures are taken to offset some of the undesired results of the system. Heightened tariffs, surcharges on imports, rebates for exports, special tourist exchange rates, and other price interventions are used in this phase. However, primary reliance continues to be placed on quantitative restrictions.

Phase III: This phase is characterized by an attempt to systematize the changes which take place during Phase II. It generally starts with a formal exchange-rate change and may be accompanied by removal of some of the surcharges, etc., imposed during Phase II and by reduced reliance upon quantitative restrictions. Phase III may be little more than a tidying-up operation (in which case the likelihood is that the country will re-enter Phase II), or it may signal the beginning of withdrawal from reliance upon quantitative restrictions.

Phase IV: If the changes in Phase III result in adjustments within the country, so that liberalization can continue, the country is said to enter Phase IV. The necessary adjustments generally include increased foreign-exchange earnings and gradual relaxation of quantitative restrictions. The latter relaxation may take the form of changes in the nature of quantitative restrictions or of increased foreign-exchange allocations, and thus reduced premiums, under the same administrative system.

Phase V: This is a period during which an exchange regime is fully liberalized. There is full convertibility on current account, and quantitative restrictions are not employed as a means of regulating the ex ante balance of payments.

NOTES

1. In this volume the term *official exchange rate* is used more frequently than *nominal exchange rate*.

2. The terms used in this volume have more frequently been the *purchasing-power-parity effective exchange rate* and the *official exchange rate on a purchasing-power-parity basis*.

3. In this volume the term *legal tariff* rather than *explicit tariff* has been used.

4. *Nominal tariff rate* rather than *implicit tariff rate* is used in this volume.

5. See the two preceding footnotes referring to the terms *explicit tariff* and *implicit tariff*.

Bibliography

Adelman, Irma, ed. *Practical Approaches to Development Planning: Korea's Second Five-Year Plan*. Baltimore: Johns Hopkins Press, 1969.

Balassa, Bela. "Tariff Protection in Industrial Countries." *Journal of Political Economy* 73 (1965): 573–594.

————. "Industrial Policies in Taiwan and Korea." *Weltwirtschaftliches Archiv* 106 (1971): 55–77.

Balassa, Bela, and Schydlowsky, D. "Effective Tariffs, Domestic Cost of Foreign Exchange, and the Equilibrium Exchange Rate." *Journal of Political Economy* 76 (1968): 348–360.

Balassa, Bela, et al. *Development Strategies in Semi-Industrialized Countries*. Washington, D.C.: International Bank for Reconstruction and Development, forthcoming.

————. *The Structure of Protection in Developing Countries*. Baltimore: Johns Hopkins Press, published for the International Bank for Reconstruction and Development, 1971.

Bank of Korea. *Annual Economic Review*. Seoul: 1948 through 1959. (Narratives in Korean, statistics in Korean and English.)

————. *Economic History of Chosen, Compiled in Commemoration of the Decennial of the Bank of Chosen*. Seoul: 1920.

————. *Economic Statistics Yearbook*. Seoul: 1960 through 1973. (In English and Korean.)

————. *Effect of Export on GNP by Input-Output Method, 1963–1968*. Seoul: 1969.

————. *The Interindustry Relations Study for the Korean Economy, 1960*. Seoul: Research Department, 1964.

————. *Monthly Statistical Review*. Seoul: Research Department, for selected months, 1960 through 1973.

————. *National Income Statistics Yearbook*. Seoul: 1953 through 1972. (Only major statistics in English.)

————. *Review of the Korean Economy* (annual). Seoul: 1960 through 1973. (In English and Korean.)

————. *Review of Price Index*. Seoul: 1961. (Narratives in Korean, statistics in Korean and English.)

————. *A Ten-Year History of the Bank of Korea*. Seoul: 1960. (In Korean.)

Bhagwati, Jagdish. "More on the Equivalence of Tariffs and Quotas." *American Economic Review* 58 (1968): 142–146.

————. "On the Equivalence of Tariffs and Quotas," in *Trade, Growth, and Balance of Payments: Essays in Honor of Gottfried Haberler*. Robert E. Baldwin et al., eds., pp. 53–67. Chicago: Rand McNally, 1965.

Bhagwati, Jagdish N., and Cheh, John. "The Share of Manufacturing Exports in Total Exports of LDC's: A Cross Section Analysis," in *International Economics and Development: Essays in Honor of Raul Prebisch*. Eugenio DiMarco, ed. New York: Academic Press, 1972.

Bhagwati, Jagdish N., and Hansen, Bent. "Should Growth Rates be Evaluated at International Prices?" in *Development Planning: Essays in Honor of Paul Rosenstein Rodan*. J. N. Bhagwati and R. S. Eckaus, eds., pp. 53–68. Cambridge: M.I.T. Press, 1973.

Bhagwati, Jagdish, and Krueger, Anne O. "Exchange Control, Liberalization, and Economic Development." *American Economic Review* 63 (1973): 419–427.

————. *Exchange Control, Liberalization and Economic Development: Analytical Framework*. Processed. New York: National Bureau of Economic Research, 1970.

————. *Foreign Trade Regimes and Economic Development: Theory and Experience*. New York: National Bureau of Economic Research, forthcoming.

Bhagwati, Jagdish N., and Srinivasan, T. N. "The General Equilibrium Theory of Effective Protection and Resource Allocation." *Journal of International Economics* 3 (1973): 259–281.

Brown, Gilbert T. *Korean Pricing Policies and Economic Development in the 1960's*. Baltimore: Johns Hopkins University Press, 1973.

Bruno, Michael. "Domestic Resource Costs and Effective Protection: Clarification and Synthesis." *Journal of Political Economy* 80 (1972): 16–33.

————. "Protection and Tariff Change under General Equilibrium." *Journal of International Economics* 3 (1973): 205–225.

Cha, Byung Kwon, et al. *Analysis of Korea's Import Substitution Industries.* Seoul: Seoul National University, 1967.

Chenery, Hollis B. "Alternative Patterns of Development." *Economic Development Report No. 163.* Cambridge: Development Research Group, Harvard University, 1970b.

————. "The Normally Developing Country." *Economic Development Report No. 162.* Cambridge: Development Research Group, Harvard University, 1970a.

————. "Patterns of Industrial Growth." *American Economic Review* 50 (1960): 624–654.

————. "The Process of Industrialization," in *Economic Development Report No. 146.* Processed. Cambridge: Harvard University Project for Quantitative Research in Economic Development, 1969.

Chenery, Hollis; Duloy, John; and Jolly, Richard. "Redistribution with Growth: An Approach to Policy." Processed. Washington, D.C.: International Bank for Reconstruction and Development, 1973.

Chenery, Hollis B.; Shishido, Shuntaro; and Watanabe, Tsunehiko. "The Pattern of Japanese Growth, 1914–1954." *Econometrica* 30 (1962): 98–129.

Chenery, Hollis B., and Westphal, Larry E. "Economics of Scale and Investment over Time," in *Public Economics: An Analysis of Public Production and Consumption and their Relations to the Private Sector,* Conference on the Analysis of the Public Sector, Biarritz, 1966, Julius Margolis, and Henri Guitton, eds. Proceedings of a conference held by the International Economic Association. New York: St. Martin's Press, 1969.

Cho, Yong Sam. *"Disguised Unemployment" in Underdeveloped Areas: with Special Reference to South Korea.* Berkeley: University of California Press, 1963.

Choi, Myong Nam, and Kim, Kwang Suk. "A Study of Korea's Export Function." A paper prepared for USAID/Korea. Seoul: November 1968.

Choi, Woonsang. *The Fall of the Hermit Kingdom.* Dobbs Ferry, New York: Oceana Publications, 1967.

Choy, Bong Youn. *Korea: A History* (foreword by Youghil Kang). Rutland, Vermont: C. E. Tuttle Co., 1971.

Chung, Henry. *The Russians Came to Korea.* Seoul, Washington: Korean Pacific Press, 1947.

Chung, Joseph Sang-hoon, ed. *Patterns of Economic Development: Korea.* Detroit: Cellar Book Shop, for Korea Research and Publications, Inc., 1966.

Cohen, Benjamin I. *Multinational Firms and the Export of Manufactures from Developing Countries: An Empirical and Theoretical Analysis of Singa-*

pore, South Korea, and Taiwan. New Haven: Yale University Press, forthcoming.

Cole, David C., and Lyman, Princeton N. *Korean Development: The Interplay of Politics and Economics.* Cambridge: Harvard University Press, 1971.

Cole, David C., and Westphal, Larry. "The Contribution of Exports to Employment." Processed. Seoul: Korea Development Institute, June 1974.

Corden, Warner M. *The Theory of Protection.* Oxford: Clarendon Press, 1971.

Desai, Padma. "Alternative Measures of Import Substitution." *Oxford Economic Papers* 21 (1969): 312–324.

Dolph, Fred A. *Japanese Stewardship of Korea: Economic and Financial.* Washington, D.C.: 1920.

Fair, Ray C. "The Estimation of Simultaneous Equation Models with Lagged Endogenous Variables and First Order Serially Correlated Errors." *Econometrica* 38 (1970): 507–516.

Fane, George. "Import Substitution and Export Expansion: Their Measurement and an Example of Their Application," in *Economic Development Report No. 179.* Cambridge: Development Research Group, Harvard University, 1971.

Federation of Korean Industries. *Korean Economic Yearbook.* Seoul: 1969 through 1971. (Narratives in Korean, statistics in Korean and English.)

Fisher, Franklin M. "The Choice of Instrumental Variables in the Estimation of Economy-Wide Econometric Models." *International Economic Review* 6 (1965): 245–274.

Frank, Charles R., Jr. "Debt and Terms of Aid." Washington, D.C.: Overseas Development Council, 1970. Reprinted in Frank, Charles R., Jr.; Bhagwati, Jagdish N.; and Malmgren, Harald B. *Assisting Developing Countries: Problems of Debts, Burden-Sharing, Jobs and Trade.* New York: Praeger, for the Overseas Development Council, 1972: 1–66.

————. "External Debt Service of Less Developed Countries: Problems and Prospects for Korea." In *Seminar on Korea's Foreign Trade and Balance of Payments in Economic Development.* Seoul: Korea University, 1971.

Frank, Charles R., Jr., and Cline, William R. "Measurement of Debt Servicing Capacity: An Application of Discriminant Analysis." *Journal of International Economics* 1 (1971): 327–344.

Grajdanzev, Andrew J. *Modern Korea.* New York: Institute of Pacific Relations, distributed by John Day Company, 1954.

Guisinger, Stephen E. "Negative Value Added and the Theory of Effective Protection." *Quarterly Journal of Economics* 83 (1969): 415–433.

————. "The Theory and Measurement of Effective Protection: The Case of Pakistan." Ph.D. dissertation, Harvard University, 1970.

Han, Kee Chun. "Estimates of Korean Capital and Inventory Coefficients in 1968." Processed. Seoul: Yonsei University, 1970.

————. *A Study on Export Promotion Measures in Korea.* Seoul: Yonsei University, 1967. (In Korean and English.)

Hatada, Takashi. *A History of Korea.* Translated and edited by Warren W. Smith, Jr., and Benjamin H. Hazard. Santa Barbara, Calif.: American Bibliographical Center, Clio Press, 1969.

Henderson, Gregory. *Korea: Politics of the Vortex.* Cambridge: Harvard University Press, 1968.

Hong, Wontak. "Factor Supply and Factor Intensity of Trade: The Case of Korea, 1962–1971," in *Interim Report No. 7304.* Seoul: Korea Development Institute, 1973.

Ireland, Alleyne. *The New Korea.* New York: E. P. Dutton and Company, 1926.

Kim, Kwang Suk. "Industrial Incentives for Export Promotion in Korea," in *Seminar on Korea's Foreign Trade and Balance of Payments in Economic Development.* Seoul: Korea University, International Management Institute, 1971. (In Korean.)

Kim, Mahn Je. *Macro Planning Model for the Third Five-Year Plan.* Seoul: Economic Planning Board, 1970.

Kim, Nak Kwan. "Effects of Devaluation on the Major Trading Commodities of the Republic of Korea." *Asian Economics* No. 3 (1972): 34–48.

Kim, Seung Hee. *Foreign Capital for Economic Development: A Korean Case Study* (foreword by Thomas M. Franck). New York: Praeger, 1970.

Korea (Republic). *Economic Survey* (annual). Seoul: Economic Planning Board, 1959 through 1971. (In English and Korean.)

————. *The First Five-Year Economic Development Plan. 1962–1966.* Seoul: Economic Planning Board, 1961. (Korean edition with English summary.)

————. *Foreign Trade White-Paper.* Seoul: Ministry of Commerce and Industry, 1971. (In Korean.)

————. *The Laws and Regulations Pertaining to Foreign Capital Inducement.* Seoul: Ministry of Foreign Affairs, 1969. (In English.)

————. *An Outline of Foreign Exchange System and Policy in Korea.* Seoul: Ministry of Finance, 1967. (In Korean.)

————. *Republic of Korea Tariff Table.* Korean Customs Association. Seoul: Ministry of Finance, 1964 and 1968. (In English and Korean.)

————. *The Second Five-Year Economic Development Plan, 1967–1971.* Seoul: Economic Planning Board, 1966. (In English and Korean.)

————. *Semi-Annual Trade Programs.* Seoul: Ministry of Commerce and Industry, for selected years. (In Korean.)

————. *Statistical Yearbook of Foreign Trade.* Seoul: Ministry of Finance, 1964 through 1972. (In English and Korean.)

————. *Statistical Yearbook of National Tax.* Seoul: Office of National Tax, 1958 through 1972. (In Korean and English.)

————. *The Structure and Policy of Korea's Foreign Trade.* Seoul: Ministry of Finance, 1967. (In Korean.)

————. *The Structure of Public Finance and Policy in Korea.* Seoul: Ministry of Finance, 1967. (In Korean.)

————. *A Ten Year History of Korea's Trade and Industrial Policy, 1960–1969.* Seoul: Ministry of Commerce and Industry, 1970. (In Korean.)

Korea Development Association. *Status and Outlook of Export Industry and Study of Export Promotion.* Seoul: 1968. (In Korean.)

Korea Development Bank. *Industrial Development and Problems in Korea.* Seoul: 1968. (In Korean.)

————. *Korean Industry.* Seoul: 1970. (In English and Korean.)

————. *A Ten-Year History of the Korea Development Bank.* Seoul: 1964. (In Korean.)

Korean Productivity Center, The Institute of Productivity Research. *The Analysis of Cost and Rate of Net Foreign Exchange Earnings of Korean Export Products.* Seoul: 1970.

————. *A Study for Export Promotion Measures.* Seoul: 1968. (In Korean.)

————. *A Study of Export Supporting Measures Through Cost Analysis.* Seoul: 1968. (In Korean.)

Korea Trade Research Center. *Measures to Increase Net Foreign Exchange Earnings from Exports.* Seoul: Seoul National University, 1969. (In Korean.)

Korea Trade Research Institute. *Projection of Import Demand and Measures to Reduce Import Demand.* Seoul: Seoul National University, 1968. (In Korean.)

Korean Traders Association. *Foreign Trade Yearbook.* Seoul: 1960. (Narratives in Korean, statistics in Korean and English.)

————. *A Study of International Competitiveness of Korean Export Industries.* Seoul: 1969. (In Korean.)

————. *A Study on the Promotion of Strategic Export Industries and Direction of Export Promotion Policy.* Seoul: 1970. (In Korean.)

Krueger, Anne O. "Evaluating Restrictionist Trade Regimes: Theory and Measurement." *Journal of Political Economy* 80 (1972): 48–62.

Kwak, Sang Soo. *Tax Policy and Tax Administration in a Developing Economy: The Korean Experiment.* Seoul: The Korean Research Center, 1965.

Lee, Duk Soo. "Analysis of Capital Cost, Selected Industrial Establishments." Seoul: Korean Economic Development Institute, 1967.

Lee, Eric Y. "The Effects of Exchange Rate Devaluation on the Dynamics of Inflation in Korea." Processed. A paper prepared for USAID/Korea. Seoul: 1973.

Lee, Hahn-Been. *Korea: Time, Change, and Administration.* Honolulu: East-West Center Press, 1968.

Lee, S. Y. *A Study of Price Comparisons between Domestic Producer's Unit Prices and International Prices.* Seoul: Sogang University, 1971.

Leontief, Wassily. "Domestic Production and Foreign Trade: The American Capital Position Re-Examined." *Economia Internazionale* 7 (1954): 9–38.

Lewis, Stephen R., and Soligo, Ronald. "Growth and Structural Changes in Pakistan's Manufacturing Sector, 1954–1964." *Pakistan Development Review* 5 (1965): 94–139.

Lim, Youngil. "Foreign Capital Influence on Economic Change in Korea." *Journal of Asian Studies* 28 (1968–1969): 77–99.

Little, Ian M.; Scitovsky, Tibor; and Scott, Maurice. *Industry and Trade in Some Developing Countries: A Comparative Study.* London: Oxford University Press, published for the Organization for Economic Cooperation and Development, 1970.

McCune, George M., with collaboration of Gray, Arthur L., Jr. *Korea Today.* Cambridge: Harvard University Press, 1950.

McKinnon, Ronald I., "The Financial Feasibility of Increasing Private Saving in Korea." Processed. Seoul: Korea Development Institute, 1973.

————. "Monetary Theory and Controlled Flexibility in the Foreign Exchanges," in *Essays in International Finance No. 84.* Princeton: International Finance Section, Princeton University, 1971.

————. "Savings Propensities and the Korean Monetary Reform in Retrospect." Processed. Paper read at Conference on Money and Finance in Economic Growth and Development, in Honor of Edward F. Shaw, April 1974 at Stanford University.

————. "Tariff and Commodity Tax Reform in Korea: Some Specific Suggestions." Processed. A paper prepared for USAID/Korea. Seoul: 1967.

————. "Tariff, Special Customs Duty and Excise Tax Reform. Processed. A paper prepared for USAID/Korea. Seoul: 1967.

Musgrave, Richard A. "Revenue Policy for Korea's Economic Development." Processed. A paper prepared for USAID/Korea. Seoul: 1965.

Nathan, Robert R., and Associates. "An Economic Programme for Korean Reconstruction." Processed. A paper prepared for the United Nations Reconstruction Agency. New York: 1954.

Norton, Rodger D. "The South Korean Economy in the 1960's." Washington, D.C.: Development Research Center, International Bank for Reconstruction and Development, 1971.

Park, Pil Soo. "Government Export Promotion Policy," in *Seminar on Korea's Foreign Trade and Balance of Payments in Economic Development.* Seoul: Korea University, International Management Institute, 1971. (In Korean.)

Park, Sung-jo. *Die Wirtschaftsbeziehungen Zwischen Japan und Korea, 1910–1968.* (Foreign Economic Relations between Japan and Korea, 1910–1968.) Wiesbaden: O. Harrassowitz, 1969.

Patrick, Hugh T. "Basic Issues of Financial Policy for Korea's Third Five-Year Plan." Transcription of an address to the *Second Seminar on Korea's Financial System,* 1971.

————. "Thoughts on Korean Monetary and Financial Research Policy." Processed. A paper prepared for USAID/Korea. Seoul: 1971.

Ramaswami, V. K., and Srinivasan, T. N. "Tariff Structure and Resource Allocation in the Presence of Factor Substitution," in *Trade, Balance of Payments and Growth: Papers in Honor of C. P. Kindleberger,* Jagdish Bhagwati et al., eds., pp. 291–299. Amsterdam: North-Holland Publishing Co., 1971.

Ranis, Gustav. "Some Observations on the Economic Framework for Optimum LDC Utilization of Technology," in *Technology and Economics in International Development: Report of a Seminar.* Washington, D.C.: United States Agency for International Development, 1972.

Ray, Alok. "Non-Traded Inputs and Effective Protection: A General Equilibrium Analysis." *Journal of International Economics* 3 (1973): 245–257.

Reeve, W. D. *The Republic of Korea: A Political and Economic Study.* London, New York: Oxford University Press, 1963.

Research Institute for Economics and Business. *A Study of Money Market and Industrial Investment Financing in Korea.* Seoul: Sogang University, 1970. (In Korean.)

Shibata, Hirofumi. "A Note on the Equivalence of Tariffs and Quotas." *American Economic Review* 58 (1968): 137–142.

Watanabe, Susumu. "Exports and Employment: The Case of the Republic of Korea." *International Labor Review* 106 (1972): 495–526.

Watanabe, Tsunehiko. "A Test of the Constancy of Input-Output Coefficients Among Countries." *International Economic Review* 2 (1961): 340–350.

Westphal, Larry E., and Adelman, Irma. "Reflections on the Political Economy of Planning: The Case of Korea," in *Basic Documents and Selected Papers of Korea's Third Five-Year Economic Development Plan, 1972–1976,* S. H. Jo and S. Y. Park, ed., pp. 13–31. Seoul: Sogang University, 1972.

Westphal, Larry E., and Kim, Kwang Suk. "Industrial Policy and Development in Korea," 1974, in *Development Strategies in Semi-Industrialized*

Countries, Bela Balassa, ed. Washington, D.C.: International Bank for Reconstruction and Development, forthcoming.

Willet, Thomas D.; Katz, Samuel I.; and Branson, William H. "Exchange Rate Systems, Interest Rates, and Capital Flows," in *Essays in International Finance No. 78.* Princeton: International Finance Section, Princeton University, 1970.

Index